SHELLS AND BRIGHT STONES

SHELLS AND BRIGHT STONES

A BIOGRAPHY OF
LEO WALMSLEY

Edited by NONA STEAD

Nona Stead

SMITH SETTLE

First published by
Smith Settle
Ilkley Road, Otley
West Yorkshire LS21 3JP

ISBN PB 1 85825 141 9
HB 1 85825 142 7

Designed, printed and bound by
Smith Settle
Ilkley Road, Otley, West Yorkshire LS21 3JP

A child went down to the sea-shore to find
Shells and bright stones, the means to happiness

From 'Lonesomeness' by Gerald Gould

*This biography is dedicated to Jack L W Hazell,
a great friend and the founder of the Walmsley Society.
It was one of his wishes that this biography be written
and we regret that he did not live to see it completed.*

Contents

Acknowledgements

The writing and editing of this biography presented a formidable task but the dedication and enthusiasm of all the contributors was such that tackling the project soon assumed a new significance.

First and foremost, I must thank Fred Lane for undertaking the Herculean task of putting into his computer all the drafts, whether typed or handwritten. Frequent requests for alterations to the drafts were met by unfailing cheerfulness and willingness. All this in addition to the chapters which he wrote with such commitment. Of the other writers, Peter Barton, Jane Ellis, George Featherston and John Watts, I can only express my deep gratitude for all their hard work.

I must make particular reference to Pauline Burdon, who gave everything she had to writing her chapter during the last stages of a terminal illness. Her courage and determination were beyond words.

My thanks to Stephanie Walmsley, not only for her very personal chapter on her life with Leo, but also her permission to use many quotations from Leo's works. A special thank you goes to Dr Sean Walmsley and Selina Craze (*née* Walmsley) for their delightful reminiscences of their father.

Last and by no means least of the contributors, my husband, Jack. His patience, forebearance and support made it possible for me to devote so much of my time to the project.

In addition to those who actually wrote for the biography, there were many who worked 'behind the scenes'. Of these, particular mention must be made of Peter J Woods, who made available to the Walmsley Society the results of many years of research into the life and works of Leo Walmsley. I also wish to express my appreciation to Frances Wilson, great-niece to Leo Walmsley, for her permission to use the information which resulted from her research into the Walmsley family history. We are also indebted to Marilyn Barraclough and Alan Roper for their investigative work. They both have the ability to glean information which may have otherwise remained unknown to us.

I wish to thank my sister, Gwen Allison, BA (Oxon) English Language and Literature, for her painstaking reading and checking of the text.

Nona Stead

Introduction

THE solitary, diminutive figure crouched motionless by the rock pool on the scaur. He was completely engrossed. He gazed intently into the pool, searching with practised eye for movement in the waving fronds of weeds at the bottom of the pool, always careful to allow no sign of his presence to alert the tiny creatures which he knew were hiding below. That day he had been 'first on', escaping from school as soon as the class was dismissed, running down the street to the Dock, down the slipway and on to the beach. Excitement had pulsed through his whole body. What treasures might he find as he searched through the debris left by the last high tide? It was always like this when he was 'first on' — with the expanse of beach and scaurs stretching into the North Sea. A thrill of anticipation tingled through his veins, urging him to start his search before the other children came racing down to the beach.

But inevitably he was drawn towards the rock pools, where he entered a miniature marine world. Time was of no consequence to him as he searched the pools for small marine animals and, if he was lucky, a crab or even a lobster. This fascination with the sea shore was to be the catalyst which started him on a literary career, for this small boy was Leo Walmsley.

His ability to focus his attention on what had taken his interest, the total concentration, the love of nature and contentment in solitude were facets of his personality which never changed throughout his life. His character was of such complexity that attempts to describe him create the most confusing contradictions.

A veneer of sophistication was apparent in his early manhood: a sophistication which he deliberately contrived when, as a rather gauche village youth, he had mixed with the more worldly students of two Yorkshire universities. It had further developed in his service in the First World War, when he successfully emulated the speech and manners of his fellow officers. His confidence grew when later he and his first wife travelled widely on the continent, and for a short period settled in London, mixing with the bohemian art set. His wife was in her element but gradually Walmsley became disillusioned and, turning his back on the artificiality of the gatherings and parties of the artists, he returned to the fishing village of his youth, living a life of the utmost simplicity.

The simple life was to provide inspiration for the books which made his name in the literary world of the thirties. His work was held in great regard by authors whose names are renowned in English literature.

Phyllis Bentley wrote of him:

> 'Leo Walmsley has filled me with shame. Our cheap artificial plots, distorting human nature to make it suit our jaded palate must go on the scrap heap. We are not worthy to be called writers if we cannot do what he has done in *Love in the Sun* and show the novel-reading public that the simple things of life are the only things that matter.'

And T E Lawrence (of Arabia) ...

> 'My sense of fitness makes me feel that all the book people should take their hats off to Walmsley ... He's a real writer. Cherish him.'

Sadly the reading public failed to heed Lawrence's counsel and Walmsley became a forgotten man. Almost. Fortunately there were people who appreciated his work, reading and re-reading his books over the years until in 1985, nearly twenty years after his death, a group came together to share their love of Walmsley's books. The Walmsley Society soon developed into a progressive and thriving association. As research into his life revealed information previously undisclosed, it became apparent that the life of the man was going to be as fascinating as his writings.

His life began in the enclosed community of a picturesque Yorkshire fishing village, virtually cut off from the surrounding area. He longed to escape and see the world. The war gave him his chance and the wider horizons which opened before him led to a most colourful life. Service in East Africa provided excitement but also horror, which he understated in his writing on the subject. The fact that he won the Military Cross but was to suffer bouts of depression throughout his life suggests more danger and suffering than he was prepared to reveal.

The sophisticated life with his first wife, a highly intelligent, spirited woman, provides compelling reading but it is his life after this era which is identified with the real Leo Walmsley. But who knows the real Leo Walmsley?

Nowhere in his writings does he reveal his true self. Although most of his books are written in the first person, he always remains a shadowy figure. He is the storyteller, skilfully keeping his own personality in the background. Whether living with his second wife in an old army hut on the edge of a creek in Cornwall, penniless but ecstatically happy, or back in Yorkshire converting a barn into a house between the moors and the sea for his growing family, he gives few clues about himself.

It was rather like looking at an unfinished portrait. Painstaking research highlighted some of the missing details and gradually the picture took shape. A life of infinite variety. A personality veering from exuberance and vigour to depression and self-doubt. Here indeed is a story without need of 'artificial plots' or characters plucked from the fertile imagination.

* * *

A word frequently used to describe Leo Walmsley books, both style and content, is simplicity. Yet in no way can this word be used in connection with the man himself. His personality was complex and his life varied. Rarely do two people see him in the same light — there always seems to be a diversity of view, reflecting the numerous facets of the man's character. It is an area which is intriguing to explore and analyse. In an attempt to convey the diversification of opinion, it was decided to adopt an unusual format for this biography. Walmsley's life, rather surprisingly, can be divided into several neat sections, quite different, but each of compelling interest. Several members of the Walmsley Society agreed to undertake a joint authorship, writing their own chapters and thereby bringing an individual slant to the life, personality and writings of the author. By using this approach, we sought to emphasize the complexity of Walmsley's character, allowing the variations of styles to suggest the many aspects of the man's psyche.

Nona Stead

PART ONE

THE EARLY YEARS

CHAPTER I

Wonders to Behold

'I HAVE a photograph, very faded, taken in Bramblewick Dock from the slipway top showing in a space between the hauled-up fishing cobles and stacks of lobster pots, a group of boys of various ages.

They are a rough-looking lot. Most of them are wearing jerseys and short trousers with long black stockings. Some have home-made jackets over their jerseys. Some have only shirts, with their braces showing. Two boys are almost in rags with bare legs and feet. One boy (and he is the smallest in the group) is in knickerbockers with an incongruous Jack Tar jacket.

Each boy wears or carries something which shows that this is a special occasion: a paper billycock hat, a toy bandolier, a wooden sword, a wooden gun. One boy has a ship's bell, another an oxhorn (one was always kept in each coble for use in fog), another a wooden rattle, like the ones the coconut-shy men had at Bramblewick Fair.

Several boys hold flags in their hands. On their jackets or jerseys, where soldiers wear their medal ribbons, are numbers of button-like discs. But the photograph is not clear enough to show that these discs are themselves photographic reproductions of the faces of heroes of the South African war. Lord Roberts, General Buller, General French, Lord Methuen, Sir George White, Gatacre, Kelly-Kenny, Baden-Powell, and, of course, Lord Kitchener.

All the boys save one are staring frozenly at the camera. It would have been a time exposure, and they have been warned by the photographer to keep still. The exception is the little boy with the Jack Tar jacket. He has moved slightly, but you can see that he is smiling. He has a chubby puckish face. He has no hat. His hair is fair, and a tuft of it grows up straight at one side of his forehead, like a brush with half of its bristles gone. He has a sturdy body.

Tied by a piece of string to his waist is a sword made of two laths. He has a tin can supported by another piece of string for a drum, a drum stick in one hand, a small Union Jack in the other.

To me that photograph is like a scene from a movie when the projector has stopped. I have only to look at it, close my eyes, and the projector starts again, everything becomes alive, the characters move, speak, shout, wave their flags. I hear the sound of the sea, the cries of the gulls wheeling over the house tops, and I am that little boy, banging my tin can drum, waving my flag, shouting:

'Long Live the Queen! Down with Kruger! Hooray — Hooray!'

This was Mafeking Day, May 1900.'

* * *

A day from the past, almost forgotten, but now the recollection was enough to bring other memories tumbling back like a torrent released from an obstruction. Thoughts flashed through his mind. He had to hold on to those memories somehow and not allow them to slip away. He knew how to use words. Writing

J Ulric Walmsley c1940, *by courtesy of Mrs J Moon (Wirral)*

Leo Walmsley as a young boy

was his living and he had caused considerable excitement in the literary world over two decades before. The faded photograph now gave him the inspiration for a book and served as a delightful introduction to the world of the young Leo Walmsley. That book, entitled *Sound of the Sea*, was centred on the author's beloved Robin Hoods bay, one of the loveliest villages on the North Yorkshire coast.

Lionel Walmsley was born at Shipley in the West Riding of Yorkshire on the 29th September 1892. The house at 7 Clifton Place was typical of the area, a small terrace house built of stone which had been almost golden when taken from the local quarries but which had turned to a drab, dark grey, almost black, as the smoke-laden atmosphere left its grim deposit. Shipley was a small township on the outskirts of Bradford and, like so many which clustered in the valleys as if sheltering from the bleak surrounding moorland, owed its existence to the textile mills which had sprung up during the Industrial Revolution.

His father, James Ulric, was an artist, trying to make a name for himself so as to provide for his wife, Jeannie, and their growing family. With the birth of Lionel, they had four sons: Ulric Bertram born 1886, Sydney Victor born 1887 and Percy born 1890, although sadly he died early in childhood. A daughter, Doris Sheila, was born in 1901. Painting for a living was not easy in the urban environment and when Ulric Walmsley heard a friend's enthusiastic description of a picturesque fishing village on the Yorkshire coast, he decided to move his family there, hoping that he would find inspiration and make his fortune.

Thus it was that Lionel, now two years old, came to live in Robin Hoods Bay, which for him remained to the end of his days 'that beloved place'. There could not have been a greater contrast with the town which he had left. Here the stone cottages retained all their golden colour and the pantiled roofs were a cheerful red. Instead of serried ranks of terraces, the quaint cottages were built one above the other in delightful confusion, as if huddled together in protection against the sea. Although the moors surrounded the village in a similar fashion to the area which the family had left, they appeared less bleak and hostile. It was a wonderful environment for a small boy born with a devouring curiosity. The sea and its shore, the cliffs, the woods with their tumbling streams — all had secret places which had to be explored.

Lionel, or Leo as he was later to be known, was so influenced by the many facets of his surroundings that one cannot help but wonder what sort of person he would have become had his father not made that momentous decision to move from the industrial West Riding.

Generations of the Walmsley forebears lived in Liverpool, so the move to Shipley, then further across country to the east coast, broke away from the family roots. Not only did Ulric Walmsley break with the geographical traditions of the family, but he also cast aside security and chose instead a precarious living as an artist. Leo Walmsley's paternal grandfather William and great-grandfather, John, had both been bookkeepers, a respectable occupation which enabled them to live comfortable lives in a traditionally middle-class area of Liverpool. Indeed, one member of an earlier generation, Joshua, was an esteemed public-spirited man who became mayor of Liverpool and Liberal MP for Bolton and Leicester. He counted Robert Stephenson and Richard Cobden as his friends and was knighted in 1840.

The maternal side of Leo Walmsley's family also had its share of businessmen and surprisingly, his mother, Jeannie, (or, to give her full name, Elizabeth Jane Rachel Cohu Dodd) took a position assisting a photographer. This, being rather unusual for a girl from a middle-class background, suggests that she, like Ulric, had a mind of her own and was prepared to defy convention. Could it be that these characteristics resulted from the Irish ancestry which genealogy reveals in both families?

It seems likely that their mutual attraction developed from an interest in art. There is no record of artistic influence from Ulric's family, but Jeannie appears to have had several relatives and ancestors with an artistic streak, including musicians and an interior designer in addition to a nephew who was an artist of some repute.

With such a family background, it is hardly surprising that the young Leo Walmsley should develop a strongly individual personality.

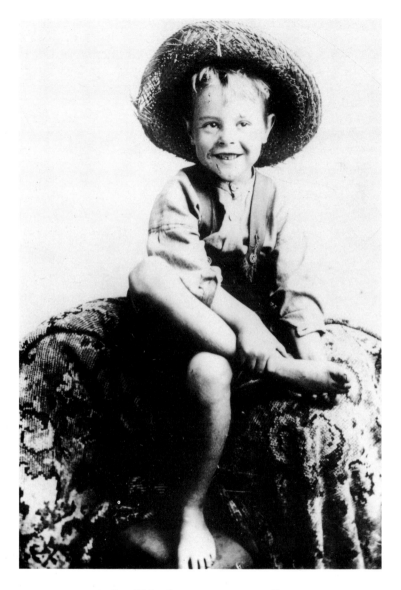

Leo Walmsley, a strong personality

The village of Robin Hoods Bay (which is called Bramblewick in his books) was a very close-knit community. It was based on the fishing industry which had gone into decline at the end of the nineteenth century. The hardships of their lives had bound the villagers together, leaving no room for sentiment or emotion. They were suspicious of the outside world, jealously guarding their privacy. This attitude extended to any newcomers to the village who were regarded as 'foreigners' and this included the Walmsley family. They had to face a barrier of hostility born of fear and a distrust of anything alien to the enclosed familiar group. To fully understand the Bay families of this period, one must appreciate the almost total isolation of such communities. Prior to the advent of the railway they had been virtually cut off from the outside world with the resultant development of a character which was dour and taciturn. Notwithstanding this, they were men of fine character, simple and honest with tremendous courage and an ability to absorb and withstand the cruel blows which life dealt them.

Gradually, Ulric and Jeannie sought to integrate and become accepted by the villagers, although Jeannie apparently on rare occasions expressed a longing for what she called 'the rush and flow of souls!' Ulric was a devout member of the Church of England while Jeannie was strict Wesleyan, although each respected the other's faith. Religious worship, always an important part of village life, and other community occasions gradually helped them towards a tolerant acceptance, but they remained 'foreigners'.

They lived in a cottage in King Street, a steep, narrow street leading down to the Dock, an open area above the slipway. The cottages, narrow and tall, lined the street, giving the appearance of a chasm with sides leaning towards each other.

> 'Above the life-boat house were rows of houses each row higher than the other, for they had been built on the slopes of a ravine, and it was the same on the other side of the dock, only here the ground was steeper, for it rose to the edge of the North Cliff, and the houses were packed close together, with only narrow cobbled alleys running between the rows except the one called Chapel Street, which had been a cart road until part of it had fallen into the sea.'[1]

Most of the cottages were of the same design, with three, sometimes four, floors each comprising one room with a steep staircase winding from ground floor to attic. The room on the ground floor of the Walmsley cottage, leading directly on to the street, was used as the shop where Ulric's paintings were on display. His wife used to help in the shop while he was outside or in his studio painting. She was also adept at framing pictures. Leo Walmsley admired his father's skill as an artist and loved to watch him painting, although on occasions when he was required to sit as a model, he found it extremely irksome and his wriggling would soon bring about an irritable dismissal.

Sitting still also presented a problem at school. In his book *Foreigners*, Leo writes of his dislike of school because it stopped him from doing things that he liked. The schoolmaster, 'Slogger',[2] expected absolute obedience and failure to give full attention was rewarded by a sharp, stinging slap across the face. Nor did the young boy find compensation in the friendship of his classmates as he was either ignored or taunted as a 'foreigner'. Of the few other boys also regarded as outsiders, he seems to have found only one that he was prepared to accept as a friend. This boy, 'Chicken', was small …

> 'He was dirty, too, and his clothes were ragged, for his father was a drunkard, and he annoyed me by following when I didn't want him, and offering me sticky sweets or bad apples or bits of pie out of his pocket, and he always looked so sad when I wouldn't take them. Yet it was something to feel that I had any sort of friends at present.'[3]

It is amusing to learn that Leo was known by the nickname 'Worms'. The local children had to improvise when playing games as no money was available for anything other than the basic essentials of life. Cricket bats were made from driftwood and footballs were inflated ox-bladders begged from the local butcher. An exciting game was devised by attaching old perambulator wheels to a soap box and making a sail from sacking - a forerunner of land-yachting?

The impression given throughout the books is that Leo was a solitary child and this is reinforced by the fact that in the books about his childhood no reference is made to brothers and sister. One explanation could be that the storylines of the two books *Foreigners* and *Sound of the Sea* are greatly enhanced when told from the viewpoint of the solitary child. However, one would expect his autobiography *So Many Loves* to contain references to his siblings, but even here the impression is given that he was an only child, the sole focus of his parents' attention. In his book *Phantom Lobster*, he refers briefly to his mother's 'immense task of saving at least her family of three sons from Bramblewick'. She refused to allow them to wear the traditional village attire of guernseys and corduroy trousers. Instead, she insisted that they wore respectable clothing and, to their mortification, the boys were dispatched to school in 'Norfolk suits, starched Eton collars (with bows), bare knees and roll-over stockings'. She also insisted that they took bottles of water to use for cleaning their slates, instead of the time-honoured spit. She also made a valiant effort to prevent their speech from lapsing into the Bramblewick dialect. In this, she had some success as, in later years when serving in the Royal Flying Corps, Leo was so dismayed when 'ragged unmercifully' about his Yorkshire accent that he determined to change his speech and 'learnt to speak quite nicely'.

Of the few photographs of his early years that have come to light, the impression given on all of them is of a bright, cheerful boy, always smiling, frequently with a decidedly impish grin. The image is of a vivacious child, full of life, with bright, sparkling eyes. He intends to enjoy life, whereas in comparison, in one particular photograph, the other members of the family show an attitude of resignation, with their mother having a severe, slightly harassed appearance, her hands seeming to have a restraining influence on Leo's shoulders.

It becomes apparent when reading Leo's books about his childhood that his mother's influence played an important part in the development of his character. Jeannie had a very strong personality and this affected the boy in varying ways. While being slightly in awe of her and reluctant to cause anger, he was also compelled by his own determination to fight her when his wishes were adversely affected. There seems to have been a close bond between them which was lacking between father and son. However, her religious fervour became so irksome to him as he grew older that it had the contrary effect of turning him against religion as practised in most churches and chapels in that era. Doubtless his mother had very good cause for her strict attitude as he must have been a difficult child to control. His father does not figure largely as a person with lasting influence, although in Leo's early years there were occasions when a conspiratorial comradeship developed between them. Obviously they had both been at the receiving end of Jeannie's strict adherence to acceptable behaviour! So little is recorded of the early life of his brothers and sister that it is unlikely that they had any influence on his developing personality.

Left to right: Sydney, Leo and Bert, with mother (Jeannie), *by courtesy of Frances Wilson*

Although he was a typical schoolboy in most respects, wanting to join in the games and pranks of his schoolmates, less than enthusiastic about his lessons, he also had an unusually developed inquisitiveness about matters which really interested him.

'I must have been born with a strong bump of curiosity. From my earliest remembered days I wanted to find out about everything that was going on around me. As those days were spent in a village on the north-east Yorkshire coast, where there were fishermen and deep-water sailors, and boat-builders and sail-makers; where there were miles of sea-bird haunted cliffs and rocky shores (with pools that teemed with marine life, and coves the tide left strewn with flotsam and jetsam in stormy weather), it is not surprising that my curiosity was concerned about things related directly or indirectly with the sea.'[4]

His environment had a profound effect on him and these early experiences were to influence him for the rest of his life. He was never bored. He loved the open vastness of his surroundings, yearning for freedom to wander and suffered frustration from the restrictions imposed on him by his mother.

'As I grew older, and mother got a little less fussy about having me out of her sight alone, my education continued apace. True that the restrictions that she imposed upon me would have made my advancement impossible had I been obedient.'[5]

This is not his only reference to disobedience. It reveals an insight into the boy's developing personality, which was so influenced by his burning desire to delve into things which interested him. One feels the compulsion which urged him on to the point where he was oblivious to possible repercussions. Punishment and anger to him were the unfortunate consequences which had to be accepted if he was found out, but if by devious means he could avoid discovery, he would take that course with only a slight prick of conscience. His mother had imposed a 'strict list of bounds' which, had they been adhered to, would have seriously limited the boy's activities, but despite his obvious love for his parents, when he knew that they were occupied, he just went where he wanted and this was invariably seawards.

At a very early age, Leo became interested in fishing, but found that the elementary apparatus which was traditionally used as an introduction was so exasperating that he was reduced to tears. It is hardly surprising that the bent pin tackle was replaced by something more sophisticated at the earliest opportunity. He struck up a friendship with Captain Bunny, who was one of the few men of whom his mother approved. He had 'twinkling eyes and a smile for everybody' and had been master of a top-sail schooner, not a 'real fisherman'. He regarded fishing as a sport and must have perceived the eagerness which the boy showed in his determination to learn all that he could about the art of fishing. It was his patient guidance which was to a great extent responsible for a passion which remained with Leo to the end of his life. Having learned the rudiments of the art of fishing, Leo spent as much time as possible perfecting his technique, whether it was offshore in Captain Bunny's small boat, or alone on the scaurs using limpets for bait. The fascination which fishing held for him led him into numerous scrapes and near catastrophes, but also opened his eyes to the incredible variety of life in the sea and on the scaurs. These hard ironstone and limestone strata jutting out to sea were of varying height and allowed the sea to flow between them, forming creeks.

'Some of these creeks were sandy or muddy. Some had clean shale for a bed, but in all, the tide left standing pools, usually with boulders or flattish stones in them. If there was sand or mud, as in the Landing creek, you got swarms of shrimps and sand-hoppers, and of course buried in the sand, lob-worms and rag-worms. In the hard bottomed creeks there were swarms of shore-crabs. The scaurs themselves were encrusted with acorn barnacles, and there were limpets too, and small mussels, and other shell-fish. All these animals were the food of the big sea fish like cod and billet and conger, which when the tide was far out, lurked in the forest of tangle, but swam shorewards up the creek as the tide flowed.'[6]

The young boy learned how to utilise the small marine animals for bait and gradually became aware of the habits and characteristics of different fish. He used various methods of fishing and was overjoyed when he could take something back home for his mother to cook. Always it was the excitement that was his motivation and we will see that, as his personality developed through adolescence to manhood, whatever interest claimed his attention, the essential ingredient was excitement. Even as a boy he had a passion for life and this was expressed in his passion for fishing. In his autobiography *So Many Loves,* Leo refers to the thrill of anticipation which, when connected with the sea, is 'enhanced by mystery … you can never see what is going on below the surface. The probabilities may be proscribed: the possibilities are as infinite as the sea itself.'

His inquisitiveness and overwhelming enthusiasm combined to produce a fascination with nature of such intensity that his awareness of his environment became razor-sharp. Although still centred on the sea, his interests diversified as he grew older and encompassed other aspects of that coastal strip, so rich in historical and scientific values. The port of Whitby held many delights for Leo, particularly the 'graving docks' where he loved to watch the sailors at work. With their boat high and dry, they would scrape the planks and caulk the seams. Apart from what he called the 'real' ships, there were the fishing boats in summer, the herring fleets from Scotland, East Anglia and Cornwall. He was enthralled by the lively atmosphere and the variety of accents, which sounded like foreign tongues to him. His quick eyes absorbed details of the fishermen's garb, the different patterned guernseys, each village and port having its own particular design. One of the reasons for this was that, as few fishermen could swim, in the tragic event of a boat being lost, a body could be identified by the design of the guernsey. Other unusual items of clothing worn by visiting crews included Tam O'Shanters, hard-felted sou'westers and brightly coloured scarves. Sometimes he saw men with rings in their ears and long hair. The bustle and colour was a never-ending source of excitement for Leo but he felt that this would pale compared with the thrill of seeing the docks of his parents' home town, Liverpool. He listened avidly to their descriptions of that huge port, which they had left so many years ago. How he longed to see it for himself.

The chance came unexpectedly when he was ten years old. His mother was struck down by scarlet fever and Leo was sent out of the way to stay with his aunt, who lived at West Derby on the outskirts of the city. His aunt and uncle were very religious and lived in a gloomy house, which was far from Leo's idea of an exotic Liverpool. His request to be taken to the docks was greeted with horror as 'the whole place was a haunt of iniquity and sin'. The religious stories and 'nice' walks he was offered soon made him determined to escape from their watchful eyes and when the opportunity arose, he ran from the house and caught a tram to Pier Head.

> 'It was the start of a day of mounting and unbelievable joy. I could tell where the docks were by the smell of them, without the sight of masts and funnels rising above the roofs of warehouses; a smell compounded of oil and smoke and tar and spices, a smell that lingers on a ship even when she is miles from land, and is accentuated rather than overcome by the briny vapours of the open sea. There were steamers, huge ones, so close to the dock walls that you could actually touch them. Some had English names. Others were foreign and they were flying foreign flags which I had never seen before. But there was no mistaking a Japanese ship, for there were Japanese sailors on her, and I could scarcely bring myself to move on to the next ship, they were so fascinating. There were Indians, too, wearing turbans; and I saw a real Chinaman with a pigtail, although he had it coiled up under his hat, and there were dozens of negroes, although to my disappointment they wore ordinary sailors' clothes. I should have preferred to have seen them wearing animal skins, and carrying shields and spears!'[7]

He wandered around, absorbing all the wonderful sights, sounds and smells and eventually was actually invited on board a steamer whose captain came from Whitby. When at last he returned to his aunt's house, in disgrace but quite unchastened, he considered that it had been well worth it!

One can assume that Leo's curiosity was a trait passed down from his mother as she was obviously a person whose strongly held opinions had been seriously considered. The reference in *Phantom Lobster* to Jeannie's aloof attitude towards the villagers gives us an insight in to her resolve to provide her sons with an opportunity to better themselves and, with considerable foresight, she realised that a good education was the way in which this could be attained. When the time came for the two eldest boys to leave the local elementary school which she had abhorred, she had saved enough money to pay for them to attend a private school in Whitby. This was an outstanding achievement and one can imagine her, over the years, putting on one side small amounts from the sale of Ulric's 'summer visitor' paintings, watching with satisfaction as her cache grew. According to Leo, her strategy was successful and her sons 'never looked back'.

His desire for knowledge, although it did not extend to traditional school lessons, appears to have been the deciding factor in Leo being awarded a special place at Scarborough Grammar School, a condition being that he should become a teacher. Through his mother's determination, he was granted an interview with the headmaster, despite the fact that the final date for the entrance examination had passed. Jeannie Walmsley was a woman of such strength of character that she did not allow this to stand in the way of what she saw as an opportunity for her son to pursue a professional career. She therefore went to the school personally in order to argue her case. Leo's personality also had an impact on the headmaster. In *So Many Loves* he wrote:

'... he must have been a man ahead of his time as a teacher, and a shrewd psychologist. First he was very kind in his manner, so that I did not feel afraid of him: then he made me talk about dad and mother, and my life at Bramblewick, and the things I liked doing and what I wanted to be when I grew up. I told him about fishing and my collection of birds' eggs, which included a cormorant's and a cuckoo's and a sparrow hawk's, and he encouraged me by telling me that he'd collected eggs once but he'd never found a cuckoo's: and that he liked fishing only didn't often have time for it.'

Mr Tetley showed the boy around the splendidly equipped new school with science laboratories, lecture theatre, woodwork and metalwork rooms for the boys and kitchens for the girls. When he was finally taken to the library, Leo was overwhelmed by the array of books. His avid thirst for knowledge had been somewhat restricted by his mother's censorship of his reading. She had banned the Charles Darwin books which he had borrowed from the local library. He had managed to read *Voyage of the Beagle* as the title gave the impression of a boy's adventure story and was admitted into the house. Leo enthused about the book and informed Mr Tetley that he wanted to be a naturalist like Charles Darwin. When he showed interest in one of the Kearton brothers' books which was in the school library, the headmaster, to the boy's delight, told him that he could borrow it. Mr Tetley must have been a very astute man to have seen the potential in the boy and gained his confidence and respect at their first meeting. Leo admits in his autobiography that he was far from being a model pupil. He played truant for nearly a week on one occasion and forged a letter from his mother but was discovered as a result of a spelling mistake. He was no doubt in trouble on numerous occasions as he had a reputation for being mischievous. However, he held the headmaster in high esteem and it was to his lasting regret that he was unable to give tangible proof that the man's belief in him was justified. Sadly, Mr Tetley died shortly after Leo left the school. The reason for his truancy was because he had been infected by yet another enthusiasm - geology, a subject not taught at the school. There is a very illuminating passage in *So Many Loves* in which Leo muses about his interest (or lack of it) in a variety of school subjects:

'It's funny to think that what made me a failure at school was studying things like geology, and astronomy, and evolution and philosophy and other subjects which were not taught at school at all. It was not the fault of Mr Tetley or any of the other masters, who were all very kind and patient. I was not a complete failure. I actually shone in chemistry, physics, geography and woodwork, and staggered each of my form-masters in succession by being top in scripture. This delighted mother and made her much more hopeful about my future. I was consistently bottom or near bottom in most other subjects. I hated every branch of mathematics. History bored me ... I was a fool of course, and later I was to regret my wasted opportunities, for it was a good school, unique in its day.'

Had he been taught geology at school, no doubt he would have eagerly absorbed all aspects of the subject. However, being resourceful (and devious as it turned out), he did the next best thing and set out to educate himself. As a result of borrowing Lyell's *Principles Of Geology* from the local library, he became 'crazy on fossil-hunting'. He spent hours wandering along the shore searching for semi-precious stones such as amber, agates and cornelians and on one occasion made the exciting discovery of a piece of mammoth's tusk 'sixteen inches long and as thick as my arm'. As the North Yorkshire coast has a wealth of fossils in the cliffs, he had tremendous scope for practical observation. By chance, he had a very rewarding meeting with a foreign visitor to the area. This was Professor Otto Overbeck, who was professor of geology at the high school in Stuttgart and was making a special study of the ammonites of the Yorkshire Lias prior to writing a book. He was most impressed by the knowledge and enthusiasm of the teenage boy and a friendship developed between them. With his parents' permission, Leo spent Christmas 1907 on a tour of the coast with the professor, who taught him more about geology than all the books he had read. What is more, the boy noticed the professor's meticulous recording of what he found and observed, a precept which was to become a critical adjunct to his own inherent curiosity.

An interest in geology was a natural progression from the childish 'scratting' on the seashore. To be 'first on' was a very exciting prospect as, providing the tide was out, he would have the whole sweep of the bay as his own little world to explore, to search for coins and other treasures. As he grew older, he became interested in other aspects of the shore and cliffs. The composition of the strata of the cliffs reveals a wealth of prehistoric detail as the sea gradually erodes the surface of the boulder clay. Careful search yielded a variety of fossilised remains, and to a boy with such a thirst for knowledge about everything which caught his interest, it was a challenge which he willingly accepted. Other more mundane matters were relegated to the background as his developing mind craved for more information about this engrossing topic.

> 'The geological formation of this region consists chiefly of soft blue shales, very rich in iron, that were originally deposited at the bottom of a tropical or sub-tropical sea, where animal life was extraordinarily diversified and abundant. In this sea lived ferocious crocodile-like reptiles whose fossilized remains are frequently found intact in the cliffs ...'[8]

The opportunities thus offered were given a new dimension after his meeting with Professor Overbeck and he studied geology, mainly through books borrowed from the local library, with such dedication that a few years later, in 1914, he had his first book, *A Guide to the Geology of the Whitby District*, published by Horne and Son of Whitby.

It is understandable that a parallel subject should claim Leo's attention as he wandered about the locality, searching for specimens from a bygone age. On the moors which stretch miles inland from the cliffs, the boy would roam regardless of parental displeasure. Although by force of circumstances he led a solitary existence during his leisure time, this had never worried him as he could always manage to find something to engage his attention. The moors with their vastness stretching into the distance held a deep fascination for him. He had heard that there had once been a Roman fort at Ravenscar (called High Batts in his books) and that on the moors there were burial places of early Britons.

> 'I had reached the moor. I had done something I had never done before, even with dad ... I aimed for what I thought was the highest point ... A peewit was circling overhead, making its queer call and I heard a curlew calling far off. A lark was singing too, in the

air … I wasn't far off the highest point now. I was out of sight of the bay and the village, even of the sea. To right and left, and behind was nothing but moor, ahead some more stacks of turf, and I guessed that when I reached them I would be able to look down on the other side. I actually ran the last few yards.'[9]

It was during a similar excursion that Leo had found a flint arrowhead, and it needed only tangible evidence such as this to arouse his highly charged enthusiasm. The whole area was a wonderland for the boy with the realisation that here, centuries ago, had lived a race of people who had come across the sea and settled, leaving traces of their way of life which could be found by diligent searching.

His character was complex, and another feature of this is revealed in the above passage. One can accept that many children have an interest in the seashore, the rock pools and wildlife, but it must be unusual for one of such tender years to have an appreciation of beautiful scenery to the degree that Leo had, creating in him an excitement which compelled him to run the last few yards of his long climb so as to gaze on that magnificent panorama. It was, indeed, the simple things of life which appealed to him and his appreciation of the beauty and importance of the commonplace was to have far-reaching effects. Years hence, as his writing skill developed, his persuasive style drew his readers along with him so that they too saw the wonder of the commonplace.

Another interesting facet of Leo's character is revealed in *Sound of the Sea*. This shows love of animals, part of his abiding love of nature. During a particularly harsh winter, huge numbers of redwings from Russia or Scandinavia were blown off course and alighted on the roof-tops and on the shore, some appearing to literally fall from the sky. Most were in a state of exhaustion and starvation and the tender-hearted boy was desperate to help them.

'I got a basket, and lined it with bits of old blanket and picked up about a dozen redwings that were too weak to fly and hurried home with them.'[10]

He and his mother kept them warm and fed them. To his great joy, most of them revived and his sadness at the death of two of them was alleviated when his father painted a beautiful picture of them, which he regarded as one of his best.

Whilst walking on the beach one day, he found a dog which attached itself to him and an immediate friendship developed between them. He called it Gyp after a book he had read and he desperately hoped that his parents would allow him to keep it if it was not claimed. Although the owner turned up, he was eventually able to keep the dog and it proved to be a much-loved companion for him on his many expeditions on the beach and on the moors in total disregard for the bounds determined by his parents.

There are numerous references to his love of animals, but there is an apparent contradiction as he records his adventures when collecting birds' eggs as a boy and later when he writes of shooting expeditions in Africa, which he found exhilarating.

Leo's boyish adventures led him farther afield as he grew older, far beyond the imposed restrictions which were ignored when it suited him. His disobedience seems to have been a combination of his overwhelming curiosity to find out more about his surroundings and a decidedly mischievous side of his personality. It most certainly resulted in a knack of becoming involved in numerous escapades, which required an agile mind for inventing plausible excuses to extricate himself from punishment. He was described as 'a red-faced and very tiresome schoolboy' by Storm Jameson, the Whitby author who was later to become a good friend. When reviewing his book *Phantom Lobster*, she recalls the morning train journey to Scarborough.

> 'The train moved very slowly, along the coast, stopping at every village, to pick up farmers, market women with their baskets and children. The children were a noisy disruptive set, the bane of porters and stationmasters. One boy who used to join the train at Robin Hoods Bay was more mischievous than any. He was short, sturdy, brown, with <u>very</u> bright eyes. His innate wickedness impressed itself even on our own hardened spirits. One morning when the train was drawn up at the station there was a terrific crash - someone in the road had overturned a load of milk churns - the noise was frightful, like the end of the world. Without troubling to look out of the window the girl next to me exclaimed 'That will be <u>that</u> Leo Walmsley!' No one disagreed with her.'[11]

Perhaps the ready use of his imagination for self-preservation was an early sign of his skill as a storyteller. Furthermore, his reputation as a mischievous schoolboy could show the beginnings of the nonconformist part of his character which gradually became more apparent in adult life. His hatred of the strict religious attitudes of his parents during his boyhood caused him to turn in later years towards what he termed Christian humanism, and an attitude he referred to as the middle-class morality of the villagers left a deep, abiding contempt for convention.

Nona Stead

CHAPTER 2

Observe and Record

AS his schooldays came to an inauspicious end, he passed the Preliminary Certificate Examination, which qualified him to take a position as an uncertificated teacher. He had never had ambitions in this direction but in consideration for his parents' financial state, he took a position briefly as assistant teacher at Guisborough Council School (Northgate Boys) on the 8th September 1911. This is revealed in the log book of the Robin Hoods Bay Methodist School, where he commenced work on the 9th January 1912.

> 'I loathed it, and I am certain that I would have chucked it and risked breaking my mother's heart by going to sea, but for a very dramatic occurrence. The Zoological Department of Leeds and Sheffield Universities had decided to open a marine biological station in the village ... and they wanted someone to act as a sort of curator-caretaker, preferably someone who knew the beaches and who would be able to assist in the collection of specimens. I got the job. They would only pay five shillings a week, but as there were no specified hours, I could still carry on at the school.'[1]

This proved to be a turning point in his life. As we have already seen, he had an incredible depth of feeling for the sea with its wealth of plant and animal life. Now, although his position was little more than that of laboratory boy, he came into contact with men whose scientific knowledge and ability inspired him to make use of the opportunity and learn as much as he could from them. Professor Alfred Denny of the University of Sheffield and Professor Walter Garstang from the University of Leeds were dedicated men, who imparted knowledge to the zoological students attending short courses at the marine laboratory. How Leo envied those students. All he was ever expected to do was to help them collect specimens and clean up after them. He never attended the lectures despite the fact that he longed to be a 'real scientist' and it was at this point that he realised the truth of his old headmaster's reasoning that a university education was vital if he were to succeed in a scientific career.

However, his position at the laboratory was to prove to be a landmark in his life. He now had the opportunity to develop his interest in marine life, making it more of a scientific study than it had been hitherto. With the advent of a senior student to undertake important research work, his life entered a new phase. This student was Sam, later to become Dr S E Wilson, who erupted into Leo's life 'with a greater force than any love affair'. Samuel Edward Wilson was an extremely forceful person, described by Leo as a 'tornado', who immediately offered very sound advice that Leo should:

> 'Read and listen to what other people said, but don't take anything for gospel until you could prove it for yourself. Be sceptical. Always keep your mind alert. Beware of dogma.'[2]

Leo was bewildered and somewhat overwhelmed by the exuberance of the newcomer, but soon became very excited by what he saw and heard. Sam had come to research *Doto coronata*, a sea-slug, and a parasitic crustacean which had selected it as its host. This hardly seems to be the most interesting of topics, but it was not long before Leo became enthralled as Sam opened a large book with coloured plates showing this and other similar marine animals. He was amazed at their beauty of form and colour and found it difficult to believe that these beautiful creatures actually existed in the scaurs and rock pools of his own bay. Typically his enthusiasm took wing and he 'had a glamorous vision of myself as a marine biologist to an expedition to the South Seas'.

The serious work began when they started to explore the scaurs, searching for specimens. Leo, knowing all the creeks and pools, was confident that he would be able to show his new friend where he was likely to find the creatures he was looking for and was mortified when Sam discovered a sea-slug in a narrow fissure in one of the scaurs. How could a man 'who had lived far away from the sea all his life come on to my own scaurs and straight away find something I had never seen'? As Sam continued to reveal the fauna to be found in the crevices, Leo realised that he had been missing a great deal which had always been there before his eyes.

> 'I was amazed, and not a little ashamed. Here indeed was the exemplification of the nursery fable of 'eyes and no eyes.' And to think that I was being shown all this on my own scaurs by a landsman.'[3]

However, he applied himself to the task before them, intent on learning all that he could and was soon completely absorbed. That remarkable curiosity was once more in evidence, for he had found a new interest about which he knew so little and his whole being was concentrated on acquiring every possible piece of information.

There is no doubt that Leo admired Sam, holding on to his every word. To a youth whose life had been restricted to the village and nearby communities, Sam must have given the impression of a man of the world, self-confident and sophisticated. Small wonder that Leo was excited about the new opportunities which opened before him. The contrast in their upbringings and early lives and the resultant attitude of Leo towards Sam leads one towards the assumption that Sam was several years Leo's senior. In fact, he was little more than a year older. We know that he was eighteen years old in 1909, when he entered Sheffield University. He received his BSc Zoology, which he was awarded in 1912, and went on to study for an MSc Zoology, which he was awarded in 1913. It is likely that it was this course of study which took him to the marine laboratory at Robin Hoods Bay. He eventually became an eminent scientist.

We have already seen how, as a young boy, Leo was fascinated by what was going on around him. As he grew towards manhood, he still retained that excitement, which had always enveloped him when finding anything new or when setting out to explore his favourite haunts. But childish excitement developed into a stronger emotion and his personality was enhanced by an incredible zest for life. The early signs revealed in the child were to become a vital part of the character of the man. What is more, his writing throughout his career is coloured by this zest for life to the extent that the reader is caught up by his infectious enthusiasm.

His teaching career continued its dreary but necessary way. By this time, he had become acquainted with a family who had settled in Robin Hoods Bay, having moved from a village farther down the coast. The father was a fisherman and two of the sons were scholars at the school. As they, too, were regarded as 'foreigners', a friendship developed which was to be of great significance to Leo's personal life and also to his future literary career. He referred to them in his books as Henry Lunn and sons John and Marney, although in fact their surname was Duke. From the beginning of their acquaintance, fishing had been the mutual interest which drew them together. Also Leo was tolerant and amused when the boys were absent from school, knowing that they were playing truant, as he had done a few years ago, to go fishing or bird-nesting. After a while, he noticed a slight diffidence in Henry's attitude towards him and realised that it was because he was a schoolmaster and 'hob-nobbing' with the strangers at the laboratory.

> 'There was no doubt that I was getting a bit superior, especially as I was now wearing, except on collecting expeditions, the flannel bags, the tweed sports coat, the open sports shirt, the fancy socks and brogues affected by male laboratory students and by Sam himself.'[4]

There is an early indication here of a sophistication which was to become apparent in a few years' time. At this age, there was no conflict between his love of nature and the simple things of life on one side and aspiration to appear worldly-wise on the other. The students with whom he was mixing had a similar outlook, although at this stage it must be admitted that he had to work harder at appearing to be sophisticated. He was motivated further in the creation of a new image as he had become infatuated by one of the girl students, Adeline. He admired from a distance, dreaming dreams yet hoping to impress, but unfortunately his calf-love was not reciprocated. The only occasion on which he thought he was making some headway ended ignominiously. A young man in a Leeds University blazer appeared with bike and sidecar and Adeline greeted him with surprise and delight, leaving Leo to face 'the pain and bitterness of my disillusionment'.

He and Sam had several rather jolly meetings with two girls from 'up-bank', who were pleased to join them for evening walks and occasionally singing popular songs of the day or hymns. The girls kept a close guard on each other and it remained 'an innocent friendship, our behaviour a model of Victorian respect-ability'. It is rather amusing to read a letter written to Sam about twenty years later in which Leo muses that because of a lack of parental instruction and 'such a blasted taboo round sex, that it's a wonder I didn't get half the girls in Bay in the family way before I was sixteen!'

Whatever other interests he may have had, there is no doubt that at this stage of his life Leo's preoccupation was with marine biology. Under Sam Wilson's guidance, he learned the importance of observing carefully and then recording in detail whatever he had seen. He followed this advice diligently and it soon became so automatic that he approached other aspects of life in the same meticulous way.

From this time on, he concentrated on all forms of study with the precision and attention to detail of the scientist. He became, in fact, a trained observer. Although he progressed satisfactorily with the practical side of his work, it soon became evident that the academic side was beyond his capability as he 'lacked the power to assimilate and remember facts'.

Sam decided that it was time to think very seriously about Leo's future. Therefore one evening they sat down to discuss the matter, Sam with a sheet of foolscap in front of him on which he started to make notes. He divided the sheet vertically and headed one side Credit and the other Debit. Several items were quickly listed on the Credit side, but on the Debit side the words 'Academic qualifications - Nil' were starkly depressing and an unusual silence enveloped the pair. Suddenly, Sam had a moment of inspiration which was to change Leo's life. The thought had occurred to him that an angle of science which they had ignored was the growing interest in popular science such as nature stories and the Kearton brothers' books. Leo could write about the marine animals with which he had become so familiar.

> 'Popular science, my boy. Writing. Articles, stories, books. There's a growing interest in science. Ever read any of those nature stories by Bensusan and St. Mars? And what about Kearton books? Don't think either of the Keartons have any academic qualifications. But don't cut into their market. Write about the things you know. Marine animals. You know the facts. Make 'em popular. You'd soon get a reputation as a naturalist. You'd make brass. Might make enough to finance your own expedition one day. South seas, anywhere. You ought to learn photography, illustrate your own articles and books.'[5]

Leo protested in vain that he could not write, but Sam dismissed any argument, insisting that he would have no difficulty in writing an article which holiday-makers from inland towns would be delighted to read as it would enliven their holiday activities. Despite being somewhat overwhelmed by this hitherto undreamed of suggestion, Leo gradually began to accept the sense of what Sam was saying. His knowledge of the area was comprehensive, having been acquired gradually over the years and developed under the guidance of professors Denny and Garstang. With the arrival of Sam Wilson and his insistence on making full use of his observational and recording skills, Leo had moved from amateur to serious scientific study. His frustration at realising that his academic ability was insufficient to allow him to read science at university had been tormenting him for months. The idea of writing about his favourite topic had a twofold appeal. Not only would it provide (hopefully) a living for him, but it would also eliminate the need for further study of what he considered to be the duller side of his zoological studies. He began to feel profoundly excited.

With his usual enthusiasm, he eagerly started to plan an article and to his delight and amazement found that 'it was easy.' His first article entitled *The Geology of the Whitby District* was accepted for publication and appeared in the *Whitby Gazette* on Friday the 25th July 1913. It was followed the next year by a thirty-six-page handbook, *A Guide to the Geology of the Whitby District,* referred to earlier. This was printed by the owners of the *Whitby Gazette*, Horne and Son of Whitby.

There is no doubt that Sam Wilson played a most important part in Leo Walmsley's life. He not only influenced him in his choice of career but was also responsible for the direction it took. In effect, it was his enthusiastic attitude to what had initially been a childhood hobby which revealed how first-hand knowledge could be developed into a serious command of the subject. It must be emphasised at this point, however, that without the necessary application and tenacity on Leo's part, Sam's inspired idea would have come to naught. Equally, it must be stressed that there were also several other ingredients which combined to produce writing of exceptional depth and quality. The events of his childhood, the wonderful variety of characters around him, the wild, romantic landscape provided him with the material for his Bramblewick stories and novels and inspired him to develop his own very individual style which weaves together the threads of fact and fiction.

By this time in his life, the boyhood interest and fascination with nature had taken a step forward. Writing many years later, he insists that his interest in natural history had always been that of the 'enthusiastic amateur, and never academic'.[6] His passion for collecting began with fossils, followed by marine animals and later by flints fashioned into arrow heads, scrapers and knives. He was incredibly fortunate that the area abounded in all these items. From time to time the cliffs surrendered remarkable specimens of fossil reptiles such as ichthyosaurus and plesiosaurus. The scaurs were one of the richest grounds in Britain for small animals and the surrounding moors were scattered with hundreds of tumuli.

He had expanded his ability to look around and regard with wonder those simple things which most people accepted without thought. He had, in fact, acquired that zest for life which his friends and acquaintances recognised as a vital part of his personality. What is more remarkable is the way in which it coloured his writing so that his depth of feeling is communicated to the reader.

> 'It was all so fascinating that I almost forgot that I was after crabs and lobsters. Stranded by the ebb were dozens of big prickly sea urchins, and starfish, some like the ones you could find under stones on a neap tide, with five arms, only much bigger, and some coloured like ripe strawberries, that had thirteen arms and were as big as dinner-plates. In the crevices among the weed which still contained water were huge anemones, the ones that the fishermen sometimes used as bait for winter cod-fishing and called scarcocks. They were more beautiful than any flowers.'[7]

Walmsley was 'as proud as a turkey-cock' when, as a result of his first interview with Harry Horne, the elder of the two brothers owning the *Whitby Gazette*, he was invited to write as many natural history articles as he liked for a payment of ten shillings each. He felt that he had got his foot on the ladder. His jubilation was crushed a few weeks later, when Sam informed him of the possibility of a post in the Malay states. Leo was incredulous when Sam was less than enthusiastic. How could anyone possibly turn down a chance to travel to the East? It was just what he had dreamed of and when Sam remarked that he would have been a far more suitable candidate if only he had a degree, he immediately started to consider a return to serious study. As the position had to be filled later that summer of 1914, they discussed the possibility of Sam taking the post and then appointing Leo as his assistant.

It was not to be, but the seeds were sown and the urge to travel to foreign parts became an obsession. This was exacerbated by meeting one of Sam's fellow students, Roland Deakin, who had been appointed as an assistant entomologist in British East Africa. How Leo envied these two men with their opportunities for foreign travel, although he accepted that it had been made possible as a result of their academic qualifications. It was yet another grim reminder of his own wasted opportunities. The three young men spent several happy days on the beach, sharing some exciting fishing experiences, one of which made a lasting impression on Leo. He dedicated *The Green Rocket,* published in 1926, to Roland with a somewhat unusual reference:

To
ROLAND H. DEAKIN,
IN MEMORY OF
A FAMOUS LOBSTER HUNT AT
ROBIN HOOD'S BAY
AND IN GRATEFUL APPRECIATION
OF AN
UNFAILING FRIENDSHIP,
MUCH KINDLY CRITICISM
AND
INSPIRING ENCOURAGEMENT.

All too soon Roland had to leave in order to make preparations for his departure to East Africa. Leo felt 'horribly depressed' and wondered if they would ever meet again.

> 'Little did I guess as the train moved out on that sunny morning in July of the year nineteen hundred and fourteen that in less than eighteen months I should be lying in the next bed to Roland in a military hospital in Nairobi, Roland then a member of The East African Volunteer Force suffering from dysentery, myself, an officer of The Royal Flying Corps recovering from the effects of my first crash.'[8]

July 1914 was a time of uncertainty and major upheavals in Europe and beyond, but in the towns and villages of England these happenings were of little concern to the ordinary people. How could they be affected by the machinations of politicians in countries of which they had little knowledge?

Leo had been appointed curator at the laboratory and still held his position as assistant master at the village school. But the declaration of war on the 4th August 1914 changed everything. No longer could he remain in what he considered a mundane situation. His country needed him and exciting opportunities were being offered by his country's leaders. Like so many young men of his generation, he responded with an eagerness which combined patriotism with his longing for adventure. On Thursday, the 10th September, he enlisted in the army at Whitby.

Nona Stead

PART TWO

WAR SERVICE 1914–1919

CHAPTER 3

Passage to the Front

THE Great War of 1914-1918 had been over for a quarter of a century when Leo Walmsley wrote 'On the whole the war was kind to me'.[1] He was not forgetting the bad times and remembering only the good times. He had always recognised and been grateful for the fact that it had allowed him to escape from a way of life that was becoming increasingly tedious and had given him opportunities beyond his wildest dreams.

When he enlisted in 1914, he could not have foreseen the horrors the war would bring nor imagine the ordeals he would have to face but, from the outset, he had felt that he was embarking on the adventure of a lifetime and nothing was going to stop him from enjoying it. He was determined to make the best of whatever Fate should have in store for him.

Dissatisfied with his job and the claustrophobic atmosphere of village life, he had for some time wanted to break out, to travel, to see the world. Now his chance had come. He could satisfy this pressing need and also gain the sort of experience he felt essential for a would-be writer. Only far from home would he find the material for the books he would write. The wonderful world he intended to explore and conquer would offer many new facets to gaze upon. Strange places and different people would excite his imagination. Believing this, he hurried to join Kitchener's New Army. Ironically, it was to be many years before he discovered that his success as a novelist was to depend on his returning to what was familiar and to a way of life that had made him the sort of man he was. Had Walmsley been sent to the Western Front, his romantic notion of what service overseas could mean would not have lasted very long but luckily he went to Africa with the Royal Flying Corps and a very different war from the one in France. Even so, ahead of him was danger, disease and terrible hardship. He was to know fear and to meet with a number of terrifying experiences before being invalided out. Yet hardly had the last shots been fired when, confined to a hospital bed, he began to write.

In *An Airman's Experiences in East Africa,* which appeared in serial form in *Blackwood's Magazine* in 1919 and 1920, Walmsley told his own story. He wrote in a light-hearted vein, giving the impression that it had all been an amusing adventure. Nevertheless, he had witnessed the unbelievably dreadful conditions faced by soldiers on the ground and, when comparing his own lot with theirs, he declares 'ours was a soft enough job'. This was an incredible understatement. Much has been written of trench warfare on the Western Front but no less terrible in its own way was the frustrating and gruelling struggle to defeat an elusive and brilliantly led enemy force in a campaign covering thousands of square miles of difficult and pestilential bush and jungle in east and central Africa. No one in the East African campaign had a 'soft job'.

Walmsley was nearly twenty-two years old when on the 4th August 1914, England declared war on Germany. What, so far, had he done with his life? Since leaving school he had been a pupil-teacher and part-time laboratory assistant. Teaching was for him a job, not a vocation. In the laboratory he was a technician, rather than the scientist he would have loved to have been. His boyish enthusiasms had developed into serious hobbies, even giving him the chance to earn a little money but, lacking formal training, he was still no more than an amateur. The feeling that he was capable of so much more meant that a sense of frustration coloured his attitude to his work and to life. As long as he remained in the village, he would be discontented. If only he had acquired a university education. If only he had money. If only something would turn up. And, as if in answer to his silent prayers, the war had come to his rescue.

When it came, Walmsley saw it as his duty to join up. His country needed him: it was a matter of honour. Within weeks he had enlisted and, like so many others, he feared the war would be over before he was in it. For him, simple concepts like 'duty' and 'patriotism' had strong appeal but he also sensed that his life might now take a new and more purposeful direction. Here was a chance to discover what he could achieve. On the 10th September, Lionel Walmsley took the oath of allegiance which was, perhaps, the most momentous step he took in all his seventy-four years.

* * *

It is not known why — or indeed if — he elected to serve with the Royal Army Medical Corps, but it would have been in his character to have wanted to succour and heal his fellow countryman rather than slaughter the enemy. Arriving at Aldershot on the 18th September, he was soon intoxicated by the good humour and cheerfulness of his comrades in arms. His letters home and to the local paper reveal that this happy frame of mind continued throughout his training in first aid and ambulance work at Sheffield. There he found the officers 'all fine' as they appeared to spare 'no pains ... to make us comfortable and happy'. 'One thing is certain', he wrote, 'there's not a man in the 33rd. [Field Ambulance unit] who regrets enlisting.'[2] And, having listened to stories of 'fiendish Hun atrocities' told by wounded soldiers, he wrote with apparent conviction 'we're fighting for civilization.' However, underlying this initial patriotic fervour was a deeper and longer-lasting excitement, for here was what he had been looking for: the opportunity for self-fulfilment.

Always ready to put pen to paper, he wrote home at length, describing his early days in the army. His style, full of contrived humour and unalloyed patriotism, now seems slightly ridiculous but his enthusiasm for his training reflected that eagerness to learn something new which had always been with him and would never fade. With the rapid expansion of the armed forces, it had soon become apparent that there was a grave shortage of commissioned and non-commissioned officers and almost any recruit found to have a reasonable standard of education was regarded as potentially useful officer material. Walmsley was made lance corporal on the 4th November and a full corporal two weeks later. On the 12th April 1915, he was gazetted as temporary second lieutenant in the third battalion,

East Yorkshire Regiment. The *Whitby Gazette* commented upon this under the headline: 'Robin Hood's Bay Man's Quick Promotion'.[3]

After this promotion and further training, Walmsley discovered that men were required by the Royal Flying Corps for training as pilots and observers and lost no time in volunteering. It had been suggested that all volunteers taken by the RFC started training as pilots and those found lacking in the qualities required were diverted to observer training. However, Walmsley seems to have been directed to observer training from the start and many years later he stated that it had been an irresistible desire to see what the land looked like from the air 'more than the obvious thrills of flying'[4] that attracted him to the Royal Flying Corps. But, whatever influenced this decision, it was undoubtedly the right one. Unaware of what the future held for him, Walmsley had from a very early age cultivated not only a keen awareness of his surroundings but the ability to interpret their significance. His natural curiosity had never allowed him to see anything he did not understand without making a determined effort to discover its secrets. Moreover, he could use a camera and could sketch with ease. He had developed most of the interpretive skills of a trained observer before joining the Royal Flying Corps. Even so, he now had to adapt them to landscapes seen from an entirely new perspective - from the air.

As a newly commissioned officer, Walmsley was on probation and in his autobiographical book *So Many Loves* he reveals a curious insight into his own character and the class distinctions of the time:

> 'Most of these men were public school and university. They ragged me unmercifully about my Yorkshire accent. I hated it because I didn't know I'd got one. But I discovered in the end that words like last and mast and fast have a long and not a short *a* … and in the end I believe I learnt to speak quite nicely.'

Not until October 1915 was Walmsley seconded to the Royal Flying Corps at Fort Grange, Gosport, Hampshire and attached to a training squadron. He was very impressed by the thoroughness of his training and wrote later, in an article published on the 27th October 1918 in the *Chicago Daily News,* that 'the observer must prove himself proficient in aerial fighting, artillery co-operation, map reading, sketching and photography'. In the same article, he also describes the sort of thing an observer had to watch out for. Among other things, this 'super detective' had to be aware of the effects of camouflage and notice those little changes in Nature which gave clues to the presence of troops on the ground. This article was one of several he wrote about this time explaining to the layman something of life in the Royal Flying Corps. Doubtless, their authenticity benefited as much from his wartime experience as from his initial training.

Having heard of the arrival in England of the South African Aviation Corps, some of whom had flown on the Western Front and also been involved in the brief encounter to overcome German West Africa, Walmsley went on to discover that, after a period of further training, they were to return to Africa. Furthermore, they were short of observers, so after completing his own training, he applied for a transfer to the South African contingent being re-formed as No 26 (South African) Squadron. He and another observer, with whom he struck up a close friendship, were elated at having their applications granted. They joined the squadron at Netheravon, Wiltshire, to be granted leave the following day to buy their tropical kit in London. What they purchased was left to themselves but the well-intentioned advice from friends, although plentiful, was full of contradictions. They accepted that a good helmet was needed as protection against the sun but they remained uncertain whether to stock up with quinine or whisky to ward off malaria. Shorts were assumed to be appropriate whereas long trousers would have afforded far more protection.

Returning to Netheravon, they learned that the squadron's imminent departure for East Africa had been postponed. Although their machines - the word usually used to describe their aeroplanes - were packed and on their way to Southampton Docks, two ancient machines were put at the squadron's disposal and a few more practice flights were possible when the persistent rain stopped. With a pilot he called 'Deerslayer', Walmsley took off to reconnoitre every railway line radiating from Salisbury station for a distance of twenty miles (32km). Of this trip he wrote:

> 'Half a mile below, the river Avon meandered snake-like towards Salisbury, a vein of lead inlaid into the dark green of sodden grasslands. Away to the west the watery sun was making an early departure into a billowy bed of reddened storm clouds. The lofty spire of Salisbury Cathedral made a conspicuous landmark to the south. Soon we sighted Stonehenge and flew right over it. I thought of the ancient Druids and their mysterious cult and it struck me that if they could see us now, like some giant bird above their heads, it would cause them to think as furiously about us as their mad circle of stones has generations of scientists. In all it would be a fitting vengeance of the Present on the Past.'[5]

Walmsley had already found history and archaeology absorbing subjects for study, but his reading had also included many nineteent- century adventure stories and at this stage in his attempt to become a writer, he shows the influence such reading had on his literary style. The picture of the English countryside he paints in his words is too colourful for modern taste but perhaps there was an excuse. It had been an emotional moment and he went on to say 'In a few days time England would be but a memory only.' Little did he suspect that it was a memory that would have to sustain him for two and a half long years.

*   *   *

The delay did not last long and on the 23rd December 1915 the squadron headed for Southampton. The vehicle convoy included light (Crossley) tenders and heavy (Leyland) lorries because the squadron had to be completely self-supporting. Their machines, canvas hangers, weapons, fuel, spare parts and maintenance equipment were going to be moved from one base to another across a large part of the African continent. The troopship awaiting them was the *Trafford Hall,* a small converted liner of 5,321 tons gross, on charter to the government. Walmsley was disappointed: he had often seen vessels nearly as large off Whitby and had been hoping for something much more magnificent. Almost alongside the stately *Aquitania,* now a hospital ship, dwarfed the *Trafford Hall.* After only one night onshore they hardly expected to be ordered on board on Christmas Day of all days but, as Walmsley wrote, 'It was a case of making the best of a bad job, which we ably did.'

The following day, the weather was atrocious. The only excitement was seeing a cross-Channel boat, laden with troops, forced to return to harbour, unable to make headway against the heavy weather. When, according to Walmsley, 'Darkness had fallen on the wettest and most miserable Boxing Day I had ever known', he joined those trying to organise 'as convivial evening as was possible under the very distressing circumstances'. However, to their dismay, they were informed that they would be sailing immediately. 'The deck', he noted, 'was cheerless enough a place in all conscience, but one had to have a last look at one's country even if the view consisted only of an unlovely black mass of brick warehouses and gaunt ugly chimney stacks.' Out they all came and the men started singing *The Anchor's Weighed* and *Tipperary*, with the surrounding ships taking up the choruses. This informal concert ended with *God Be With You Till We Meet Again*. 'It was simply wonderful', wrote Walmsley, philosophically, 'the farewell of soldier to soldier. Even to the man who will have nothing of religion there is something about an occasion like this that reaches down to his soul and strikes a chord whose existence he would previously have denied'.[6]

With an 'insolent hoot', the tug cast them off and for a while, in the lee of the land, they watched the flashing of signal lamps and the occasional sweep of searchlights. Soon they were in the open sea, darkness all around them, pitching and rolling down channel, the rain and spray obliterating all beyond the saloon windows.

Entertainment was forgotten as seasickness took its toll of nearly everyone. Walmsley, a seasoned sailor, did not go below immediately but enjoyed the exhilaration and excitement of departure. When he did retire, there was so much loose gear chasing back and forth across the cabin floor that he got very little sleep; he was glad to get on deck the next morning as below deck even he began to feel affected by the unceasing movement of the ship. Invigorated by fresh air, he preferred to admire the magnificent spectacle of a brave ship battling against raging seas. Finding words inadequate, out came his sketch book.

Nevertheless, Walmsley kept a journal of his voyage, entering everything of note, from the problem of shaving while the ship rolled to his impressions as he first set eyes on foreign lands. So violent were the seas that the small escorting warship soon bowed out on the assumption, Walmsley conjectured hopefully, that in such weather there was no fear of submarine attack. Beyond Brest, the gale moderated so that the Bay of Biscay seemed actually to welcome them. It was time to get to know his fellow travellers.

'Our crowd consisted of South Africans (many of them Dutch), a few East Africans and the remainder, like myself, who had joined up from other Squadrons. Most of the South Africans had gone through the German South West campaign under our present Commanding Officer [Major G. P. Wallace] and many were still tanned by the desert sun. Of the East Africans the District Commissioner [2nd Lt F. W. Brett formerly an Assistant District Commissioner] and the Hunter [assumed to be 2nd Lt W. D. M. Bell, a renowned shot and big game hunter] had both come home specially to learn to fly and from all accounts they'd learned it very well. Another East African had been rather badly mixed up with a Jack Johnson [a 5.9 inch anti-aircraft shell] with the result that he was still suffering from shell-shock.'[7]

Very eager to find out what might be in store for him, Walmsley plied these South Africans with question after question. They already knew something of the fighting qualities of the askaris led by their German officers but put at six months the maximum duration of the forthcoming campaign to clear Africa of her last remaining German colony. Out came the maps for the 'District Commissioner' to point to Mount Kilimanjaro, at the foot of which lay Taveta, now in German hands, but where he had once been stationed. They were not to know that this would be the first area over which they would be flying and the point from which the army would begin its thrust into German East Africa. Walmsley found that these taciturn South Africans had something of a Yorkshireman's 'hear all, say nowt' philosophy but few could resist his genuine interest in them and their flying experiences. Later he was to fly with some of these pilots and got to know them well: — captains Creed, Turner and Van der Spuy; lieutenants Clisdal and Emmett and second lieutenants Albu, Bertram, Brett and Howard.

The shipboard New Year's Eve concert produced a lot of unsuspected talent and the morning 'its usual crop of aching heads'. Two days later, at 5am, land was sighted. It was no longer cold and in thin night attire they rushed on to the deck to see and smell the beauty of Las Palmas. There in the harbour, much to Walmsley's surprise, was a Whitby ship. She proved to be the *Hawsker*, whose skipper, Captain John Mills, was an old friend from Robin Hoods Bay. For the troop ship, it was only a coaling stop but Walmsley managed to get ashore and then to the *Hawsker* to exchange news of home.

On the 11th January, a visit from *Neptune* ensured that even in wartime 'crossing the line' was a ceremony for the initiated to enjoy and the 'victims' to remember. A few days later, the dramatic scenery of Table Mountain came into view but, to the disappointment of all, they sailed on past the cape. To preserve the memory of this awe-inspiring coast, Walmsley committed it to his sketch pad. They did, however, stop at Durban, which they reached on the 22nd January, and Walmsley managed to go ashore. Having filled his mind with images of darkest Africa as portrayed in the adventure stories of his youth, the modern town and cultivated surroundings were a sad disappointment, but he had not much longer to wait for his expectations to be realised. On the last day of January 1916 the troop ship dropped anchor in the wonderful land-locked harbour of Kilindini, the port for Mombasa. They had arrived in East Africa. Here the unknown awaited them all but the excitement of the men as they disembarked left little room for any nervous speculation.

Once ashore, the RFC contingent under the command of Major G P Wallace, a South African, was directed immediately to the Uganda Railway terminal. From there, it was a painfully slow journey to Voi, where the squadron would transfer to the new military railway taking them to Myubuni. They were about 120 miles (190km) inland and within sight of the snow-capped mountain of Kilimanjaro which rose nearly 20,000 feet (6,000m) above them and dominated the skyline for many miles around. The uncomfortable journey had not ended until late in the afternoon of the next day so it was a relief to see a camp ready to welcome them and a newly prepared aerodrome.

The need for aerial reconnaissance over enemy lines was becoming increasingly urgent but it was several days before the aeroplanes came up from Mombasa and then, to add to the frustration, it was discovered that the propellers for the BE2cs were missing. The six spares, one of which was broken, were not the right type but had to be modified to fit. Improvisation was something they were going to have to get used to very quickly, and within eight days of their arrival, they were ready to test the first machine. The test flight, early the following morning, also became the squadron's first aerial reconnaissance over enemy territory. For this doubtful honour, the two lightest airmen were selected to go so, with Second Lieutenant Lionel Walmsley as the observer, Captain G S Creed took off. After only just clearing the trees at the end of the airstrip, it took them nearly half an hour to reach 600 feet (180m). The thrill and excitement felt by Walmsley as he looked down on Africa for the first time could not hide the fact that not only had the aircraft to prove itself, but both he and his pilot had an important job to do. The engine was misfiring regularly but they carried on, to be met by machine gun and rifle fire over Salaita Hill. It was annoying to have no effective means of retaliation but Walmsley emptied the magazine of his Colt automatic in the direction of the enemy's trenches. He was to discover later that his 'attack' was described by a German journalist as 'heavy machine-gun fire'! On the flight back, a complete engine failure occurred a quarter of a mile from the aerodrome but they glided to a perfect landing and to safety. It was the 10th February 1916 and the squadron's operations against the enemy had begun.

The war in Africa had already been going on in rather a half-hearted way for eighteen months. What had been happening during this period? At what stage in the fighting were aeroplanes introduced and with what sort of machines had No 26 (SA) Squadron been equipped? What was the nature of their task? These are questions which need to be considered if Walmsley's service with the RFC in East Africa is to be seen in its true perspective.

The plight of the German colonies in Africa was seen as virtually hopeless from the outset. They were surrounded by alien territory but their small standing armies, mainly African askaris with German officers, were well trained and boasted a fair number of machine guns although most of their rifles were ancient. Because they were effectively isolated from the Fatherland by the British Navy, the Germans could muster additional troops only from the native population and would soon face the serious problem of replacing ammunition and adding to their weaponry. They succumbed fairly quickly in Togoland, Cameroon and South-West Africa, but in German East Africa, thanks to their military commander, their meagre resources were marshalled in a very much more effective manner. They were quick to improvise, readily adapted to living off the land, made a point of capturing ammunition and weapons whenever possible and were comforted by the fact that no naval blockade of such an extensive coastline had ever been completely successful. Most of the advantages lay with the British Expeditionary Force for, although it took time and inefficiencies abounded, this force could be kept supplied with most of what it needed to fight the war. Moreover, the British could offer their wounded, sick and war-weary soldiers rest in pleasant areas within their colonies which the war had hardly touched and could bring in trained reinforce-ments to maintain, and even increase, the strength of their armies in the field. The outcome was inevitable.

Even so, the Germans in East Africa were to give the British far more trouble than they expected. Their commander, Colonel, later General, Paul Emil von Lettow-Vorbeck, was an exceptional man. Knowing that he could never defeat the British, he reasoned — correctly — that if he could employ tactics that would keep a large number of British and Colonial troops tied up and unavailable for transfer to the Western Front — where the main battle for supremacy was being fought — he would be rendering the Fatherland an invaluable service. Initially, as the war in Europe was draining allied resources almost to breaking point, the British were unwilling to give the East African 'sideshow' a very high priority. This played into Lettow-Vorbeck's hands and he took the initiative and moved into British territory, occupying the small town of Taveta and a few strategic points nearby. From here, he was within striking distance of the Uganda Railway, which ran from Mombasa to Nairobi and beyond. These attacks on British soil met with considerable success and were acutely embarrassing to the British. Engines, rolling stock and tracks were blown up in hit-and-run raids and the native workforce terrorised.

As early as November 1914, the British had planned to stop Lettow-Vorbeck by landing a large force, mainly Indian, at Tanga, an important town, port and rail terminal on the German East African coast, about eighty miles (130km) south of Mombasa. This attempt to regain the initiative and force the Germans to surrender became a complete fiasco. After suffering heavy losses and abandoning most of its weapons, the demoralised invading force fled back to its boats. This shameful episode in the history of the British army appalled the War Office. It sacked the general but the damage had been done. The Germans helped themselves to large quantities of modern weapons and ammunition. Later, they added to their fire power by managing to salvage ten 4.1-inch (10cm) guns from the *Konigsberg,* the Imperial German Navy's cruiser put out of action on the East African coast by the British Navy in July 1915. Not until the arrival of the South African General Jan Smuts in February 1916 did the initiative pass into British hands.

At Mombasa the *Trafford Hall* had not been the only ship unloading. reinforcement troops — many from South Africa — and large quantities of equipment were amassed at the railhead to be swept inland by train. But the arrival of No 26 (SA) Squadron of the Royal Flying Corps was a new and vital contribution to the revitalised army soon to be put at Smuts' disposal

*   *   *

The squadron's strength consisted of twenty-eight officers, twenty NCOs and 161 men divided into three flights, each with at least three operational aircraft, but rarely, if ever, could the squadron boast these numbers. In fact, their active strength abroad never seems to have exceeded 100 men although the numbers on every station were augmented as officers found native servants indispensable and other natives were employed for all menial tasks. Only eight aircraft, BE2cs with seventy-horsepower engines, accompanied the squadron to Africa but three months later a consignment of eight Henri Farman F27s arrived. Both types of aircraft had been developed before the war at a time when reconnaissance and spotting for the artillery were regarded as the only feasible roles for military aircraft. They were not designed to carry machine guns or bombs and when these were added as an afterthought, they impaired the aircrafts' already unremarkable flying qualities.

The BE2cs and Henri Farmans had two cockpits, with the observer occupying the front one, but in the Henri Farman, with its engine and propeller mounted behind the wings, the observer had an unimpeded view from the very front of the forward-projecting nacelle. Both aircraft were very slow and on the Western Front the BE2c acquired a notorious reputation as 'Focker fodder'. Even so, in the hands of a few of the more skilled pilots, it managed to do some very useful work before better aircraft became available. The Henri Farmans, with their more reliable and 140-horsepower engines, were no faster but, with a framework of steel tubing, were more robust than the usual wood-framed aircraft and could carry more weight. Slow and not conspicuously successful in France, the Henri Farmans had been relegated to training duties. It was no secret to Walmsley and the rest of the squadron that their machines were 'obsolescents' from the Western Front. The seventy-horsepower engine of the BE2cs gave them a maximum speed of about 65mph but all accepted that the machine was easy to fly and inherently stable. These characteristics, together with the machine's light construction, were to prove a blessing in disguise as the pilots gained experience of flying conditions in Africa. In fact, such was its stability that on a steady course it could be flown 'hands off'. If the engine failed, which it often did, it could be controlled to glide steadily earthwards. Even if a forced landing over dense jungle became necessary, the stick could be eased back when the canopy of trees was but a few feet away and with a bit of luck the aeroplane would make a soft pancake landing in the tree tops. The machine would then crumple and slowly fall before coming to rest. Pilot and observer were then free to climb down suffering, perhaps, more in mind than body.

When giving an account of his experiences in *Flying and Sport in East Africa,* which Blackwood published in 1920, Walmsley refers almost exclusively to the exploits of the BE2cs. It was in this type of aircraft that he carried out almost all his reconnaissance work. He expressed a strong dislike for Henri Farmans because 'for one thing it is horribly cold and again the observer's seat is a particularly uncomfortable one'. Nor, in his experience, did the wider field of view it gave compensate for the feeling of vulnerability. He felt free to voice his opinion, safe in the knowledge that, as his small stature and light weight made him far more suitable as an observer in the under-powered BE2c, he would rarely be called to fly in Henri Farmans. To read Walmsley's book is to gain the impression that most of the work of the RFC was done by BE2cs. But Captain Van der Spuy, who, fifty years on, wrote an autobiography, *Chasing the Wind* (1966), and included a chapter on his service with the RFC in Africa, stated 'With the exception of the few Navy Voisins and some BE2c's … the same old Henry (sic) Farmans we had used in the South-West African campaign did the main job.'

But this assertion by Van der Spuy is questionable. Out of the first eight Henri Farmans delivered, only three serviceable aircraft could be constructed and the situation was little better throughout his time in East Africa. True, with their greater payload, the Henri Farmans were more useful for bombing raids than the BE2cs but reconnaissance work was to prove of more value to the army. Van der

The BE2c plane flown in East Africa

Spuy viewed this campaign from the cockpit of the Henri Farmans, which he enjoyed flying, but Walmsley's experience had been longer and more varied. Strangely, this campaign, and in particular the part played by the RFC, has never been free from controversy and it will be necessary to return later to the views of the very few who, like Leo Walmsley, published their own story.

In East Africa the main function of the aeroplane was reconnaissance. The Germans had no aircraft so aerial combat was not envisaged and none of the aeroplanes was fitted with machine guns. This meant a valuable saving in weight and, apart from rifle fire and the occasional anti-aircraft shell, reconnaissance work could be carried out unhindered. The observer, and to a lesser extent the pilot, could concentrate on gathering the information asked for by the commander-in-chief and the general staff. Obviously it was desirable to know where the enemy was and what sort of defences he had prepared and to try to get some idea of what he intended. For this, flights over enemy territory were essential, as was the identification of targets for our artillery and subsequently for directing fire. But unlike the war in Europe, this campaign was to be a very mobile affair and to fight effectively over such hostile terrain units of both armies were often deployed in widely separated columns. For this reason, it was necessary for the commander-in-chief to know exactly where his own men were and to keep them in touch with each other. Aerial reconnaissance could do valuable work here, and by carrying message bags, useful information and vital instructions could be dropped to field commanders.

Although cameras were used and gave some good results, they were often in a state of disrepair. A lot of the equipment was out of date and badly packaged plates did not stand up to the rigours of the tropical climate. Most of the time the squadron was without a competent photographic officer and the facilities for developing the plates were frequently non-existent or too primitive to be relied upon. Hence the sketching of observed features was common practice. Although less accurate in depicting some detail, this method had certain advantages. A better idea of relative heights could be recorded and the results were available more quickly.

Unfortunately, there was still a reluctance to accept aerial reconnaissance as the best means of gathering information about enemy movements and intentions in the British army. Only a month before the outbreak of war, none other than General Sir Douglas Haig had recommended the use of cavalry for this purpose and dismissed the usefulness of the aeroplane. Amongst many senior staff this attitude was to die hard and was still in evidence when No 26 Squadron first arrived in East Africa and was to cause some ill feeling.

That there would be opportunities to drop bombs on the enemy had been foreseen and a good supply of twenty- and fifty-pound (9 and 22kg) bombs had been shipped to Mombasa. Ways and means were devised for carrying a few bombs so that suitable targets might be attacked. BE2cs could only do this on shorter flights when full fuel tanks were not essential and no camera was being carried; but the more powerful Henri Farmans could always carry a few bombs. Unluckily, most of the initial supply of bombs was unstable, having not travelled well, and posed too great a risk to airmen and machines used. But this was just one of the squadron's problems. Delays in the delivery of aircraft, the poor condition of many on arrival, inadequate spares and spares of the wrong description all added to the frustration, yet they still managed to keep enough machines airworthy to meet most of the army's demands.

*   *   *

General Smuts arrived in Nairobi on the 23rd February 1916 to take over the command of the British East African Expeditionary Force but just before his appointment, a fierce attempt was made to dislodge the Germans from British territory. This time General Malleson had the benefit of reports from several reconnaissance flights over Salaita Hill, the German stronghold that he proposed to attack on the 12th February. Sadly, on the day it was another disaster as the British were repelled with very heavy losses. Walmsley, who had risked his neck on the RFC's first flight, complained bitterly:

> 'For many months our reconnaissance reports were frankly discredited. Thus at Salaita Hill, a line of rocks described by airmen as a 'dummy' trench, and clearly shown as such on an aerial photograph, was bombarded continuously; while the real trenches, likewise indicated by us, were left severely alone. In the same engagement South African infantry was led straight into a line of carefully concealed trenches which Inglis, one of our observers, had accurately mapped and described some hours before.'[8]

Fortunately as the war progressed they were to get commanding officers with more understanding of, and sympathy for, the role allotted to the squadron.

Happily, when British and Dominion troops began to push forward, morale was lifted and the very positive and useful contribution made by the squadron started to gain recognition. Even so, the preface to Walmsley's book about his time in East Africa makes it clear that he would have expected more. And even General Northey, writing the introduction to the book, felt it necessary to state 'I never agreed with those writers on the East African campaign who have suggested that, owing to the wildness of the country and density of the bush, aeroplanes were of little use.' Unlike many critics of the campaign, he had fought in East Africa and perhaps he too resented the way that all their efforts were devalued as the war in East Africa was still being dismissed as merely a 'sideshow'. The arrival of General Smuts signalled the start of a new and more optimistic approach to the struggle ahead. He inspired the men he led. On the 8th March 1916, he went on the attack and started to push the Germans back through the Taveta gap and out of British territory. He knew he was up against a determined and resourceful enemy and that the way ahead led through incredibly difficult terrain. But he also knew that the unrelenting sun and tropical rains that alternately scorched and soaked his men would make life just as uncomfortable for his enemy. Both armies would suffer when watercourses ran dry or the monsoons turned the flatlands into swamps. Danger and disease would plague the German troops no less than his own. But his resources were far greater than his enemy's and there would be no slackening of effort. He was confident that the Germans could be defeated in a matter of months.

But the redoubtable Colonel von Lettow-Vorbeck had other ideas. His aim was to prolong the struggle, keep the British troops occupied and make it as difficult as possible for them. In this, he succeeded and only after the armistice had been signed did he and his undefeated army lay down their weapons.

Peter Barton

CHAPTER 4

Wings over East Africa (1916–1918)

EVEN before experiencing the thrill of that first flight over enemy positions, Walmsley had found plenty to excite his interest in the insect life invading his new living quarters. Drawings of these started to fill his notebooks and he blessed his good fortune in having been sent to a naturalist's paradise. He soon realised that flying was not going to be a full-time job; flying conditions were proving difficult and unpredictable so that most of the flights had to be restricted to early morning or late afternoon. He could foresee few other duties coming his way so looked forward to having plenty of time to do what he loved most - pursue his interest in wildlife. Thus he began his series of African notebooks, which also allowed him to exercise his drawing skills and develop his writing talent. But he soon found that Nature had another side to her and one that demanded constant vigilance. Lions and other wild animals were plentiful but were more often heard than seen. The greater menace came from the myriad of small bugs and fearless insects. These would make life a misery and were far more deadly than any human enemy. Insects enjoyed exploring all the aero-engine orifices and, unless checked, the results were likely to prove disastrous. The rapidly growing termite heaps had scarred the already rough surface of the aerodrome and termites were threatening the legs of Walmsley's bed and were to bring down one of the hangers by eating through the guy-rope pegs.

To everyone's relief, the arrival of Smuts had set a different tempo to the business of war. More reconnaissance flights over the Taveta gap were called for and this time Walmsley enjoyed lobbing a hand grenade into the Salaita Hill trenches. Smuts attacked with such determination on the 3rd March 1916 that the Germans were thrust back through the Taveta gap and had to abandon Salaita Hill to avoid being cut off. Just as the Germans were being forced into their historic retreat, Walmsley went down with a bad bout of dysentery. The ambulance train took him back to Voi and then to Nairobi, the capital of the British colony, where he spent nearly a month in hospital followed by a pleasant week recuperating on a settler's farm.

In his absence, the war had moved into German territory and he had to travel forward to Kahe, where a new aerodrome was being prepared near the River Pangani. Boarding a supply train and finding all the wagons full, he perched himself on top of one of them and prepared to enjoy the journey. Ahead, snow-topped Kilimanjaro dominated the skyline. Unfortunately, smoke and cinders from the engine spoiled some of the fun, and on the second leg, from Taveta to Kahe, much of the track, wrecked by the retreating enemy, was under repair. At one point part of it slid sideways as they passed over it. Miraculously the train was not derailed. On his return, Walmsley found himself supervising musketry practice on the range for a few days and on the 1st May he was appointed meteorological officer.

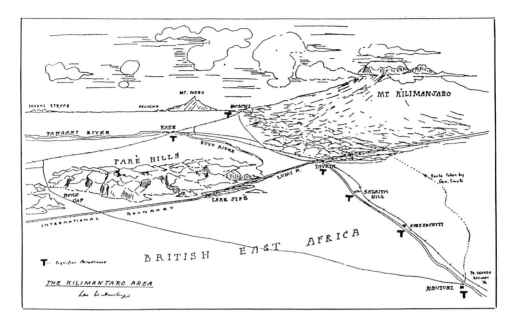

Bird's-eye view of Kilimanjaro area, drawn by author, **T** signifies aerodrome

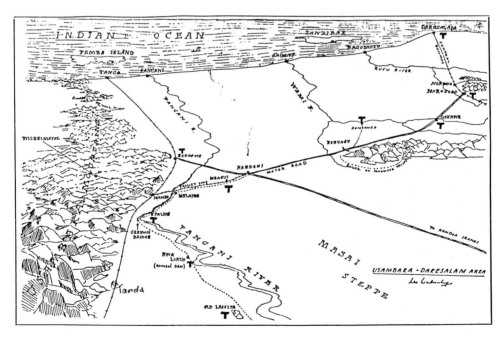

Bird's-eye view of Usambara-Daresalam area, drawn by author, **T** signifies aerodrome

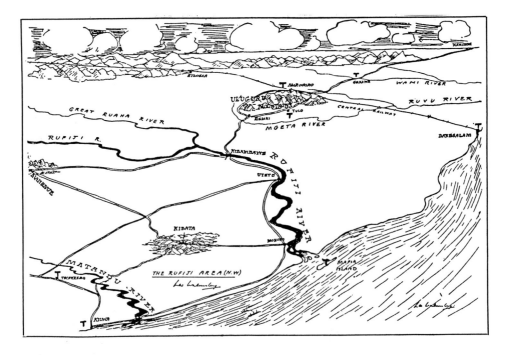

Bird's-eye view of Rufiji area, drawn by author, **T** signifies aerodrome

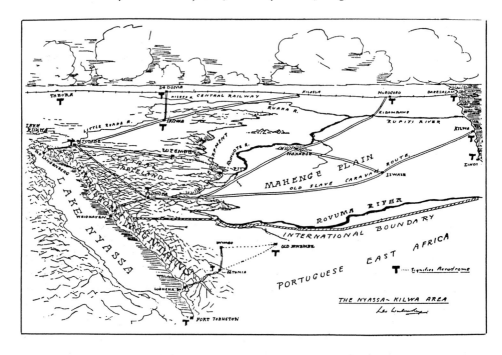

Bird's-eye view of the Nyassa-Kilwa area, drawn by author, **T** signifies aerodrome

The squadron was now on the western side of the Pare mountain range and southwards ran the Tanga railway with the river never very far away. Ahead lay swamps and patches of impenetrable jungle, but also less dense areas of bush with the occasional clearing. Too often a clearing would prove to be a trap as camouflaged machine guns opened raking crossfire. The atmosphere was heavy and damp, the smell often foul. It was an area so uninviting that even the natives had never settled it. The advance was never as fast as Smuts wanted but disease was claiming more victims than bullets. Later it was calculated that for every one killed or wounded in battle, thirty men went sick. Mosquito nets and quinine were more valuable than weapons. Yet here, from Walmsley's point of view, was all that excited his interest and after only three days in the area, he was writing a letter home that would allay any fears that his family may have had:

'Dear Old Ma,
Here we are at last in German East, and it's a land flowing with milk and honey. The honey, however, seems to attract a deuce of a lot of other things, chief of which being that dear little animal the mosquito. We're in a low swampy plain flanked by a tremendous river and, but for the sun, you'd swear you were on an English farm. The scenery by the river is exquisite - all that a tropical river should be - palms, papyrus and trees hung with gorgeous creepers amongst which sport scores of pretty little monkeys and hosts of rainbow-hued birds and insects. In the shallows wallow dozens of 'crocs' and 'hippos' and in the river itself are tons of fish. … Somehow or other the sun doesn't seem so hot here as the ground glare is absorbed by the rich, meadow-like grass. We're still living very comfortably, ham and eggs and fish for breakfast and buck meat, potatoes, cabbage, mealies (green maize), bananas, mangoes and granadillas for lunch and dinner. Of course there is a far more interesting variety of animal life here. The weaver birds you have seen pictures of - they're here in millions and gorgeous humming birds and kingfishers. There are huge cranes, pelicans and hornbills and an endless variety of smaller birds. The least said about the insects the better. The side of my neck is at present a purulent mass … caused by the beastly Nairobi fly which has infected me with 'herpes' commonly known as shingles.'[1]

Optimism was still high and he added:

'This show promises to last quite a long time yet, but I think there's every chance of my being home somewhere about September.'

The tireless Smuts demanded superhuman efforts from his men as he led them forward in his attempt to force Lettow-Vorbeck to stand and fight. At the same time, he had another detachment racing to outflank his enemy and force him to surrender. Clever though Smuts was, he reckoned without his ingenious opponent. Had the hard-driven troops on the ground read what Walmsley had written they would have thought him mad! The footsloggers were beset with appalling difficulties, not made any easier by the fact that rarely could the transport deliver adequate supplies to ensure that they were reasonably well fed and properly clothed. In contrast, although the squadron's bases were never far behind the front line, it could be supplied more easily so it had less to grumble about. But it, too, was often short of the equipment — spares, fuel and machines — necessary to keep it a fully efficient fighting unit.

As May drew to a close, the spring rains ceased, and in the course of the next three months, the Germans were forced to retreat down their light railway to Same and then to Morogoro on the Central Railway. On the way, they destroyed bridges, the track and anything that might have been useful to their pursuers, but every now and again turned to fight very effective rearguard actions. With their superiority in machine guns, they inflicted heavy casualties on the British. The 4.1-inch (10cm) guns rescued from the *Konigsberg* had a range far greater than any artillery supplied to the British, so at regular intervals the Germans could send over a few shells — ammunition was short — from a distance that they knew would attract no retaliation. The aeroplanes, in addition to their reconnaissance activities, could drop twenty- or fifty-pound (9 or 22kg) bombs on German working parties, on trains, track and railway bridges. But once the enemy heard the noise of approaching planes, everyone scattered although it took a while before the natives ceased to be mesmerised at the sight of these 'big birds' dropping their 'eggs'. Usually aimed at transport, most of the bombs fell wide of their target. Nevertheless, they could still cause damage, maim and kill. One direct hit was recorded, blowing the engine of a train to pieces and killing the driver and several military passengers. At this stage, Walmsley, returning from missions, did not find it too difficult to forget the war. The natural beauty of his surroundings was there to enjoy:

> '... the Pangani river meandered like a mighty silver serpent making its weary way to the sea. Although nearly fifty miles away, Kilimanjaro still managed comfortably to block out one-third of the northern sky, and one's eyes were drawn towards it as if by some magnetic influence.'[2]

Francis Brett Young, a doctor with the British Expeditionary Force and already an aspiring novelist, weary after another day sweltering under the sun, was affected in a similar way. In his book *Marching on Tanga* (1917), he recalls taking a rest and looking up with pleasure to see Kilimanjaro rising 'like a gigantic ghost'. It was the only snow-capped peak in the Kaiser's Empire and was never again to be in German hands.

*   *   *

Trailing the advancing army, the squadron was forced repeatedly to find new aerodromes from which to operate. Three more landing places had been brought into use between Mbuyuni and Kahe but they soon had to move to a new aerodrome, which had been prepared about fifty miles (80.5 km) farther south. The convoy of lorries carrying all the squadron's equipment started off, not on roads — there were none — but on poorly defined tracks. Walmsley joined the convoy.

> 'The dust was terrible, and so fine it penetrated our clothing, and formed a nasty muddy deposit on our perspiring bodies.'[3]

They arrived late in the afternoon and the machines flew in before dusk. During the next three days, reconnaissance and bombing raids were carried out from sunrise to sunset. Now the Germans had taken to marching at night so were even more difficult to spot so, apart from keeping an eye on their own advance, there was little of military significance for the airmen to see. After only three days, they were ordered to move again. This time Walmsley was to accompany Lt E C Emmett on a reconnaissance flight and then land at the new aerodrome. The reconnaissance was straightforward but finding the new aerodrome was not. Reluctantly, they came down to 200 feet (60m), fearing the effect of the strong whirlwinds they were encountering that were drawing up everything, including the aircraft.

> 'The machine was tossed about like a feather, and suddenly ... we were nearly shaken out of our seats by a fearful knocking in the engine. Emmett switched off ...'[4]

They landed safely on a narrow patch of grass only 100 yards (90m) long and fifty yards (45m) wide. Leaving the pilot with his machine, Walmsley was lucky enough to come across the last truck of the squadron's road convoy and so managed a lift to the aerodrome, ten miles away. The breakdown gang was dispatched to Emmett but it was two days before he turned up.

'The new aerodrome was called Old Lassita,' wrote Walmsley, 'for no other reason than that this happened to be the only name on the map within a radius of twenty miles.' The mosquitos 'fairly rolled you out of bed' warned the mess sergeant. At no time was a doctor attached to the squadron and malaria was beginning to affect several of their number, so Lt Pawson, assuming a slight knowledge of medicine, tended the sick. Fortunately no one developed the dreaded black water fever and they were all thankful that another move was ordered. A menace of a different sort awaited them at Kwa Lokua. In the middle of lion country, they decided that 'Daniel's Den' was a fairer name for their new camp.

For the week that they stayed there, they were kept very busy. The Germans had dug themselves in some distance ahead where river and railway met, to cover the inevitable approach of the main British force. Reconnaissance flights discovered the enemy's preparations and detailed sketches of their positions were made. These were forwarded to the staff headquarters, but in the event this did not stop another punishing rearguard action, again slowing down the British advance. The Germans fell back on Mkalamo and were going to pick up the Mombo-Handeni trolley line, which would take them farther south in the direction of Morogoro, their temporary capital.

Flying over Mkalamo, with Second Lieutenant C R Bertram, Walmsley was leaning over the side of his cockpit to take a photograph:

> '... when a terrific bump caught our right wing. In a second we were in a nose-dive, spinning as we went earthwards like a leaf falling from a tree. It was a horrible sensation. My belt, of course, was unfastened, and while I hung on like grim death to the struts, my map, notes, and photographic plates went streaming out behind ... Bertram, however, kept his head splendidly. Switching off his engine as soon as the spin commenced, he at last managed to pull her out - not, however, until we were hardly more than 800 feet above the Huns.'[5]

This was their first experience of being fired at by something heavy and Walmsley recorded it as exciting. He was not to know that only a few days later Bertram and his observer were to be killed in a crash; a tragedy which was to cast a gloomy spell over the squadron. To Francis Brett Young, these airmen seemed 'strangely remote and secure ... in the silvery sky'. There must have been some appreciation by those on the ground of the hazards of flying but the efforts of the flyers were seen almost as an irrelevance. They tended to be judged on their effectiveness in silencing the enemy's big guns, wrecking trains and destroying bridges, so the soldiers were not often impressed. Few would understand that bombing was a difficult art: science had yet to be applied to the question of accuracy and the damage that the small bombs could do was very limited. Soldiers could only assess the value of reconnaissance from how effectively it was applied and errors were common. Young was to remark that 'Colonel Dyke lay sweating under an awning with bundles of maps and airman's sketches and reports. It was a pity neither were very reliable.' But all sources agreed that the official maps were often useless so the problems of imposing on them reconnaissance details can be imagined. When Young came across 'an engine and a pair of trucks terribly wrecked' he thought of the Flying Corps but rather grudgingly admitted that the sight 'did something to heighten their prestige, which was lower than it need have been, seeing that their only targets in this bushy world were the tops of trees'.

On the 8th June the squadron again moved. When Walmsley saw the bedraggled state of those who arrived by road, he was thankful to have been flown in but only a few days later, he was sent forward to find another aerodrome site. Near Mkalamo he employed forty 'boys' working under a sergeant to level the ground. Nearby, the Pangani river drew him to its banks and he was delighted to see the fishermen using wicker traps similar to those used back home to catch crabs and lobsters. He was finding the jungle an exciting place — as long as there was no fighting to be done! The work completed, he reported back to learn that a site near Handeni and the enemy had been found. No one had any difficulty naming the unwanted aerodrome, which was immediately christened 'Walmsley's Folly.'

The preferred site, Mbagui, had once been under cultivation and before any aircraft dare risk a landing, local labour had to be recruited to tackle the Herculean task of 'ironing' out the furrows. The machines arrived a week later but the surface was still fairly rough and several were slightly damaged on landing.

Suspecting that the Germans were preparing strong positions at Ruhunga, about forty-five miles (70km) south of Mbagui on the motor road to Morogoro, Smuts planned yet another outflanking movement. Unfortunately, cloudy weather hampered aerial observations so there was less to do and Walmsley had to admit that on some flights he was getting bored. It was now that the stability of the 'Old Bee' (as the BE2c was affectionately known) offered an extra bonus for, as long as conditions were not too bumpy, it was possible to write letters or just read. Even the pilot could relax.

Walmsley was at Mbagui for only a couple of weeks before suffering his first serious attack of malaria and had to be sent back to the field hospital at Mbuyini. He recovered sufficiently after two days to be sent on to Mombasa for further treatment and a short convalescence. At last, after six months, he was to see the town he had gazed upon from the decks of the *Trafford Hall*. The picturesque old streets and bazaars had their attraction but the sea beckoned. Out on the coral reefs he was in his element. Dear old Robin Hoods Bay had nothing like this. The brilliant colouring of so many fish. The sea urchins, sea anenomes and starfish were bigger and the exotic beauty of so many species beggared belief.

Fit again, Walmsley found it hard to turn his back on all the restful beauty that he had been enjoying so much but before leaving, he was lucky enough to find and hire the priceless Maganga. His previous servant had gone into hospital but now he had discovered one whom he said 'stuck to me throughout the campaign and proved to be a most faithful slave'. A slave! It amused Walmsley to refer to him thus but in truth Maganga was a devoted servant. It would have been surprising if Walmsley had not written about him with touching affection: Maganga became a friend and one to whom he owed his life.

* * *

On the 7th July, during his absence, the only three serviceable Henri Farmans flew into Mbagui to join the four BE2cs. It was their first appearance at the front but almost immediately one of the BE2cs was wrecked, thereby reducing the squadron's active force to only six aeroplanes. The month that followed was a very busy one with twenty-seven bombing attacks carried out and a total of three and a half tons of bombs being dropped.

At the end of July, Walmsley returned to Mbagui in charge of a convoy of ten supply-laden Leyland lorries that had arrived in the country on the 3rd July. The convoy was to ignore the Taveta gap and take a more direct route through the Pare mountain range. Writing home, he described something of the journey:

'We came through a pass in the Pare mountains from Mbuyuni and then miles and miles through the bush into German East. The game was simply wonderful ... The way the lions roared round the camp every night made one feel a wee bit sleepless at first, but soon we became quite used to it. The mountain pass was very exciting as for nearly three miles we wound round the edge of a tremendous precipice at the bottom of which babbled a clear, ice-cold stream. We lived on venison, eggs, milk, bananas and mealies bought from the natives.'[6]

His thoughts were on home and he goes on to describe a path through a glade saying '... you could swear you were in Mill Beck Wood'. He then complains that it is three weeks since they had received mail and the grumbles continue:

'I do wish you'd send out some of the things I ask you to — I don't think it's much trouble to wrap up a *Yorkshire Post* occasionally or a few old magazines. Or perhaps I'm having such a jolly good time of it ... Honestly, I'm beginning to think you people at home refuse to consider this a war at all out here. I can assure you that, although the risks are equal, the Tommy in France doesn't suffer one quarter what our Tommies out here are suffering. They don't know what it is to march twenty-five miles in a baking sun, through a perpetual cloud of dense alkaline dust, with a quarter ration of salt bully beef for food and half a cup of filthy water to quench the thirst of hell, their heads bursting with malaria and at the end of it all they have to fight a fiendishly cunning enemy who never shows himself out of this cursed thorn, who hides his machine guns in ant heaps or in the trees ready to pour out from them their jet of death on to our unsuspecting troops ... No, please don't underrate the war in Germany's last colony — it's as live a show as any.'[7]

A typical grumble from the serviceman overseas? Yes, but not without some justification. Walmsley gives a brief, but completely accurate, description of what it was like to be following Smuts. Almost at the same time Francis Brett Young was saying this, and much more, when writing *Marching on Tanga*. No one who ever went through that war, or any historian who later wrote about it, found it possible to paint a more cheerful picture. Having described the food he had just enjoyed, he had to add, 'Naturally, in the Flying Corps we live like lords compared with the infantry, but we too have our little discomforts.' His hut was infested with 'jiggers' so he elaborated on this 'little discomfort':

> 'Jiggers are minute fleas which hop on to one's foot, find a nice soft, cushy place, usually just under the toe-nail, bore a hole and deposit a bag of eggs. These hatch into larvae which grow fat at the expense of one's toe. Eventually they get fed up and go to sleep and when they awake they are real jiggers and have no end of a game inside the nest. Most of us object to our toes being used as public incubators so we have the eggs taken out, before they hatch, by a native. He does the job very neatly with a thorn.'[8]

He penned an amusing sketch to illustrate the point. As well as an infested big toe, it shows a milestone inscribed to remind all that Bay (Robin Hoods Bay) was many thousands of miles away. His postscript reveals that some of his scribbling had found a market. He asks for an article of his appearing in the *Sunday Chronicle* to be sent out to him.

The Germans also managed to receive fresh supplies, but theirs came from two successful blockade runners and were to keep them in the field for many more months to come. Probably as a consequence, aeroplanes flying over the Ruhungu area met with a concentration of anti-aircraft fire — known to the flyers as 'archies' — not previously experienced. The Germans had modified some of their field guns and, not unnaturally, were trying to deny the British an unhindered aerial view of their defensive positions and troop movements. This made the airmen more wary but their work went on. For the enemy it was an admission that an army supported by aircraft possessed many advantages. And, not wanting to risk exposing their big guns from the *Konigsberg*, they resorted to firing them mostly at night and during the day kept them camouflaged and silent whenever the sound of aircraft was heard. But deception was a game that two could play. While operating from Mbagui, the squadron diary entry for the 3rd August reads:

> 'Capt. Van Der Spuy, Henri Farman, with 2nd. Lt Walmsley as Observer, on reconnaissance of the country east of the Handeni-Turiani road. This reconnaissance took in the entire area of the country on our left flank and had the secondary object of deceiving the enemy as to the direction of our forthcoming advance.'[9]

Unfortunately, the ruse seems to have failed but it so happened that this flight was Walmsley's first in a Henri Farman and he relates the experience vividly:

> 'But it was not until we got into the air that I began to appreciate the real discomforts of this machine. Because of the mountains near by, the air at Morogoro is very bumpy, and as soon as we got off the ground we were tossed about in a most nerve-racking fashion … my pilot Van der Spuy, had to exert his full strength at times to pull the controls over to neutralise these bumps, and there were occasions when I could swear we should never recover.'[10]

On landing there was an even greater shock to come:

> 'When the machine was examined several parts were found to be badly strained, and the steel bolts securing my seat to the *nacelle* were shorn completely across.'[11]

Firmly in his mind's eye was the vision of the sudden plunge downwards when their goggles were suspended in the air above their heads. With a shudder of utter horror, he recalled the number of times that he had unfastened his belt to lean out of the cockpit for a better view of the ground. It flashed through his mind that one day he could find himself out of the cockpit, high and dry in mid-air. This experience did nothing to help him overcome his dislike of Henri Farmans.

Other official entries for August 1916 also make interesting reading:

'Lt. Clisdal, with 2nd. Lt. Walmsley as Observer, started on a reconnaissance. When they were a few miles south of Handeni, however, the engine began to miss and the pilot turned back. At a point six miles from the aerodrome the engine gave out entirely. This necessitated a forced landing in the bush. The machine, a BE2c, was completely wrecked and the engine very much damaged. Both the pilot and observer were unhurt. The engine failure turned out to be due to magneto trouble.'[12]

In *Flying and Sport in East Africa*, Walmsley makes no secret of the fact that he was often afraid yet he tries, without notable success, to treat this particular incident with humour:

'The observer is privileged to close his eyes when the final crash comes, and so curling up my legs I waited without enthusiasm for the fireworks.'

Fortunately, their descent had been watched by dozens of awe-struck natives who gathered to help themselves to souvenirs so the two survivors felt themselves justified in demanding chickens, eggs and milk in exchange! And on the 19th August the squadron report reads:

'Lt. Carey-Smith, (BE2c), with 2nd Lt. Walmsley as Observer, on a reconnaissance to Morogoro on the Central Railway. Prior to this Intelligence Reports had announced that preparations had been made at Morogoro to repel aircraft and on this occasion numerous anti-aircraft guns were in action when our machine was over the town.'[13]

On the 24th August, with the same pilot, on a reconnaissance eastwards along the Central Railway the report reads 'four bombs were taken and dropped on an enemy camp situated on the Railway.' On the last day of the month Walmsley again accompanied Van der Spuy in his Henri Farman. Spotting about 300 hostile askaris just two miles ahead of our advancing column, a message to this effect was dropped to our troops. The report also adds, 'A message, addressed to the G.O.C. describing the country and road leading south-west from Pugu was dropped over our troops at Msumbisi.' In this manner, the routine collection and transmission of intelligence formed a vital but unglamorous part of the squadron's work.

Not wishing to be outflanked at Ruhungu, the Germans abandoned their positions and continued southwards, Walmsley was sent with a small convoy of three cars and about two dozen natives to establish a forward aerodrome for the squadron. Through the bush and tall forests, the going was rough and the absence of wildlife uncanny. Here the tsetse fly reigned supreme and the way was littered with dead transport animals. This vicious insect added to the misery of the men, but fortunately with less drastic results.

From the foot of the Nguru mountains, they struck eastwards as ordered but found the going almost impossible. It was perhaps thirty miles (50km) to the Wami river and it was nearly dark before they arrived at the Komsanga site. Here it was comforting to see a detachment of friendly troops building a bridge nearby. Preparing the surface of the aerodrome proved another very difficult task. At the end of the day, leaving only a small force to protect the bridge, they all slept well. An hour before dawn bullets were flying in all directions. Still clad in his flimsy silk pyjamas, Walmsley admitted to being horribly frightened. With few rifles and no bayonets, their chances looked hopeless. Under direct enemy fire for the first time, he realised that he was not going to be the hero he had imagined himself when he joined the army. He grabbed his rifle but very quickly the welcome noise of the guard's maxim gun opening fire could be heard and to everyone's relief the attack petered out in a matter of minutes. The danger had been slight but the shock had been most unpleasant. With the exact whereabouts of the enemy unknown, it was decided to abandon this site. Another was found at Dakawa and from here the squadron could follow the enemy's withdrawal to Morogoro.

Every attempt by Smuts to outflank the Germans failed. It surprised Lettow-Vorbeck that Smuts showed a lack of imagination by always employing this same strategy. The Germans were not going to be brought to surrender at Morogoro nor to halt their orderly retreat. The railway station and their supply lines out of Morogoro were attacked and Walmsley claimed that in a dive his machine reached nearly 100mph before circling round to drop its four bombs. One turned out to be a dud but one hit a building full of stores, blowing everything up. Flying over Morogoro the next day, Walmsley, again with Carey Thomas, could see no signs of life in the town. It appeared to have been deserted. A rude awakening came in the form of a violent explosion on their tail. Then another: they were being shot at! It was 'a very nasty sensation' wrote Walmsley. 'My hair began to stiffen and cold beads of perspiration trickled down my brow.' From contentment to fear in a second. Walmsley, having finished his observations, urged the pilot to head for home. Unperturbed, Carey-Thomas thought it more important to locate the gun but to Walmsley the extra five minutes spent circling the target seemed more like five years.

Following the line west towards Kilossa, they found themselves flying over more open country until the Mpapua mountains were reached. As they turned back, Walmsley spotted a line of occupied rifle trenches overlooking the road along which our troops were expected to advance. Enclosing a message in his handkerchief and loading it with cartridges, he dropped it as near to the road as he could, hoping that it would be seen and so prevent our troops from being ambushed. With fuel running low, they set course for home.

When the Germans evacuated Morogoro, the native population remained and so too did the German women and children — 'A fact which shows that the Hun still believes the English soldier to be a gentleman'[14] wrote Walmsley. This virtue was sorely tested when the incoming soldiers and airmen found that they had been left a disgusting legacy of filth to clear up from accommodation vacated by the enemy. Walmsley had been the first to fly over the town and could take satisfaction from seeing the damage caused by the bombing. Now, unsuspectingly, he wandered through the streets that he had studied and mapped from the air and only his relative weakness saved him from moving a booby-trapped trolley he had a mind to push along the light railway. Later, a bigger and stronger native was not so lucky.

After 400 of the natives had been pressed into service, the enemy's large parade ground made an excellent aerodrome. The Germans were supposed to be making for Kissaki, to the south of the Uluguru mountains, and a British column was in pursuit. In a few graphic sentences, Walmsley leaves his readers in no doubt that fighting and flying in East Africa was no picnic:

> 'Thank Heaven, I never had to march on the western route to Kissaki. Flying over it was enough for me ... No one was in a better position to appreciate the terrible hardships that these men were enduring than ourselves. Road there was none, water was scarce, food was unobtainable except in minute quantities ... The maintenance of supplies was an impossible task ... The whole of the country was clothed in dense elephant forest ... continuous for nearly forty miles, and in that stretch there is not a square yard where a machine could be landed or even crashed with safety. The trees grow to an immense height, the surface of the ground is hilly, and abounds in deep ravines.'[15]

The news of Walmsley's promotion to full lieutenant came through but he was growing depressed as the September rains curtailed the number of reconnaissance flights. The effect of a ten-day idle spell was to set his nerves on edge and he later volunteered to join 'B' flight at Tulo. After a hair-raising car journey down from the Uluguru foothills to the Rufiji plain, he was glad to see Carey-Thomas in charge but the dried-up swamp which was the aerodrome did not impress him. Flying again with a pilot he knew well meant that he could enjoy life and now 'the call of the air is like the call of the sea — irresistible to those who hear it'.[16]

For a month there were not many days when Walmsley did not go on at least one flight. What the enemy was doing between the Mgeta and Rufiji rivers was uncertain. Targets for the artillery had to be identified and the pooling of gathered information allowed some good maps to be drawn. Had radio been used to direct subsequent shelling, greater accuracy might have resulted but the equipment — frequently out of action due to the ravages of insects — had been on the vehicles unable to reach Tulo after heavy rains so another form of signalling had to be devised. Using pre-arranged codes indicated by coloured Very lights fired from aircraft, the artillery adjusted its aim. It was fascinating work and the damaging and demoralising effect it had on the enemy justified the work of the observers. Some of this had to be done under extreme difficulties owing to frequent and heavy rain-storms so it deservedly brought commendations. Bombs could be dropped and a new type devised. A petrol-filled tin cylinder would, by means of an added explosive charge, ignite on hitting the ground. Dropped on sun-dried elephant grass, the conflagration was both spectacular and effective.

One flight with Mossop, 'a skilful and daring airman', nearly ended in tragedy. Taking a chance on flying through the many clouds now so often confronting them, they kept on course. This time, the mist changed to rain on entering one cloud and they found themselves in the thick of it. The expected light did not loom ahead and they were flying towards the Uluguru mountains. Walmsley demanded that the pilot throttle back and, as they glided down, the trees finally appeared on the steep slopes 400 feet (120m) below. Another minute and they would have flown straight into the steep mountain side.

Worries about the reliability of the engine were always present and when it started to splutter, the tension increased dramatically. After one such incident, Walmsley took himself hunting to calm his nerves, but on returning to the camp, found that most of the accommodation had been burnt to the ground. For Walmsley, this was more than just an unfortunate accident: it was a calamity. All his kit had been destroyed, together with his shotgun, field glasses, cameras, more than 100 films and, most precious of all, his wartime diaries. For any man under a similar strain for so many months and often less than fully fit, the shock would have been severe but it was too much for the highly strung Walmsley. Those diaries had meant everything to him. He collapsed with a nervous breakdown and was immediately sent back to Morogoro on his way to a splendid convalescent home on the island of Zanzibar.

The Central Railway and Dar es Salaam were now in British hands so Walmsley hoped to enjoy a rail journey to what had been the capital of the German Colony. In the event, he had to travel on top of the coal in the engine's tender, sharing this uncomfortable perch with several others, but at Dar es Salaam he found a small whaler to take him to Zanzibar. Walmsley never revealed how his nervous disability affected him but it does not seem to have prevented him from soaking up the pleasure of new sights, sounds and smells along the way. From the Sultan's Palace, no less magnificent now as a convalescent home, he ventured out to explore the island's countryside. After a month of rest, Walmsley was declared fit.

Returning to the mainland, Walmsley crossed in an Arab dhow, so adding to his cherished experiences. His orders were to report to a new aerodrome being prepared at Kilwa Kissiwani, about 130 miles (200k) down the coast. Supplied with three new BE2cs, the flight was to assist the army in pushing the Germans inland. On one occasion, Carey-Thomas, on reaching dense forest, brought his machine down to 1,000 feet (300m) and, having spotted a few trenches, Walmsley began sketching. Without warning, the engine stopped. With visions of ending up a mangled corpse, Walmsley curled his legs under his body 'in order to keep them out of the way of the engine', loosened his belt, an action which he justified as 'a wise precaution in case the machine was badly smashed up', closed his eyes and waited. Just in time, the engine spluttered into life and, with shouts of joy and relief, they began to climb away. Safely back, they found the carburettor choked with 'a thimbleful of a peculiar red mud'. As the mechanics regularly cleaned and checked fuel leads, everyone was puzzled. When Second Lieutenant Osman took the same machine and experienced the same problem the next morning, further investigation was called for. The inside of the petrol tank had never received its anti-corrosion treatment. Some harsh words were said about careless factory workers who could have caused the loss of a valuable aeroplane and possibly the death of the crew.

Christmas was near but the prospect of Christmas fare being on the table looked remote. Supplies and mail had not appeared for weeks and all bottles had been drained. The faithful Maganga ventured out to return with two fine geese, which Walmsley's instincts told him had not been paid for. At the last minute, the flight commander flew in with a 'heavenly cargo' of food and drink. Now there was everything to ensure that Christmas 1916 would be a merry one. Feeling happy after a wonderful Christmas dinner, Walmsley suggested that perhaps they could fly some of their surplus cigarettes to the besieged garrison at Kibata. Into a sandbag went 6,000 cigarettes and newspapers together with a message of good cheer. Walmsley took off with Lieutenant Howard and, ten minutes after spotting and making notes of an enemy trench complex, they easily picked out the fort and at 400 feet (120m) threw out the surprise package.

Not surprisingly, the cheering soldiers in the fort had scattered quickly, thinking the fool of a pilot must imagine that he was bombing the enemy. Grateful to the Flying Corps as they must have been, a bottle or two of the whisky or champagne being consumed in the flight's mess might have been even more welcome.

Whisky was regarded by most as an essential prophylactic and by one particular pilot as the only one. He was a good pilot, but when the supply of whisky occasionally ran out, his hand on the joystick was not as steady as Walmsley would have liked, although neither of them came to harm. It was unfortunate that many years later, after this story had appeared in *So Many Loves*, it was picked up by Byron Farwell when writing *The Great War in Africa* (1987) to argue that not only were the aircraft used by the squadron poor but the 'aviators did not seem to be first class either'. In fact, few pilots were more experienced but, in common with many authors, Farwell seems not to have read Walmsley's account of the air war in east Africa or consulted squadron records. Fighting off all manner of diseases with inadequate supplies of drugs meant that no possible precautions or comforting remedies could be ignored.

With a considerable section of the German East African coast now in British hands, it was thought that the enemy would be boxed in between the main force pressing it southwards, the force pushing on it from the west and the coastal forces. At its back would be Portuguese East Africa, an ally of the British. Viewed optimistically, the end was in sight. Meanwhile, the rain that followed Christmas had turned the aerodrome into a lake. Another site had to be prepared on the hillside and the mess moved to drier quarters in the town. With no flying possible, Walmsley could dabble in a little amateur archaeology by exploring some of Kilwa's ancient sites. With the new year, flying recommenced.

For Walmsley, the highlights of the January 1917 flights were sighting one of the enemy's few remaining 4.1 guns taken from the *Konigsberg* and dropping a bomb near enough to put it out of action. But that month it was distinctly frightening trying to land and take off from Tschermo, a new forward aerodrome which proved far too small. Inevitably, sickness took its toll and for a spell the flight's only fit pilots were Howard and Clowe with Walmsley the only fit observer. The rest of the squadron, now elsewhere, was not much better off but it did send another officer. He was a pilot new to East Africa and it was Walmsley's responsibility to accompany him in the air and to help him to get his bearings.

In flew Mossop from Tulo one day to surprise them with the news that he had come to collect General Hoskins, who was to take over from General Smuts as commander of the British Expeditionary Force. General Smuts relinquished this post on the 20th January 1917. He had driven Lettow-Vorbeck more than halfway across German East Africa yet had failed to defeat him. Back in England, Smuts managed to give the impression that he had virtually won the battle for East Africa. It was not true but this was the sort of good news that England desperately wanted to hear. Not surprisingly, those left behind were not in the best of spirits as they were well aware that the promised victory had not come. Although it now seemed certain that Lettow-Vorbeck was no longer strong enough to pose a serious threat, he still had a few surprises up his sleeve. He was more and more to resort to guerilla tactics to harass his pursuers and keep them guessing. It was, however, reassuring for the squadron to know that Hoskins was a general who had great faith in the Royal Flying Corps.

At the end of the month, Walmsley succumbed to the strain and was sent back to Dar es Salaam and to hospital. The ambulance journey depressed him still further because accompanying him was a captain of the King's African Rifles, who was wasting away from the debilitating effects of malaria and dysentery. He had fought the enemy in France and East Africa only to be defeated by disease. Before the ship had reached Dar es Salaam, the captain had been buried at sea.

On his discharge from hospital, Walmsley was surprised to receive orders to report to the officer commanding A Flight, Captain G W Hodgkinson ('Hodge'), at Iringa, some 250 miles (400km) inland. Without realising it, Walmsley was about to start the final phase of his service in East Africa. He was to join General Northey's force, which had started off in Rhodesia and had been trying to push the Germans eastwards towards Smuts.

*   *   *

It was the onset of spring 1917, the height of the rainy season, and the wettest for nearly thirty years. To complete most of the journey, Walmsley was able to travel to Dodoma on the Central Railway. Facing him then was a 100-mile (160km) trek southwards over the wide, flat plain across which the Great Ruaha river meandered. The river had flooded many miles of country and was soon likely to be impossible to cross. Still feeling very weak, Walmsley had collected two Ford light lorries, had them specially overhauled for the journey, and was determined to make the effort. For the first forty miles (64km) the going was surprisingly good but an enforced stop with carburettor trouble gave Walmsley another opportunity to take his gun into the bush, looking for game and extra food for his men. The convoy then pushed on, passing many stranded vehicles and occasionally having to dig its own out of the mud. A tropical thunderstorm made life very uncomfortable but Walmsley thought the lightning magnificent. Abandoning the idea of getting any farther with the cars, they sent them back to Dodoma with a request for more robust carriers. When the replacement transport arrived, it turned out to be six donkeys with the same number of natives but, to their surprise, they proved to be less troublesome than the mechanised vehicles. The pontoon across the Kisego river was still working but, against all advice, Walmsley pressed on towards the Ruaha floods.

At times they were up to their waists in muddy water. To keep them moving, the porters had to be threatened, sworn at and intimidated by the occasional pistol shot, but not physically struck. Walmsley was not surprised that they wanted to desert and he felt sorry for them as the water softened their bare feet, making them vulnerable to thorns and sharp stones, but they had to reach the bridge. With Maganga's help, he struggled on in the grip of fever. In this mood he was not pleased when one of the mischievous boys swam underwater to grab the leg of a porter. Shrieks of 'Mamba! Mamba!' (crocodile) created such a panic that it took Walmsley and Maganga half an hour to get them all on the move again. The bridge, normally fifteen feet (5m) above the water, was almost afloat.

'The roadway of the bridge had long since been washed away, and now nothing was left but logs and branches, on which one had to balance while the water swirled past one's legs. The whole structure groaned and vibrated in the terrible force of the current, and it only required a moderate-sized drifting tree to smash it up completely. I was now feeling horribly weak, and had it not been for Maganga's support I should have been washed away a dozen times. It took us fifteen minutes to get across, and when I at last felt the firm but wet and muddy earth underneath my feet, I heaved a great sigh of relief.'[17]

In true adventure book fashion the bridge collapsed only hours later. There were three more miles of flood to wade through before they could camp on dry land. Word had been sent forward and a motor ambulance turned up to collect Walmsley. Caring little about the rest of the journey, he arrived at Iringa with the mail and stores. Of this ordeal he was to say '... but thanks to Maganga's wonderful nursing I pulled through all right.'

On arrival at Iringa, Walmsley found the flight re-directed to General Northey's headquarters at Njombe, another 150 miles (250km) nearer Lake Nyasa. Urgently required, the only two available BE2cs flew to Njombe but Walmsley was left to follow with all the flight's equipment.

For the rough trek across unknown country, 100 porters were put at Walmsley's disposal. When they understood what was expected of them, nearly all pleaded sickness, but this was cured by the simple expedient of stuffing the mouth of the first patient with crystallised quinine, a loathsome concoction. After this, no second patient appeared. The nearby Little Ruaha river presented them with their first problem. The ox taken along to provide meat rations could not be persuaded to board the pontoon made of empty petrol tins and escaped down river. Few seemed to regret the animal's disappearance, the natives having such implicit faith in the 'boss' to keep them fed.

After the first few miles, they began the steep climb into the Iringa hills. On the high tableland the ground was unexpectedly swampy and the rains closed in on them again as they trudged on to find somewhere to rest for the night. In the wet morning mist they were bitterly cold until the sun appeared but the rain soon resumed and by the end of the day they were both cold and hungry but had reached the halfway mark.

As pre-arranged, a string of porters from Njombe turned up and the Iringa boys were sent back. Nearly 6,000 feet (1,800m) up, the extensive plateau lacked signs of habitation by either man or beast. It varied from park-like land to grassland and in the rain the uncomfortable monotony was relieved only occasionally in Walmsley's eyes by the sight of a clear bubbling stream with wooded banks. For one three-mile (5km) stretch heads were bent against driving hailstones. Each evening a halt was called and, thanks to Walmsley's gun, there was a fair variety of food to cook and enjoy around warming camp-fires. As usual, before turning in, they found the energy to talk and sing, and sometimes on such occasions the natives danced. Highly amusing to all were the efforts of Walmsley to pull a tooth. The patient seemed unperturbed and it was Walmsley who needed a 'tot' before tackling the job. After great exertions, many tries and an extra 'anaesthetic' or two, the offending tooth yielded. The next day, despite a thunderstorm and icy winds, they pressed on to reach their final destination before dark. The welcome received made the extra effort well worthwhile. However the high, bleak aerodrome site at Njombe did not look too promising, but for Walmsley a long and tiring journey across the breadth of German East Africa, some 500 miles, had ended at last.

The weather prevented them from getting airborne for nearly a week and then Walmsley joined 'Hodge' for a flight back towards the much lower eastern plains. Disregarding the virtually useless official maps, they flew on using information given by Captain Sutherland, an African explorer. Too high for aerial observations, they came down to 3,000 feet (900m) and were surprised by a shell bursting only a few hundred feet below them. Finding three enemy camps, Walmsley was given time to make his sketches before 'Hodge' tried out a new bombing contraption. To a frame beneath the wing thirty-six grenades had been attached and twelve were dropped on each camp before turning for home.

It was something new to have to climb to an even greater height to reach the aerodrome, but then to see ahead the top of the escarpment hidden by a dark mass of thunder clouds was an unpleasant shock. Now was the time to test the climbing power of the BE2c's improved ninety-horsepower engine by taking her above the cloud and most of the mountain range. But in the rarefied atmosphere, it took nearly half an hour to reach 7,000 feet (2,000m) before they could look across the top of the clouds. Setting a compass bearing for Njombe, they basked in sunshine and blue sky as they flew just 100 feet (30m) above snowy white billows. From a known mountain peak they checked their direction but just where was the aerodrome? Assuming that they were close, they were about to descend when the fuel gave out. Horrified, they could only glide down and hope to come out of the cloud whilst still at a reasonable height. Three minutes later greenery penetrated the gloom and there below was the familiar sight of their hanger. Jokingly, 'Hodge' congratulated himself on a superb bit of cross-country flying, but Walmsley thanked his lucky golliwog mascot.

Rain continued to hamper operations but when Army Intelligence reported the German force under Captain Wintgens in the neighbourhood of Lake Rukwa, 150 miles (240km) north-west of Njombe, it was essential to have this checked. This posed a new problem. It was likely to be a five-hour trip but the aircraft's fuel tanks gave only four and a half hours' flying time. Somehow, more petrol had to be carried, so two extra two-gallon tins were squeezed into the observer's cockpit. After an hour or so, the petrol in the tins was to be syphoned off into the main fuel tank, which happened to be under the observer's seat. No one had told Walmsley to remove the fine gauze filter from the fuel tank so much of the petrol refused to enter the tank and spilled on to the cockpit floor, first soaking Walmsley then running out to where the red-hot exhaust pipes ran alongside the fuselage. To avoid everything catching fire, 'Hodge' hastily dived to cool the pipes. The petrol evaporated so quickly that Walmsley felt his backside freeze. There was now no chance of completing the reconnaissance so they turned back. The following day, having sorted out the problems and fixing a cycle inner tube, in the form of a spout, to each petrol tin, another attempt was made and this time the refuelling went without a hitch. The result was a record flight of over five hours but they saw nothing. Army Intelligence directions had been wrong.

The remoteness of their operations made it difficult to order or receive any supplies so when the aviation petrol ran out, they had to repeatedly pass motor transport petrol through chamois leather filters. They could not risk any speck of dirt blocking the fuel line and luckily the end-product proved satisfactory. Bombs had to be home made, with dynamite added to petrol tins filled with nails and other potentially lethal bits of metal.

*   *   *

Fearing an invasion of Nyasaland, General Northey decided to send a detachment of troops into Portuguese East Africa and ordered Captain Hodgkinson to support it from an aerodrome at Fort Johnston on the southern tip of Lake Nyasa. Only one BE2c, with Walmsley as the observer, could be spared. Hodgkinson flew the 100 miles (160km) to Weidhaven, a lakeside settlement, dismantled the machine and waited to be collected. With a sergeant and four mechanics, Walmsley's task was to bring the remainder of the flight's gear overland to Alt Langenberg, on the northern tip of the lake, where it could be loaded on to one of the steamers. On their way down the lake to Fort Johnston, they would pick up Hodgkinson and his machine.

Walmsley's party climbed slowly towards the Livingstone mountains. Sweating during the day, they endured bitterly cold nights as they struggled to 9,000 feet (2,750m). A charging elephant caused near panic but potentially more disastrous was Walmsley's attempt to find a moment of peace and quiet away from the main party. The mist came down suddenly and he lost his footing. Only his camera strap, catching on a tree stump, saved him from plunging over a precipice. Fortunately Maganga became worried and went looking for his master and heard his screams. He was just in time to drag the half-stunned Walmsley to safety. It was on this trek that some porters lightened their burden by emptying the petrol cans before the climb, refilling them with water near the end of the trail. Luckily this clever deception was discovered before any serious damage could be done but valuable fuel had been lost. Their ordeal nearly over, the sun warmed their aching limbs as they descended to Alt Langenberg to load up the lake steamer *Gwendolen*. Calling at Weidhaven on the way, it took four days to reach the far end of the lake.

At Fort Johnston a few more days were required to prepare the aerodrome and gather information about enemy activity. Taking off for the first ever flight across Lake Nyasa, Hodgkinson and Walmsley headed for Portuguese territory. Somewhere out there was a well-armed German force and Northey's troops badly needed reliable maps before they could locate and pursue the enemy. Flying over uncharted terrain, this was an opportunity for the airmen to demonstrate how useful their map-making skills had become. Almost instinctively, they had been acquiring these as a means of self-preservation, for without the skill to map-read the earth and use a compass they could easily have just disappeared in the vastness of the African wilderness.

The day started pleasantly enough as they became the first to fly over Lake Nyasa. Nearing the Livingstone mountain range, the severity of the 'bumps' surprised them both. While 'Hodge' struggled with the controls to stop the machine going into a spin, the terrified Walmsley - the airmen were never supplied with parachutes - expected to be thrown out any minute. To make matters worse, the 'Old Bee' was not climbing too well and as they flew into the gap between two peaks, the sides of the mountains closed in and the trees came up to meet them. In the gap, barely 100 yards (90m) across, there was no room to turn but soon lightness loomed ahead and the next minute they emerged into sunlight and open space. Much relieved, they flew on to complete their reconnaissance work but found signs of only one German patrol.

Returning over the mountain, a strong smell of petrol alarmed Walmsley. Near the carburettor the petrol pipe was leaking badly but it was out of Walmsley's reach. Knowing that they could ill afford to lose any petrol, something had to be done. Walmsley climbed out on to the wing and, leaning back into his cockpit, could just reach and hold the pipe firmly enough to stem the flow. Soaked with petrol and close alongside the red-hot exhaust, he dared not imagine what would happen if his clothing caught fire. He hung on grimly until a few minutes later the engine stopped as the last drop of petrol was used. Fortunately, they had just crossed the mountains and were able to glide down to a lakeside landing. The usual crowd of natives gathered but Walmsley spotted one with an old penny-farthing bicycle. This he commandeered and, swallowing his pride, rode off shakily, a source of much amusement. After an uncomfortable fourteen miles (23km), he reached the lake and civilisation. A couple of days later the 'Old Bee' was brought in. The fuel pipe was repairable, otherwise she was undamaged.

Rarely were flights over East Africa routine but this one had been an extraordinary one and the citation, dated the 25th July 1917, awarding Leo Walmsley the Military Cross reads:

> 'During five hours flight over the enemy's lines the petrol pipe burst near the carburettor. Lieut. Walmsley acting as Observer behaved with great gallantry and coolness, attempting to stop the leak in spite of the great danger of fire, eventually enabling the pilot to land safely in a mealie patch in our lines. This Officer has done invaluable work throughout the campaign and was mentioned in despatches by General Smuts.'[18]

The reconnaissance flights were over wild country and forest-clad mountains where there seemed to be no signs of human habitation. The animals had this to themselves but a variety of tracks showed up from the air. If these ran straight, they were followed. They could, perhaps, lead to an enemy encampment. Extra tins of petrol were always carried so, with no bombs, they could only hope to scare the enemy by diving and firing a few rounds from their pistols. From time to time, the possibilities of a forced landing and the chances of survival troubled their minds. If flying time was running out, sketches had to be completed speedily and the turn made for home. After five hours, the tanks would be dry and once or twice it took the last drop to see them safely to the aerodrome.

Once more, they needed to get closer to the enemy and Walmsley sailed from Fort Johnston for Lungwena Bay to start looking for a site near Mtonia, which had been occupied by the British troops. For the first time, they would be flying from an aerodrome in Portuguese East Africa. It was a few miles inland from Lake Nyasa and required the efforts of 700 African women to clear the site of vegetation and termite hills. When ready, a message to Fort Johnston brought 'Hodge' flying in. Joined by Walmsley, the two airmen resumed their aerial surveys until it was necessary to move forward again. The army had been asked to prepare a landing place at Mwembe, also in Portuguese territory, and when 'Hodge' and Walmsley approached it they could see a strip only 150 yards (130m) by twenty yards (30m) in the centre of the camp marked with a huge white calico letter 'T'. Only the flight commander's skill brought the machine down to land safely.

After a few more flights, Hodgkinson had to fly to Ssongea, about 100 miles (160km) over the border, in German East Africa. Walmsley was left with three days of rough walking back to the lake for a boat to Fort Johnston. Collecting the flight's equipment, he sailed for Weidhaven where he was given the news that 'Hodge' was missing. There was no better news when Walmsley reported to General Northey at Ssongea but there was now another BE2c awaiting collection from Iringa. With 'Hodge' lost, there was now no pilot so Walmsley volunteered to act as navigator if a pilot from Iringa would fly the machine back. Taking a car, he arrived at Iringa in the grip of fever only to find Blackburn, the new pilot, also suffering from malaria. Their flight to Ssongea had to be postponed for a few days but they were pleased to learn that Hodgkinson and his passenger were safe. The new aeroplane was required urgently and neither pilot nor observer were properly fit when they decided to take off. It was soon obvious that the new machine was not behaving itself as they could gain no height so they turned towards the aerodrome, some two miles (3km) away. Below them were nothing but trees.

'Soon the altimeter was reading 100 feet, and the little hand was flickering backwards ... 90 feet ... 80 feet ... 70 feet ... A big tree suddenly loomed above us ... Blackburn banked steeply and avoided it, only to find another behind ... I saw the fat trunk of a baobab 100 feet away ... we dived steeply ... there came a terrific crash ... the starboard plane [wing] whizzed over my head like a sail of a windmill ... then came a great darkness.'[19]

From Walmsley's recollections of the crash, they appear to have flown into the ground rather than glided down gently and the consequences were far more serious than the previous crashes he had survived. In fact, Walmsley was to write later that apparently the pilot had fainted and fallen forward on to the 'joystick'. A strut and some rigging pinned Walmsley under the wreckage but the shaken Blackburn managed to struggle free. To add to their problems, a breeze was bringing a small bush fire towards them and the petrol-soaked wreckage. Blackburn's frenzied activities stirred Walmsley into semi-consciousness and, with superhuman effort, the wing was levered up and the dazed Walmsley was dragged free. He fainted again, but when he finally came round it was to find that the fire had burnt itself out. Blackburn, who had gone for help, returned with a doctor and, although Walmsley's injuries were not so serious, appendicitis was suspected and, what with malaria and the onset of dysentery, there was only one place for him. With hospital treatment, his injuries and unpleasant disorders were soon mended but the shock he had suffered put an end to his flying days, and was something only time could heal. But Walmsley carried the mental scars for the rest of his life.

Over a prolonged period the combination of exhaustion, illness and both physical and mental strain had finally taken its toll. Throughout the campaign, Walmsley had admitted that every dangerous situation — and there were many — made him sweat with fear. He never claimed to be a hero, just an ordinary chap doing his duty and accepting whatever risk that might involve. In *So Many Loves*, Walmsley wrote 'My nervous system had gone all wrong' but on exactly how it affected him, Walmsley is reticent. He remained a further six months in Africa and seems to have spent most of his time in and out of hospitals, convalescing and on 'light duties'. At first he was sent to South Africa, travelling in a hospital ship from Mombasa to Cape Town. Returning some weeks later to Dar es Salaam, where No 26 Squadron now had its headquarters, he was well enough to travel by train to Durban and complete the journey by sea. At Dar es Salaam, on the 4th September 1917, Walmsley was removed from the squadron's strength.

* * *

Although Walmsley must now have been free to return to England, it was almost six months before he stepped off the Cherbourg to Southampton ferry to greet the English spring of 1918. His interesting journey home, seemingly organised by himself, began from Dar es Salaam, where he took passage in a ship sailing through the Red Sea to Suez. He did not go through the canal but travelled overland to Alexandria and the nearby RFC training establishment at Aboukir. Here he noticed with excitement that ancient stones from Cleopatra's summer resort had been used for some of the buildings. His light duties gave him plenty of time to explore and he even took himself much farther south for a sightseeing tour of Luxor. A spell in a Cairo hospital suggests that he was probably still suffering from recurrent bouts of fever and depression. Finally he left Alexandria for the Italian port of Taranto to begin his own 'Grand Tour', which allowed him to enjoy some of the best of Italy and France.

If he now seemed to be having a good time, who could begrudge him this? He had been in Africa for more than two years and seen more active service than many. Francis Brett Young lasted only nine months before he returned home ill. The South African flyer, Van der Spuy, with whom Walmsley had 'enjoyed' his first flight in a Henri Farman, had taken himself off to England after just one year. Smuts had done a great job but in January 1917, after one year, he too quit Africa. His false claim that the war by that time 'may be said to be over'[20] was echoed years later by Van der Spuy, who for some reason wrote 'At the conclusion of the East African campaign in 1916, No 26 Squadron Royal Flying Corps returned to England.' He, but *not* the squadron, returned to England. Perhaps he felt the need to support Smuts, his illustrious fellow countryman. He also wrote 'Without aircraft, the East African campaign would have lasted much longer.' But it was the armistice, not the aeroplane, that brought the war to an end. Even then, it took a few days for the news to reach Africa, and Lettow-Vorbeck did not lay down his arms until the 21st November 1918. How could Smuts and Van der Spuy have not known this? Walmsley and all those who remained with the British Expeditionary Force certainly did.

Almost inevitably the sheer scale of the war in Europe and the numbers involved meant that the African 'sideshow' would be overshadowed. Perhaps another reason for this was that the majority of troops fighting in Africa were not from Britain. And later, from the unfair comments Walmsley heard or read, he must have wondered at times whether the dangers and hardships faced by all those who served in No 26 Squadron had been worthwhile. He knew the value of its work should not be judged by the number of casualties or material damage inflicted on the enemy. Almost always the main purpose of BE2c flights was reconnaissance but they did drop a few bombs. The heavier Henri Farmans were sent more deliberately to bomb the enemy but they too spent most of their time on reconnaissance. But especially worth remembering when the squadron's contribution to the East African campaign is assessed are the little-known activities of Flight 'A' stationed in the vicinity of Lake Nyasa. Lieutenant Walmsley and Captain Hodgkinson were very much part of the campaign in that remote corner of Africa.

However, just before his book was published, Walmsley was gratified to find that even Lettow-Vorbeck, while claiming that bombing had caused no crippling damage, did not deny that the aeroplanes had caused himself and his men many problems. And General Northey showed his appreciation when he wrote of the immense value of the reconnaissance work carried out by the squadron:

> 'Each flight was made with a definite object which was generally fulfilled ... For making sketch-maps of unsurveyed country, for obtaining details of the topography, mountains, rivers, swamps and other military obstacles, for bombing and otherwise directly attacking the enemy's camps or porter convoys, and for keeping up communication between wide-spread units of a command, the aeroplane fully justified its use.'[21]

Because he was invalided out early, Francis Brett Young's stirring account of *Marching On Tanga* was available to readers while the war raged and attracted great interest. But judging from the sales, it would seem that by the time Walmsley's book had reached the public, interest in the war may have faded. Nevertheless, he must have felt very proud when General Northey offered to write an introduction for *Flying and Sport in East Africa* and, generous with his praise, took the opportunity to recall the formidable task undertaken by Walmsley and his pilot:

> 'He and his Flight Commander, Captain Hodgkinson, M.C., were among the bravest of our brave airmen. If they were not daily facing the dangers of the enemy aircraft and guns, they encountered other odds every time they flew.'[22]

The war had provided Walmsley with the greatest adventure of his life but it had left its mark on him. He returned to the less exciting life of a civilian, having survived more than a dozen crash landings, been mentioned in despatches four times and been awarded the Military Cross.

Leo Walmsley was just one of the many unsung heroes of the First World War.

Peter Barton

PART THREE

THE WHIRLWIND YEARS

CHAPTER 5

The Homecoming

WHEN Leo took that last step from the soil of East Africa on to the ship, his active service was over. He had come a long way from the gauche young man who had eagerly enlisted to see the world and seek adventure. Never in his wildest dreams could he have anticipated the results of his action. His experiences had such a profound impact on him that they were to affect him for the rest of his life. As with most servicemen, he was a changed man by the end of his military career. He had taken full advantage of the opportunities for adventure, accepting that he had to endure physical and mental ordeals as well as pleasurable excitement. The lively spirit of his youth remained but with it had developed a restlessness, which became a noticeable facet of his personality. The carefree attitude of his boyhood had been replaced by a tendency to depression, which on occasions threatened to overwhelm him. The horrors of his wartime ordeals were never to be completely erased.

On his return to England, which appears to have been in early July 1918, he found, rather to his disgust, that he had been given a desk job. This was not as unfortunate as it might have seemed. He was to serve with military intelligence with the Royal Air Force, which was formed by a merger of the RNAS with the RFC on the 1st April 1918. It was here that he first met Harold Brighouse, author and playwright, who played a major part in setting up the propaganda section of military intelligence, with responsibility for presenting news and stories of the war in a way considered suitable for public consumption. While working in military intelligence, Leo had the opportunity to develop further his writing and oral skills. He found that he had a talent for public speaking and he put this to good use.

Mainly through the Lecture Agency Ltd in London, he was offered many engagements throughout the country. His previous teaching experience before the war had no doubt given him a good grounding for this task. The lectures were very well received wherever he went and he delighted his audiences with many serious and amusing stories about his flying experiences and his travels throughout Europe. To him, the most important of all were his stories about Africa. From his first sight of that country, it had cast a spell on him, creating within him a depth of feeling which at times verged on the obsessive. Despite being plagued by recurring attacks of depression and malaria, the nostalgia remained. In *So Many Loves* Leo writes:

'... evermore virulent than the bug of malaria was the bug of Africa itself, that terrible yearning to be back.'

His love of Africa was to last for many years and it did, in fact, play an influential part in his development as a writer and gave inspiration for original ideas that he

Leo Walmsley, late 1920s

was to try to develop later. Short stories centred on Africa were followed by full-length stories. He had a limited success with them, but they did serve him as a form of apprenticeship.

The newspapers reported his lectures and proclaimed that he was 'gifted with that fluency of speech, lucidity of expression and power of graphic description which, plus a fine sense of humour, go to make a popular lecturer' and 'a racy lecturer ... For real humour it would be difficult to surpass the lecture Lieutenant Walmsley delivered.'

The lectures, often accompanied by lantern slides, were presented as an entertainment, but there was also a more serious purpose behind them and that was recruiting for the RAF. A recruiting officer was usually conspicuous in the lecture hall. Despite his own experiences, Walmsley painted a rather glowing picture of life in the service. One report of a lecture in Hereford ends with:

'The whole lecture was greatly enjoyed. Lieut. Walmsley closed with a very hearty invitation to young men of 17 years and 10 months to avail themselves of the opportunity now afforded them of joining the R.A.F. They would find it a fine sporting life. He minimised the danger. It was not the death trap existence some would make out. There was a great future for commercial aviation. Aircraft had in it all the elements of a great career.'

The last sentences at least were prophetic.

He had already started writing about his flying experiences and was determined to finish this at the earliest opportunity. Initially *An Airman's Experiences in East Africa* was published in serial form in *Blackwood's Magazine* but within a year it had been expanded into a complete book which *Blackwood* published in 1920. To his actual flying experiences Leo added reminiscences of game hunting, which accounts for the somewhat strange combination of activities in the title *Flying and Sport in East Africa*. The immaturity of his writing is noticeable, particularly in the early sections of the book, but it is interesting to note a gradual change to a slightly more mature style towards the end of the book. He was, of course, an inexperienced writer at this point and would have benefited from editorial advice, which could have resulted in the production of a very important record of the East African campai n. What is more, had his personal wartime diaries and sketches survived, their inclusion would have elevated his book into a unique depiction of that field of conflict.

He also sent contributions to newspapers and other periodicals about a variety of subjects, many of which were visionary, thought-provoking and proffered ideas that were often in advance of the current thinking. His fertile brain came up with ideas for using aerial photography for far more than just map-making. It might be applied to carrying out surveys of archaeological sites or mapping navigational channels through reefs and sand banks in shallow waters, or even finding the shoals of fish to aid the fishing fleets. He envisaged long flights being possible by the aeroplanes of the future and people travelling by this means on pleasure trips, carrying mail, theatre companies and produce to and from Africa.

In his efforts to popularise flying and in his relation to the RAF, he spoke out for fairer treatment of ex-servicemen and suggested ways of smartening the uniform and the need to retain the use of the pigeon post, 'the winged life savers' used for communication, in seeking help by the crew when the plane had crashed. For a year or two, these and other causes, such as teachers' pay and status were tackled with his usual enthusiasm.

Leo had started his lecture tours on the 20th August 1918 at Whitby Coliseum and during the following few days visited other Yorkshire towns in the area. Later he went to Bury and Horwich, and south to Bromley in Kent. In 1919 the lectures continued at such diverse venues as Newcastle, London, Dublin and Rochester, the latter being at a very important moment in his life.

The young man, whose longing for adventure had precipitated him into the war, had survived. His experiences had been more hazardous and exciting than he could ever have dreamed of. He had seized his chance and now that the 'adventure' was over, he would make full use of what his enquiring mind had accumulated during those eventful years.

Frederick W Lane

CHAPTER 6

On a Shoestring

AT 11.30am on Thursday the 16th October 1919 at the age of twenty-seven,
Leo Walmsley married Elsie Susanna Preston,[1] five years his junior, at the
Paddington Registry Office, London. Throughout her life she preferred
to call herself Suzanne.

The circumstances in which they originally met each other are still a mystery
but it is said that Leo's first meeting with her was in South Africa. He was there in
1917, convalescing after his last, and near fatal, aeroplane crash. There is a tradition
in the Walmsley family that he met her again in London while waiting in a queue
outside a cinema. Soon after this reunion they decided to marry.

At the time of their meeting again, Leo was still in uniform and actively touring
the country lecturing, the theme of his lectures being his experiences in East
Africa and the RAF. Many of the lectures were in the North East but he also went
to Dublin and to the south of England. On the day before he was to marry
Suzanne, he was asked if he would lecture at Gravesend in Kent as the original
speaker was taken ill and could not attend. There is an interesting report in
the local paper with the headlines 'Historic Sunday School — Anniversary at
Gravesend.'

> 'Sunday was a significant occasion in the history of Princes Street Congregational Church,
> Gravesend when services were held in celebration of 118th anniversary of the Sunday
> School and Bible Institute ... The Superintendent went on to say that Lieut. Leo Walmsley,
> M.C., the distinguished airman, who did such admirable work in East Africa during the
> war, had come forward and would treat them to a story of his flying experiences. Lieut.
> Walmsley had come at great personal inconvenience. He was going to be married on the
> morrow at 11.30, and to make sure that he didn't lose his fiance he had brought her with
> him that evening ...'

Leo and Suzanne would seem, to the onlooker, to have had little in common in
their family background, character, or interests, but that they were much in love
is not in doubt.

Leo's family struggled to make a living, whereas it would seem that Suzanne's
family was reasonably well off. His educational opportunities had been good, as
we have already discussed, but because he did not like school and was rebellious,
he did not make the most of his chances. Although there is no record of Suzanne's
education, it would seem that she was well educated, had a vivid imagination, had
a considerable interest and proficiency in languages, and was well read in French
and Spanish as well as being fluent in both. She had an avid appreciation of the
arts and was intellectual in her outlook. Leo seemed to have little interest in his
appearance whereas she had always dressed well, sometimes in a personal adaptation

of the latest fashion, but more often in her own style that was in contradiction to the fashionable trend. Leo was good-looking and had an attractive personality while Suzanne, although not unattractive, was not considered to be beautiful. She had a pleasing personality, was cultured and knew how to make herself look attractive. Leo was charming and friendly and had the sort of personality that attracted friendship and help when he needed it. Whilst they were so very different, they had two things in common that sustained them during the years they were together, love for each other and love of adventure.

It is tantalisingly difficult to establish facts about their life together from Leo's writing and Suzanne hardly ever talked about it. He seems to have taken great care to conceal her identity and their marriage but why he did so is unlikely ever to be known.

It is known that he contemplated writing a book about their life together. It was said by someone who knew them both well that if that book about their married life had been written, it would seem that an obvious title for it would be 'Fever Chart'. They had always, it seemed, suffered from an acute restlessness of body and mind. They were constantly on the move, living in no one place for more than six months. But why? It was not merely the desire for a geographical change of scene. It was not merely financial exigence. No matter how hard up they had been, they had always managed to steer clear of debt until the St John's Wood period. The problem, he felt, was very subtle. It was a problem of the times, of universal significance!

In Walmsley's writing, published and unpublished, Suzanne remains a shadowy enigmatic figure and is often referred to as my *wife* or disguised by the use of such pseudonyms as *Joe, Helen, Claire* and *Billy*. Even in his own personal diary he used his pet name *Wendy* when referring to her. He was *Peter Pan* and she his *Wendy*, a whimsical aspect of his personality.

He was reticent about talking about her to anyone, even his subsequent wives, and as far as they were concerned, she might never have existed.

Correspondence reveals that Leo kept in contact with her long after they were divorced and he was with his second wife, Margaret. A letter written by her on the 25th March, 1944 from 12 Woodstock Close, Oxford, where she was temporarily staying with the Blunden family, indicates that this was the case. The letter is in answer to Leo's reply to a previous letter that she had sent him. Her letter refers to Leo's autobiography, *So Many Loves*, and to privacy about her past and also to the break-up of his marriage with Margaret, which will be referred to in a later chapter. It also contains references to her own activities and thoughts and the possible reason for their eventual separation. The 'man from Australia' to whom she refers is Doctor Harrop, one of her husbands subsequent to Leo.

'Dear Leo,
It was kind of you to reassure me about the auto-biography. I have not had a public life, or at least only a very limited one, but I still have to earn money, and the world that pays one salaries still has a different standard for men, so one has to be reticent about one's past. No, I had no idea of any unhappy circumstances when I wrote, and am still quite ignorant of your tragedy. I do most sincerely hope nothing awful has happened to you. When things were most difficult for me I used to find it consoling to think I had made someone's

life happy, or at least contributed, if only by getting out of it. You must remember that I have been out of England for many years, and am really only trapped here by the war. I know no one in our old set, it was purely a co-incidence that I came here for a time when my husband was forced to leave England without me. Now I am quite too bewildered to realise the whole tragedy. It was so unnecessary. They had been waiting eighteen months for someone for that job, and he was the right man, and for the sake of giving him an extra month to recover from flu, they sent him away ill and alone, and now he is dead. Although we had been together for about two years, we had only just got married to fulfil the necessary formalities of passports etc. It is just possible that the British Council will send me alone there or somewhere in Africa.

It really does not matter what you say about me in the book — as far as I am concerned. As you say, it is not the facts, but the form which matters. If it suits you to say or think I am an intellectual, the truth is of no importance. Actually I am an incorrigible vagabond, and have only used my rather meagre intellectual equipment to get myself around the world wherever I wanted to go, a bit of an effort sometimes, but, "for to admire and for to see … It aint never done any good, but I can't stop if I tried."

The things I do very well are not things one earns one's living at — swimming and sailing boats. But I managed to have some wonderful bits of life and often wished you had been there. Once I went with an old Dutch retired skipper and one Javanese sailor in a small boat across from Sydney to the Philippines and cruised about among a hundred isles. Sometimes I did well in life and sometimes I had to starve. The latter never worried me too much, and I often thought how you would have enjoyed bits of it.

Thank you for not replying to the "man from Australia". He is the only person I ever met who definitely wanted to do me any harm, and he has several times made a very good attempt.

I think your books are very fine. I like their rhythm. I like the form in which they grow, and the sense of life they leave one with. You shouldn't worry about what Sylvia says — she is almost what I should call a pure intellectual, and as such, must be an imperfect critic of anything.

Fishermen at War still remains for me to read.

I don't know what I shall do next. If the world was open it would be different. If I had a quiet place, and cheap, I should get through this piece of work about two lives starting, one in Italy, the other in Spain about 1935, coming together through a series of strange adventures, to end, or to have ended in Ethiopia. A pity not to do it but I am not a writer, so can't work in any place or under any conditions. If I don't do this, I may get a job as a stewardess, so as to be off again. I don't seem to have any physical fear, and death is before me today as a white sail on a windy day.

No, I don't think our marriage came to an end through intellectualism, but rather through the less romantic medium of india rubber — no good for a young woman's first and most complete love, but this is something one had, unfortunately no way of knowing when I was young. It was a difficult time to be young in, without the protection of Victorians and Edwardians or the straight information of the moderns. However, one tried to have courage, and I suppose that is all anyone can do.

Probably I shan't ever recover from what has just happened. I feel curiously stunned and without my usual initiative. I hope you are not truly unhappy, and that all will go well with you.

Suzanne.'

It seems that he might also have met her occasionally when he was away from home visiting friends and his publishers. There is no evidence that this was anything but a continued friendship and concern for someone he had once cared for a great deal and who had shared an important part of his life.

In the late 1940s she went to Fowey, Cornwall, living there for a while with her mother, and a letter to Leo dated the 26th September 1947 seems to imply that she would have chased after him to London if she had known that he was there. Friends of Leo who were in Fowey at the time were convinced that she wanted to get back together with him, but so many years had passed and he did not want to become involved with her again.

Leo and Suzanne suffered from the general restlessness of their generation. The First World War had finished and there did not seem to be any role for the young people. So, like many of that generation, they became immersed in the somewhat mad, frivolous and superficial life that it seemed would provide happiness.

There were the artificial stimuli of party-going, dancing, lively music and extrovert fashions and the groups of intellectuals. For those who were fortunate enough to be financially secure, this artificiality would not matter, but Leo and Suzanne had little money and were constantly on the move, sometimes to escape their creditors.

It was a time of great posing by the 'artistic set' and those who considered themselves intellectuals. Leo and Suzanne at this time were not immune from the influences that surrounded them. Some years later, when Leo was having doubts about his art of writing, he wrote to fellow writer Harold Brighouse (author of *Hobson's Choice*), who replied with a letter of his accusing Leo and Suzanne of being great posers and Leo of using his chosen occupation as an excuse for a lack of success in other areas.

> 'Artist? Forget it, my dear Leo. About 90% of your failures and your troubles arise from the artist's pose. I've never had any use for that pose myself. Writing's a job of work. There's always dissatisfaction at not working, whatever the job is. Ask any unemployed. We're cursed by a conviction we ought to work. I think I'm for a slave state which compels work for a few hours a day. But this poppycock about art! Rubbish, pernicious rubbish! You've made it your constant excuse for the evasion of responsibilities and it isn't a valid excuse. So far as I can see, you are working, which is splendid. Art be damned for a tale…
>
> But, of course, Leo, you posed and Suzanne posed. She achieved at times a grotesque artificiality. She didn't discourage your poses and I hope Jerry [Margaret] hits you on the head if you try to weep on her lap and tell her you're a thwarted genius. I hope she's a young woman of a strong sense. You badly need laughing at. If she can do that she'll make you happier than Suzanne did.'[2]

At one time or another they lived in such places as furnished rooms in a ten-roomed villa near Genoa, a stone cottage near Robin Hoods Bay, a single room in Pimlico, a luxurious studio flat in South Kensington, a maisonette in West Kensington, a villa in Ilfracombe, the Palace Hotel in Torquay, and an ex-army hut near Exmouth. For periods of varying duration, they returned each year to Robin Hoods Bay. Interspersed with these moves were travels in Europe, West Africa and North America, mostly undertaken together.

He had taken Suzanne to Bay a month or two before they were married and there was a report in the *Whitby Gazette* in August 1919 which said:

> 'Lieutenant Leo Walmsley and a lady friend, with a special combination of spoon and spinner bait, in an hour's sail across the Bay, landed two stones of fish, including a cod weighing six pounds and many mackerel, billet and codling.'

This was probably on a visit to Leo's parents in preparation for the wedding and he had taken the opportunity to introduce Suzanne to his great passion, fishing. Over the years he never lost his love of Bay but Suzanne hated it. She hated the cold of the East Coast and longed to be where it was warmer. She also missed the lively life among the intellectuals and the art set. She was, however, not entirely isolated from the art world in Bay as Leo's father was a competent artist and the picturesque setting of the area attracted many artists who were, or later became, famous.

For a while in the earlier part of their married life together, they lived in a stone cottage in Bay called 'Lantern Cottage'. Leo later renamed it 'Waratah' after a ship of that name disappeared without trace, presumably as he was having problems at that time and wanted to disappear from his creditors without trace.

There is a foreword to his novel *The Silver Blimp*, which was published in 1921, but he must have started it in the cottage in Bay over the winter of 1919/20.

> 'We planned that we'd write this book in the long winter months, over our own fireside; so that, while existing in a land of snow and fog, we might live in a land of eternal sunshine — our beloved Africa. Thus it was written; in a little stone cottage on the edge of the Yorkshire moors, with the cold rain beating on the windows, and the sea-wind a-howling; a bright red fire on the hearth, cracking and spluttering; our dog Peter asleep on the mat. Could I do otherwise than dedicate this, my first work of fiction, to her who sat beside me, critical, suggestive, helpful always - my dear wife?'

They must have been very much in love for Suzanne to have stayed there, in the place she considered so cold and unpleasant.

Leo and Suzanne set off on their first real adventure together in the summer of 1920. It had to be a modest one as Suzanne had no money and he had only a little of what he had saved out of his gratuity on discharge from the Royal Air Force.

They decided on a cycle-camping tour of Normandy and Brittany and then on to Paris. They bought a tent and bicycles and set off, the idea being that they would continue south to the Mediterranean coast, find a fisherman's cottage and stay there for the winter so that Leo could write. Leo wrote about the holiday on his return and started it with:

> 'Our cycle-camping tour in Western France was born, not of reading the alluring advertisements of Thomas Cook and the South-Eastern Railway Company, but of sheer downright necessity. The lease of our house terminated on the last day of May; there was no prospect of getting so much as a decent sized fowl house until September; hotels, barges, army huts, dug-outs, boarding establishments, caravans, were all for various reasons impracticable. England had become too small for us; we must clear out. But where, *where* should we go ?'[4]

Some three years later Leo wrote again about the same holiday but changed the story. This time he starts with:

Leo and Suzanne on Filey beach

'Could there possibly be a more delightful way of spending a glorious summer-time of year than on a cycle-camping holiday with ones wife in Rural Normandy?

Think of the romance of it! The wrapping of your furniture in pale pink shrouds, the exchanging of your money into crisp French notes, the swift rush of the boat express, the setting foot in a foreign country, the leaping on to cycles, the call of the long French roads, the smell of peat fires and new-mown hay, the taste for Normandy butter and Camembert cheese, the open care-free life, and the dolce far niente - particularly the dolce far niente ... All of which explains how it came about that on a fine evening in early June last year a young couple were to be seen sprawling on the grassy bank of a Normandy Road somewhere within fifty miles of the historically famous town of Falaise
I was the man and the girl was my wife.'[5]

Although the holiday gave him ideas for his writing, it was not a success.

'From the morning we mounted our bikes in Rouen for the first stage of the journey to Lisieux it rained almost without stop.'[6]

Because it rained practically all of the time they were there, they did not enjoy themselves. Suzanne wanted to give up the tour and head for Paris and live there for a while. She thought it would be good for Leo to live there, giving him the opportunity to meet other writers and artists. Leo's thoughts were elsewhere.

'How I longed for Africa, the sunshine, the clear vistas, the sound of drums instead of the eternal lowing of Normandy cattle, for black people instead of gloomy-looking peasants who seemed more under the weather than we were ...'[7]

Leo had an attack of fever and was laid up for a week in an expensive hotel. They discussed what they should do and Leo compromised on a plan to go to the coast first, then by train to Paris if they had enough money. At the coast he would like to meet the fisher people whom he had heard so much about and to see the famous marine zoological collecting grounds at Roscoff.

They eventually arrived at Roscoff[8] and as their money was running low, they decided to stay there a while in a *pension*, to enable him to write some more articles to help their financial situation. While they were there, he heard that his book *Flying and Sport in East Africa* had been published and had received a good review in *The Times* reviews of 'Books of the Week'. A publisher contacted Leo and offered an advance of £100 if he would write a boys' adventure book based on his East African experiences. He accepted and now that his finances looked a little healthier, he and Suzanne took the train to Paris.

When they arrived in Paris, they made for the Latin Quarter, to a studio of an art student whom they knew. He was studying marine biology. They were immediately in the authentic atmosphere of the art colony. They went from studio to studio, looking at pictures and sculptures. Leo admitted that he knew little about 'modern art' or art cults. Cezanne, Gauguin, Picasso, Mattisse, Epstein, Mestrovic, James Joyce, Wyndham Lewis, Ezra Pound had meant nothing to him and he was bewildered by it all. They joined in the studio parties and drank beer, vodka and absinthe in the open-air cafes and went to the music halls, opera and ballet.

> 'Claire (Suzanne) was in her element. She could speak French like a native, and I am sure she would have been content if we'd found some sort of apartment and settled down for at least that winter. But our money was nearly gone. The life we were leading was too distracting for work. I was at a disadvantage having only my Scarborough school knowledge of French (How I cursed again my wasted opportunities) and often at a party when everyone was talking or arguing excitedly about art, the tobacco smoke mingled with the fumes of alcohol was so thick that you could hardly see across the particular studio we were in, that terrible nausea for Africa would come over me, and I'd have a fierce longing to be off.'[9]

Leo at last found life there too distracting for work so they returned home.

Frederick W Lane

CHAPTER 7

Films and Travel

SOON after returning, Leo decided that he needed to be by the sea to write his boys' adventure book. As Suzanne did not like Robin Hoods Bay, they went to Ilfracombe and lived in a small furnished house called 'Brimlands' in Hillsborough Road. Neither of them liked it there so when the book was finished, they moved back to London and took a furnished maisonette on the Chelsea side of Fulham. This move would have been in the autumn of 1920 or early spring of the following year.

Leo's publishers wanted more adventure books for young people but he realised that, unless he could produce them at a great rate or could get more money for them than he was currently offered, he could not make a living from them.

It was at this time that his interest in cinema films was reawakened and he reflected on their future and what they could portray. Previously in 1919 he had written what would turn out to be prophetic ideas for a newspaper, extolling the virtues of 'A New field for the Cinema-man'. He was often ahead of his time in his thinking.

'By means of the cinematograph most of the great geographical wonders of the world have already been brought within armchair reach of the general public. In the luxurious comfort of a modern theatre it is now possible to view the world and lonesome ice-parks and snowfields of the Antarctic, the luxuriant tropical forests of the Amazon and Central Africa, to make a tour through the wonder cities of India and Japan, to gaze at the rolling prairies of the West, to thrill at the majestic grandeur of the Stanley and Niagara Falls, to look into the sulphurous crater of some world-famous volcano.

But the rapid development of the aircraft during the last few years has thrown open to the cinema man an entirely new field for operations. It will be some years yet before flying comes within the means of the ordinary man and woman as a regular mode of travel, but by means of film it will be possible to experience at any rate some of the artistic joys of aviation ...

A very effective type of cinema camera has been evolved and tested by the photographic section of the R.A.F. however, and as soon as civil aviation comes into its own, doubtless this machine or a modification of it, will be employed for taking thousands of feet of the air-view, not only in England but in all parts of the world ...'[1]

He had seen films of Africa but thought that they lacked form and, above all, a story. They simply presented the facts. Leo conceived the idea of not simply showing animals in their native haunts, but of giving a complete picture of tropical Africa by showing how all the creatures that lived there were subject to the one great law, that of survival.

With his usual unbounded enthusiasm, he developed a mass of ideas for films. His agent suggested that he write them down and he would submit them on Leo's behalf to various wealthy people who might fund an expedition to film in Africa. Leo put his ideas down on paper in the form of a film script, having first bought and studied a book telling him how to write scenarios. Suzanne was as excited as he was and was already wondering where and how they would go to East Africa. He was worried about her enthusiasm but dared not tell her of his fears that conditions there would not be suitable for a white woman. The place abounded with mosquitoes and tsetse flies and there was great danger of malaria and other equally unpleasant diseases. He had already formed the idea that he could leave her somewhere in a healthy area such as Nairobi in the highlands whilst he went off to make the film.

Leo submitted his scenarios to his publisher and then waited. There were weeks of waiting with no sign of any progress. He continued with his writing, getting more despondent about the lack of progress on the filming proposals. He even contacted well-known people in the public eye such as Lord Northcliffe and George Bernard Shaw. The spring of 1921 came. They remained at Fulham, he finished *The Silver Blimp*, the story that he had started earlier in the cottage in Bay and throughout the summer wrote other stories and articles for newspapers and magazines and on occasions gave lectures. Meanwhile, he kept up a dilatory correspondence with his great friend, Dr Sam Wilson.

Suzanne was in her element.

'Claire (Suzanne) liked town and was happy. She'd got some sort of job in a small West-end picture gallery specialising in modern art and she was meeting a lot of interesting people. She was also attending courses in art and criticism at University College and was going to the School of Oriental Studies. We went to all the shows we could afford, especially the Old Vic, and concerts at the Albert and Queens Hall and at the smaller halls in the West-end, and of course we went to the movies. I learnt to appreciate the music of Beethoven and Bach and Schubert and the sculpture of Epstein whom we often met in a little bohemian Club in Beak Street together with his famous model Dolores ... I was becoming quite a highbrow myself but I used another "club" which was in complete contrast to this, and was a constant stimulus to the life of adventure I yearned for. This was an old fashioned coffee house called Groom's at the Strand end of Fleet Street, where a room was reserved every week day for managers of the combined literary and lecture agency, and men for whom the agency acted. Some were stay-at-home people like Will Owen the cartoonist, Hamilton Fyffe, who later became editor of the *Daily Herald*. But often famous explorers came in, and it was there that I met Sir Ernest Shackleton, Captain Worseley and Evans of the *Broke,* Frederick Villiers, the famous war correspondent, and H.W. Nevinson.'[2]

They both went to dancing classes and it is more than likely that it was she who would have insisted that he learned the latest dances. Leo hated being in town when the weather was fine but trips to Richmond and Hampton Court and a boat on the river compensated a little. During these outings Leo looked longingly and enviously at the anglers along the river banks.

They continued to mix with intellectuals and artists and Leo was conscious of the effect that this was having on his own personality and outlook. He felt the need to escape from this lifestyle from time to time, hence his visits to Groom's. Sir Ernest Shackleton and the other men of adventure once again stimulated in him the life of adventure for which he yearned.

Tenaciously he pursued his idea of filming but time passed without any apparent results and he was tired of waiting. He then tried the American and British film companies in Wardour Street and became so desperate that he even approached a German film company. He did this with some embarrassment because he intended to film in territory in Africa that the Germans had lost during the war. All this without any satisfactory results.

He then thought of another approach. He had previously been accepted as a Fellow of The Royal Geographical Society because of an article he had written for its journal. The president at the time was the explorer Sir Francis Younghusband and Leo went to see him and discussed his ambitions for an expedition to make films. Sir Francis approved of the ideas that he had outlined to him but thought that financing such an expedition would be very difficult. Leo did not hear anything from Sir Francis until early the next year and then on Monday the 6th January 1922, a letter arrived asking him to go and see him. A new film company, Solar Films Co, had been formed with a view to making natural history, geographical and films of scientific interest in places all over the world. Its first expedition, to be led by Sir George Lampton, was to travel across Africa from Dakar on the west coast, via Lake Chad, to Timbuktu and on to Mombasa on the east coast, filming and collecting animals on the way. Leo was offered the job of field naturalist and he would be paid £20 a week during the expedition with the possibility of royalties, books and articles and paid lecturing if the expedition was a success.

Whilst awaiting further developments, he finished an article for *Herbert Strang's Annual* about the wonders of the seashore and worked on his new book, *The Lure of Thunder Island*. He and Suzanne went dancing and visiting friends and Leo also did some lecturing. It was decided that Suzanne would not accompany him to Africa but would stay with Sir George's wife at Hyeres in the south of France.

On Friday the 3rd February he caught the train at Kings Cross and went back to Bay to see his family and collect the things that he needed for the expedition. He returned to London on the Sunday and on Thursday the 9th February he said goodbye to a very upset Suzanne at Victoria Station and, with other members of the expedition, left on the 8.30am train for Paris and Bordeaux. On Friday the 10th February they boarded the boat for Dakar.

The expedition was beset with problems from the start and these continued until it at last reached the town of Bamako (now Mali) on the 15th March 1922. At Bamako the final blow came when it was notified on the 22nd March that the Solar Film Company had run out of money and gone into liquidation.

On Tuesday the 4th April a telegraph cable was received, telling Leo that he could not continue and had to return home. He arrived back in Dakar on Sunday the 9th April, travelled to Rufisque and sailed from there on the *SS Oria* for home, arriving at Victoria Station at 5.50pm on Monday the 1st May. Even the journey home was not without incident as some animals that members of the expedition were bringing home were gassed by stokehold fumes and died.

During the enforced separation from Suzanne, he had been thinking of her constantly, and there were many entries in his diary showing that he was worried about her and missing her very much. A memorandum in the diary says:

'There are several disturbing factors in this expedition - the greatest of them the love for my wife and the sorrow of leaving her. Yet the law of confirmation holds. The anticipation of our reunion is the greatest thing in all my dreams.'

There is also an entry written whilst he was in Dakar which reads, 'Very homesick and full of love for W' (Wendy).

He was not sorry that the expedition had come to a sudden end as it meant that he could return to her earlier than expected. His diary also shows that he was writing whenever he could and was particularly engaged in working on *The Lure of Thunder Island*, which he was pleased with but was finding difficult to write.

Whilst Leo had been away, Suzanne had faithfully received one half of his salary, as had been agreed before he left, and this had been paid until the film company had gone into liquidation. She had been having a good time staying with Sir George Lampton's wife. They had been to Florence and Rome to see the art galleries and museums and had met a lot of interesting people, mostly painters and sculptors. Suzanne thought it might be a good idea if they both went and lived in Italy as food and lodging were so cheap there. Leo knew that their finances were so low as to make this impossible.

They took a furnished room at 17 Matheson Road, Kensington, and Leo started work on another book. He found it hard to concentrate on his writing as he was longing for further adventure. He had made up his mind that he would go anywhere for a reasonable amount of expenses and payment for his writing. Suzanne suggested that they might buy a caravan or donkey and travel through such places as Provence, although Leo, remembering their unfortunate experiences during their travels in Normandy and Brittany, was very doubtful about the idea. Leo tentatively put forward the idea to the editor of the *Wide World Magazine*, which had already published some of his stories in 1920 and 1921. To his surprise, the editor liked the idea of them travelling with a donkey and would give him an advance and take a series of at least six articles. They were to go to the French Pyrenees on their adventure.

On Saturday the 24th June 1922 they left Matheson Road for the last time and went to stay in a hotel. A decision had already been made not go back to Matheson Road on their return. They caught the train to Paris at Victoria Station at 8pm on Monday the 26th June. It was a very cold day and the sea crossing from Dover to Bologne was extremely rough. Suzanne was very ill. When they arrived in Paris, they took the opportunity of seeing the sights and even went to the Folies Bergere. They eventually arrived in Bayonne, in heavy rain, on Thursday the 29th June and stayed at the Grand Hotel. They purchased a white donkey named Blanchette and a small cart. There is a considerable amount of humour in the account of their adventures in the story that Leo wrote called 'Three Asses in the Pyrenees', which appeared in the *Wide World Magazine*. Leo and Billy (Suzanne) have gone to see a M Francois to buy the donkey.

'He disappeared behind the cottage and returned two minutes later with the most remarkable looking animal I have ever seen.

"Oh! isn't she perfectly sweet?" my wife cried.

Her coat was as white as that of a dipped sheep; her back was so flat that you could have laid a tea-service upon it, and in place of a mane she had a curious swelling that looked like a bolster with a fringe of hair coming from the seam of it.

"Good heavens!" I cried to my wife. "She's got dropsy!"

"It does look funny doesn't it?" she answered. "But isn't its face perfectly sweet?"

"This is Blanchette," said M. Francois. "Did you ever see so beautiful a she-ass?"

"But what's wrong with her neck?" I asked, pointing to the bolster. "Surely that is a disease?"

He laughed. *"Mais non,* that is the grease! She eats — ah, there never was an ass so fond of her food as Blanchette! She eats the mice."

"Mice?" I echoed in astonishment.

"No; he means maize," Billy put in …

I got up on Blanchette's broad back and turned her head down the path. She was full of beans, or maize, or mischief, and set off gaily. We reached the gate safely and turned round.

"Gee up!" I said kicking her flanks with my heels, "let's see what you can do."

She did — nobly. A second later we charged into Billy and the two men, scattered them and brought up stock-still in front of the kennel, with my left foot dangling almost into the jaws of that horrible dog! I suppose it was the finest chance the brute ever had. He growled and made a flying leap at my leg. He missed the flesh but got the front part of my trousers and held firm. I yelled, kicked Blanchette with my right foot and rained blows upon her neck, but she would not stir an inch. Evidently she was in league with the dog.'

They eventually set off through the Pyrenees and arrived at Lourdes on Thursday the 27th July. The whole story was serialised in *Wide World Magazine* from December 1922 until July 1923 and is also described in *So Many Loves*. Leo includes a lot more exciting adventures in his story 'Three Asses in The Pyrenees' than he records in his diary which he kept at the time so it is difficult to sort the fact from the fiction. For instance, in the story he recalls a situation when they camp by the River Saison and Leo decides to go in the water and bathe naked. The current is very strong and he gets washed down-river. He eventually gets safely to the bank farther downstream and climbs out, unfortunately near some women on the bank washing clothes. They see him naked and run off and he 'borrows' a petticoat to cover himself. The women find out and accuse him of stealing it. The whole farcical situation continues until finally he gets back to his tent. In his diary there is no reference to any of this. Of course, he could have omitted to make such notes, but it is unlikely that if the events he describes actually took place, there would not at least be a cryptic note to jog his memory later. There are a number of other situations in the story which are again not referred to in his diary and others that can certainly be recognised from his notes. It would seem that he may have relied on his writer's talent to embellish the story to make it more interesting to the readers.

They arrived at Lourdes at the end of the adventure and Leo found the torchlight procession of the pilgrims a wonderful experience but was revolted by the commercialism and exploitation of the sick people and visitors. His upbringing had not endeared the usual views of religion and religious practices to him. He was very upset when he saw the faces of a brother and sister of a sick child looking anxiously at their sick sister, in expectation of a miracle, which for them did not happen.

Just before they returned home, via Paris where they spent a few days, Leo was told that Harmsworth, the publisher of the *Red* magazine, had accepted one of his stories about a shore-crab and would pay him twenty guineas. When they arrived back, his agent told him that the magazine editor had liked his work and was ready to accept further stories. He was a little disappointed that *Red* did not have the prestige of some of the other magazines but it was a useful source of income. He hoped that his agent would be able to get his work into the American market as the rates for books and stories were much higher than in Britain, and there was the possibility of a story being made into a film. He had to wait nearly twelve years before that dream could be realised.

He was writing many stories and articles, mostly nature stories, some written at 'white heat' but with complete sincerity. They were interesting and he was getting them accepted for publication.

His visits to publishers in the Fleet Street area of London allowed him to savour the noisy, racing and slightly crazy world of publishing, with its flavour of paper and scent of printers' ink. He was excited by all this and fully appreciated the feel of the beautifully printed and illustrated heavy gloss paper of the high-class magazines. What did it matter if his stories at this time were in the cheaper range of magazines? At least he had at last got his foot on the ladder of success in the world of literature.

He was working hard and earning quite a lot of money, but he and Suzanne were managing to spend it as fast as he made it. Suzanne wanted to live in Chelsea but the nearest place they could find to this was the top floor of a mansion house, 15 Roland Gardens, South Kensington, that had been converted into maisonettes. The rent was enormous and furnishing, even on hire purchase, was expensive. However, the address was impressive and there was a telephone and they thought they could manage to live there from his anticipated income. Suzanne was disappointed that Chelsea had very little in common with the Latin Quarter of Paris. There were no open-air cafes and restaurants where you could sit and talk and there did not seem to be any studio parties. Suzanne longed to return to this sort of life again and to be in Paris or Italy.

Frederick W Lane

CHAPTER 8

Art and Disillusionment

IT was summer 1923 and they decided to go on holiday to Devon for a fortnight. They stayed on a farm near Chagford. Bad weather seemed to follow them around and it was wet and foggy and they were glad to return to London. September came and Leo had already written a number of nature stories for *Red* and its sister magazines, *Yellow* and *Green*. He realised that, although you could change your animal and your scene, the theme must be essentially the same so he decided to move away from nature stories and write about people instead. The change-over was not easy. The editor of *Red* did not like his first effort as the hero and heroine were 'immoral' because they lived together without being married, and he thought that this would shock his lady readers. Having finally decided to make the change, he wrote some adventure stories, leaving out 'the love' aspect and these were readily accepted by the publisher.

It was at this time that Suzanne was distracted from her immediate yearning for Paris and Italy. They went out to dinner in a restaurant called the 'Good Intent' in the Kings Road, Chelsea. It was not bohemian but was occasionally frequented by artists. Leo said that you could tell them by their black stetson hats and long hair, or if they were women, by their disregard for fashion.

> 'We were having dinner when a very striking looking girl came in and sat at a table close to us. She wore a black hat, and a black Italian cloak, but when she took this off it revealed a brightly coloured dress cut with a tight bodice and a long flared skirt in the Medici style. Her hair was raven black, her face pale, and she had dark eyes. Everyone in the restaurant looked at her but she wasn't flustered. It was clear she was used to being looked at. But I was soon looking at her for a very different reason. I knew I had seen her before, and shortly she chanced to look towards our table and instantly she gave me a smile of recognition. Before I could rise she came towards us. It was Barbara Hepworth, but if she hadn't given her name I don't think I would have recognised her for it was the summer before the war when her father, the Borough Engineer to the West Riding, with wife and family of three daughters and one boy, had stayed at a cottage close to the laboratory for several weeks, and Sam and I had become friendly with them. Barbara, then only a schoolgirl had been making a collection of seaweeds and Sam had identified them for her in the laboratory.'[1]

Barbara was at the London College of Art in the school for sculpture, studying for the 1924 Prix de Rome. Suzanne was delighted when Barbara took them both to her studio near Fulham Road. The studio was full of drawings, mostly nudes, but there was a stand with an unfinished model in clay of the head and shoulders of a woman, life-sized. Leo did not know much about this form of art but sensed that it was good.

It was the start of a long friendship, especially for Suzanne. During the time that they were close friends she and Barbara visited Robin Hoods Bay together. Barbara used to rent Beachholme, a cottage with its foundations almost in the sea. She and her friends used to have wild parties there and Suzanne and Barbara could be seen strolling about, looking very elegant in their fashionable dresses and large brimmed hats. This must have given the inhabitants of Bay plenty to talk about.

Now that they had again entered this art world, they were able to meet other artists like Henry Moore. Leo admits that he felt out of his depth in the discussions going on around him about the 'modern' and other forms of art. They talked about Chinese, Tibetan, Egyptian, Assyrian and Aztec art. Leo and Suzanne made 'an almost weekly pilgrimage' to the Chinese room in the British Museum mostly, one presumes, at Suzanne's bidding as she was much more informed about such matters than he was. They did not often show any interest in his writing, which he considered particularly unfair as they had the run of his larder and drinks almost every night, and this was earned out of his work.

At least once a week they had a bottle party and the student artists would turn up in fancy dress, and they would dance. On these occasions there would be no talk of art, which was a relief to Leo. On one occasion, when in the midst of a gathering with Barbara and some of her friends, Sam Wilson appeared unexpectedly at the door and joined them. Sam talked about Leo's writing, to the embarrassment of the others, as they realised that they hadn't been fair to him. Sam was proud to have made suggestions which helped Leo formulate some ideas on the way to proceed with his writing during their days together in the laboratory in Bay. Sam told the assembled crowd, 'I always said he'd be a writer. He's got the gift. Heredity partly. You know, of course, that his father was an artist?'

At this time, he was again yearning for Africa and was annoyed that there were several big game films running in London that he considered were not as good as the one that he had planned to make. He was longing to make another attempt at filming but his agent said that he would be a fool to do so as he was just establishing a reputation for writing.

Suzanne was anxious for Barbara Hepworth to win the Prix de Rome prize as, if she did, they were all going together on the long-deferred visit to Italy. Unfortunately she was denied the prize as it was won by Jack (John) Skeaping. The Walmsleys decided to go to Italy anyway and just after the Easter holidays in 1924 they set off. They travelled by train direct to Lausanne in Switzerland, and Leo wanted to stay there to do some climbing and fishing in the mountain streams. Suzanne was on edge to get to Florence and persuaded him to leave the next morning.

> 'I had never seen anything quite so lovely as the scenery we passed in the train after leaving the Simplon Tunnel. We passed quite close to Lake Maggiore. The weather was fine but not too hot, and there was a breeze which filled the coloured sails of many beautifully shaped boats. There were wooded islands with romantic looking castles and villas on them, and to the north of the lake huge snow-capped mountains. And there was to me something unsatisfying about this scenery. It was theatrical, too beautiful to be real. It was like looking at an endless succession of Academy pictures by the best English landscape painters and it made me almost long for something ugly.'[2]

They reached Milan, which was quite a contrast. It was a major industrial city and he thought it was ugly. However, with its busy streets, smart cars and polite well-dressed people it was to him invigorating and had an air of prosperity.

They went on to Florence and found accommodation at a first-class hotel, within sight of the River Arno and the Ponte Vecchio, with its houses and shops built on the arches. Both Leo and Suzanne liked and spent a lot of time visiting the art galleries in Florence, which were thronged with tourists, mostly English, American and German. Leo felt that he could not really appreciate any serious work of art if he had to gaze at it with other people around. He needed to study it in solitude. He had no doubt that Suzanne was completely sincere in her interest but what defeated him was her capacity for admiration and ecstasy that she derived from looking at one picture then passing on to the next 'like a bee among flowers'. She did not like his attitude towards art.

> 'Claire (Suzanne) resented what she called my marine biological theory of aesthetic appreciation. I was not certain that I was right about it and am not now. She accused me of being bored. I was not bored exactly, but even after we discovered that we could see the galleries in relative solitude if we went immediately at opening time, I felt that there were far too many galleries for one town and far too many masterpieces in them, and that I was being stuffed.'[3]

Nothing new ever bored him, but he felt submerged in art — there was just too much — and soon they got to know quite a crowd of artists and art students. He was pleased that they were mostly English or American so he could at least understand the language they spoke, even if the subject was fairly incomprehensible to him. They all dined and drank together in Florence's best-known artist restaurants and went to studio parties. Suzanne loved it all and thought it would be a good place to live for a year at least. Leo was beginning to tire of the life and started to feel a longing to be back in England but told Suzanne that they should see some more of Italy. They went on to Rome, a place that Leo had always wanted to see after he had discovered that there had been a Roman fort on the cliffs at Ravenscar, near his boyhood home: a stone had been found there with carved lettering and this was displayed in the Whitby museum. Leo was beginning to worry about money and knew that he had to do some work. As it was very hot and expensive where they were, they decided to go northwards to the Ligurian riviera. First they went to Rappallo and then on to Santa Margarita and finally settled in Porto Fino near Genoa, where, after two nights in a moderately priced inn, they found a furnished villa and took it for the rest of the summer at a rent of two pounds a week. It was a beautiful place with fewer artists, who were of the more staid and traditional type. There was no great excitement about the place and it lacked the liveliness of other places to which they had been.

> 'Porto Fino was what the guide books call an artist's gem. It reminded me in one respect of Bramblewick. Its original native houses were packed so close together along the water front that there had been no available sites for hotels and boarding-houses and the old part therefore was unspoilt. The houses were tall and many storeyed. Their walls were lime-washed with tints of red, yellow and blue. The harbour was deep with the water clear and usually dead calm so that it mirrored the houses and the olive orchards on the hills that rose above the port in the same way that pool in Dad's best selling subject had mirrored the red roofs of Bramblewick. There were fishing boats in the harbour and their sails were of almost every conceivable tint. Wherever you stood near the harbour or on the rocks at each side or on the hills above, Porto Fino made a perfect picture.'[4]

Leo found the life there much more to his liking but Suzanne wanted to go back to Florence. He began writing again, particularly as he was now very worried about their financial situation, and Suzanne, in anticipation of returning to Florence, taught herself Italian.

Suzanne wrote to Barbara Hepworth as she had received no reply to her letter since leaving England, and asked her if she would come and stay. When Suzanne received the answer, she was staggered. Since losing the Prix de Rome to Jack Skeaping, she wanted to see this man who had beaten her to the prize. Having been introduced to him by Henry Moore, she immediately fell in love with him and they were going to be married.

At the end of the summer, around September time, they returned to Roland Gardens and carried on with their usual lifestyle. Leo had met Jack Skeaping and liked him. He did not think he was as good a craftsman as Barbara, but considered that he had great skill. He was also a very lively character, getting things done quickly and then moving on to something else. Barbara in comparison was slow, almost stolid, but he believed the better artist.

In 1925, Leo was commissioned by the Cunard shipping line to write a pamphlet on the pleasure of first-class travel on the new Cunard liner the *RMS Aluania*. The return date was unspecified, which suited them well as he had another good reason for making the trip. He had received a letter from an American magazine editor, who was interested in the serial rights for a new book Leo was writing called *Toro of the Little People,* which was a story about a pygmy chief.

Mr and Mrs Walmsley together with a number of other well-known names, including Vaughan Williams, Lettice Cooper and Storm Jameson, set sail on the maiden voyage of the *Aluania* from Liverpool to Quebec and Montreal on the 24th July. A note on Cunard-headed paper, 'R.M.S. Aluania Montreal, 2 August 1925' was passed to 'All Cunard Representatives and Agents', introducing them to Mr and Mrs Walmsley as valued patrons of the Cunard Line and stating that any information, advice or assistance that they could give would be greatly appreciated. It was signed by the purser. The ship arrived in Montreal about the 5th August. Although they enjoyed the trip, the pamphlet, which was the reason for their voyage, was probably never written as no trace of it has ever been discovered.

Leo wanted to see the publishers about his book but, being August, they were out of town. They were offered, for as long as they liked, the use of a 'shack' beside a lake in the Laurentian Mountains, north of Montreal. The 'shack' was in fact a more than adequately furnished bungalow and they had little expense beyond that of the cost of food. Here Leo finished the book and sent it off to the New York publisher. They stayed until the freeze-up came and with it a letter from the editor saying that the book was no good.

Very worried, they made their way back south and arrived at Grand Central Station with just enough money to pay for the taxi to the Washington Hotel. Leaving Suzanne there, Leo walked to the offices of the magazine at the end of MacDougal Street. He found the editor in and set about desperately trying to persuade him to reconsider his decision.

The editor was not to be moved easily. He sent for two of his staff, who, like himself, had read the story and he asked, 'How well do you remember *Toro of the Little People?*'

Each remembered it in some detail.

'Very well', said the editor. 'It has left an impression lasting now for several months. I'll buy it.'

Leo returned to his wife with a cheque for 750 dollars in his pocket. The story was published in the American *Adventure* magazine on the 20th March 1926 and a few months later was published in book form on both sides of the Atlantic. Harold Brighouse in his book, *What I Have Had*, comments that this was a characteristic of Leo's authorship in the twenties - two Atlantic crossings for two in return for a pamphlet, the fortuitous Canadian hospitality, the almost penniless arrival in New York, and the self-rescue by salesmanship.

It is surprising that Leo never seems to have used the experiences of this visit to America and Canada in any of his books. The only known story that has any connection with this period is a work of fiction which appeared in the *Harmsworth All Story Magazine (Formerly The Yellow Magazine)* in March 1927 and again in *The Woman's World* (Chicago U.S.A) in July 1927. It was called 'Sanctuary' and subtitled, 'Two tired hearts find Sanctuary in the cold solitude of the Canadian Forest.' It starts with a description that Leo must have based on his stay in the mountains:

> 'It was one of those innumerable lakes which, like pools of cooled but still untarnished metal flung from the burning firmament of a primeval sky, are laid into the dark green folds of the Laurentian Mountains, northwards of Montreal. But on that fascinating map of the Lake and Mountain system with which the C.P.R [Canadian Pacific Railway] lures the jaded city dweller to the joys of the summer camp, Lac St. Esperit had no mark or name to indicate its geological existence.'

It could be said that this fictional story expresses some of the strong feelings that Leo always had for the protection and conservation of the environment. Although the story is a romance, its underlying theme is the protection of wild animals from unnecessary hunting — giving them sanctuary in an area safe from the hunter. Leo had hunted whilst in East Africa and was a lifelong angler. He suffered from the same paradox that many anglers have, in that, although he 'hunted' fish, he later came to hate the killing of animals merely as a 'sport'. He, like many anglers, either kept the fish he caught for food or returned them safely to the water from which they had been taken. At some later stages in his life, the catching of fish became a necessity to help feed his family.

It was in September 1926 that Leo's *The Green Rocket* was published. This is now one of the rarest of his books. It was strangely enough published in serial form in the *Red* magazine under the title 'The Barbed Forest' and was introduced as 'a new novel by Leo Walmsley'.

In November of that year, the Walmsleys moved to 24 St Annes Terrace, St Johns Wood, London. It was a large, four-storey, terraced house of the Queen Anne period. There were two rooms on each floor and a basement with three rooms. There had originally been a garden at the rear but some previous occupier had built over it to make a billiard room with top light. The Skeapings moved into the lower floors and used the 'billiard room' as their studio and installed an aviary, which extended the full length of the studio. As Suzanne had been left some money by a distant relative, they decided to renovate the top two floors, which they occupied as the place was in a bad state of repair. They had to install electricity as originally there was only gas. Leo used a rear attic room as his writing room and continued writing for the *Red* magazine, having dropped nature stories for 'straight' fiction. He received more money for these but they took him a lot longer to write.

The Skeapings were becoming well known, their fame was spreading and their work was increasingly sought after. A millionaire even bought some of their work. Leo was a little envious of their success. No 'pot boiling' work for them in order to make ends meet. It seemed to Leo that the Skeapings had only to touch a piece of clay or stone to start transforming it into something beautiful. Was this not better than having to struggle with your mind and imagination to earn a living?

Sam Wilson, who had long been out of touch with Leo, wrote to him and asked him to meet him. Sam brought along his new wife and also announced that he had got an appointment as professor of zoology at the Royal Veterinary College. Leo was glad to see his old friend so happy and making a success of his life. He did not feel that he was achieving much success himself and was thoroughly fed up with the type of stories that he had been writing. He had exhausted the subject of animals and Africa. He was sitting in his attic room, listening to the sounds of the animals in Regents Park Zoo floating in on the wind. They aroused a feeling of adventure, not literary emotion. He started thinking of his early days in Robin Hoods Bay; of his friend, the old captain whom he used to help with his boat; of fishing on the scaurs; calm summer seas and raging winter gales; the Mill Dam, the becks, the woods and the moors. Then he thought of it as it was now, with hundreds of visitors, the fishermen he had known dead or retired and most of the boats used for pleasure only, and no longer for serious fishing, and felt that he had no wish to go back there again.

A sudden blow came when he heard that the Amalgamated Press had been sold and its new owners were to discontinue many of its publications, including the *Green* and *Yellow* magazines. Although the *Red* magazine would continue, they already had too many stories and would not be needing any more for at least a year. As many publishers were having difficulty, it would not be easy to find a new market for his work. As if this were not enough, in late January 1928 the Skeapings decided that they would go to Florence for the spring and perhaps the summer and would not be returning to St John's Wood.

'Then one day (it was late January) the Skeapings announced that they had decided to go to Florence for the spring and perhaps for the summer, and that when they returned they would find a larger studio, as both of them intended to tackle big carvings. They suggested we might like to go with them, and Claire was very willing because it had been a gloomy rainy winter and she was longing for sunshine, and there would be no point in staying on in St. John's Wood if Jack and Barbara were not coming back to it. We could either let or surrender the lease and store or sell the furniture. I certainly did not want to live in St. John's Wood any longer, but I did not wish to go to Florence. So Claire decided she would go with Jack and Barbara, and I decided to go to Bramblewick. There was no quarrel. We all parted good friends. But it was the end of our marriage.'[5]

Leo stayed on in the house for a short while then returned to Bay, where later he met, and became very interested in, Margaret Bell-Little. A friend of Suzanne's wrote to her in Spain, where she was living at the time, and told her of the liaison and that, if she did not want to lose him, she had better do something about it. She hurried back to England but it was too late to do anything about saving the marriage. Leo and Suzanne remained separated until, on the 14th November 1932, they were finally divorced.

This chapter in his life had been a great adventure. It had established him as a writer, had given him material and a library of experience that was to influence his thinking and his work. Despite the break-up of the marriage to Suzanne, he still thought of her kindly. That he did so is apparent by the dedication of his book *Three Fevers* to her when it was published in 1932. The dedication read,

'To Suzanne in the wind of a Bramblewick Spring.'

Frederick W Lane

PART FOUR

THE FOREIGNER RETURNS

CHAPTER 9

Their Protagonist, the Sea

WE cannot be sure why Leo returned to Robin Hoods Bay in 1928 rather than staying in London or going elsewhere. Certainly there was nothing to keep him in that high-pressure atmosphere of art once Suzanne had gone with the Skeapings, and indeed he admits that he was glad to be out of London. Also, he may have been in debt. The publishing houses were no longer buying his stories and he had little other income. An early draft of *Phantom Lobster* shows a debt-ridden writer travelling north, protesting the need to be free of pressure in order to write the bestseller which would pay his creditors.

But why his native Bay? In some ways his return can be seen almost as a rebirth. He had soon realised that he had thrown away a good education and his life in the last twenty years had not led anywhere. His war service had been commendable but his new career of writing had failed along with his marriage. Perhaps he instinctively went back to his childhood and started again. Although he had said the village was dead when he and Suzanne had lived there briefly, he had earlier realised that he did love the place and would one day want to get back to it.

He rented a fisherman's cottage which had been let to him for five shillings per week. He did not seek accommodation with his family, nor did he often see them. Indeed, Fran Storm, a local man who was a boy during this period, asserts that members of Leo's family were seen about much more than Leo. This may give us a clue to his mood at the time. A marriage breakdown was a much greater social stigma at that time. He admitted that, as a result of his war service in Africa, his 'nervous system had gone all wrong' and that on his return he felt rather sorry for himself. Probably quite depressed, he preferred to hide away 'down bank' and avoid contact with people. This was probably good policy, as Robin Hoods Bay had changed, but not so much that his free spirit would be welcome and in some ways it was a harder place in which to be an outsider than it had been previously.

The old roistering days of the lively fishing village had largely gone despite some of the old families remaining. But only two of these were active fisherfolk, the Dukes and the Storms. The successful sea captains had mostly moved 'up bank' to the new villas and the village largely lived off the summer letting trade and the increasing number of day trippers. The centre of gravity of the village was moving 'up bank', leading to some antagonism, as Leo shows in his book *Master Mariner*, when he refers to the moving of the Methodist chapel to new premises.

To an outsider, the village could seem dead and empty. Those who even then retired to the coast found out how cold it could be and how easily the road and railway links over the high moors could be blocked, but there was plenty of life of a sort. The village supported most of the shops which one would expect even in a small town at that time — two post offices, two bakeries, two butchers, several

The old coastguard station, Robin Hoods Bay

grocers, a chemist, two tailors, three shoemakers, a fish shop, sweet shops and a farrier. It even had its own independent, albeit expensive and unreliable, gas-works. Its living and sense of purpose still came from the sea, despite the growth in holiday trade. It had long supplied men for crews in the merchant navy and this continued. Ships with Bay connections would sail close to the village and sound their sirens. The womenfolk would wave blankets in reply. There was a coastguard station and a lifeboat which was 'a symbol of the spirit and community of the village.'[1]

Yet, by 1929 the lifeboat had to be manned by the few remaining fishermen and other volunteers. As Leo pointed out in a *National Geographic Magazine*, 'What strikes the casual visitor is the extraordinary absence of young men ... Bay is a town of women and old men.' Losses in the First World War and the decline of fishing had only reinforced this tendency to matriarchy.

Leo knew only too well the sort of women who ran the village. In *So Many Loves*, he describes two educated daughters of an 'up bank' sea captain:

> 'Despite their villa, their nice clothes and their disdain of the "Down Bank" villagers they were at heart true Bramblewick. Their forebears on both sides were of the same tough seafaring stock. They were hard and close and quite unimaginative.'

In general the community had an air of respectability. There had not been a single case of divorce in the village and it was unusual for Leo to lock his door at night. Entertainment revolved around the churches and chapels, while friends might arrange musical evenings. Men had bowls, billiards and the *Shipping Gazette*. The cinema and radio had not yet had much influence.

Even as a child, he had been aware of the veiled hostility which the villagers had towards outsiders or 'foreigners', and he sensed that undercurrent of resentment was still there thirty years later. He always seems to have kept a chip on his shoulder about this throughout his life. On one of his last visits, he is said to have remarked to a crowd in the Laurel Inn that they were 'all foreigners', to which one customer replied that while he had chosen to live in Bay, Leo had chosen to live elsewhere.

Part of the trouble was not just that he was a foreigner. He and his brothers, under his mother's influence, had remained different, never embracing the Bramblewick spirit. Leo realised later that this patriotism 'came from an intense pride of a people in themselves and in their place'.[2]

There were not many families amongst the few hundred inhabitants and this clannishness reinforced the attitude which they adopted. Yet Fran Storm insists that the old villagers were not really interbred and that any newcomers were judged on their merits. Leo and his brothers were prepared to bow to the inevitable, to learn the local dialect and how to swear. But his mother's pride, snobbery, puritanism and solid Lancashire strain made her resist all her sons' tendencies in this direction. His father never seemed to fear this village miasma. Leo wrote rather cruelly when his father was still alive and living in Bay:

> 'Between him and all miasmas (and most realities) was the impenetrable blanket of his own illusions.'[3]

Like his son, Ulric Walmsley could dream dreams of inventions bringing a fortune and his wife had to be practical.

Yet the slights on his parents, a snobbish mother and a bohemian father, give us another clue to his state of mind at that time. We recall Ulric's hopes of getting his portrait seen, via the vicar of Fylingdales, by the earl of Mulgrave. Fran Storm recalls sitting beside Mrs. Walmsley on a bus and being pushed off the seat by her so that she could offer it to the headmistress, who otherwise would have to stand.

Leo had by this time rejected such 'respectability'. He was always something of a loner, probably by nature and the more so as a result of having to stand against both his mother and Bay folk. The religion of the respectable he had long ago rejected and their solidness would not get through to his somewhat romantic inherited Irish temperament. Although a very effective observer of people and a user of them in his stories, he was not ultimately vastly interested in his relationships with them. That he hardly ever mentions his family, especially his brothers and sister, is significant. A visitor once asked his sister why Leo always gave the impression in most of his writing of being an only child, and was told 'because he always wanted to be one!' Like many loners, he took criticism badly, was not easily able to laugh at himself, did not easily forgive, and did not readily forget. This attitude also applied to the villagers. They too did not readily forget or forgive; his behaviour and his attitude towards them remained deep in their memories, to be passed on to following generations. No doubt like many of those who have suffered ostracism

The Dock, Robin Hoods Bay

and bullying, he resorted to underhand tactics. In all probability, he used his mouth as a means of both attack and defence. A story still told in the village illustrates the antagonism felt by the local people. In what was most likely a boyish prank which went wrong or an act of retaliation to taunting, Leo was held responsible for one of the boys losing the sight of an eye. According to the story, Leo had thrown lime with the catastrophic result of this serious injury. There was no court case and apparently no action taken against Leo, but he was not allowed to forget. Yet despite this deep-seated prejudice, there was a grudging acceptance of him when he returned to the village. Fran Storm recalled that he 'found it hard to believe that this was the little scoundrel I'd heard so much about!'

Leo does not give us any account of a split with his family, whether there was an argument, or whether he just let relationships drop. But his writing in *Phantom Lobster* is certainly bitter and in *Foreigners* no better. In this period, and he was over forty years old, he could still see his childhood with the eyes of a child. His book *Sound of the Sea* shows a mellower picture and a respectful understanding, for instance, of the old vicar, which he was not capable of in the 1930s.

Nor ultimately do we know how forcibly he put over his views, which, in the wake of George Bernard Shaw and T E Lawrence, were something of an anathema to most Bay people. Some people considered that at that period he could be a verbal bully and had to be stood up to. It is not surprising perhaps that even today

a lot of those Bay residents who actually knew Leo confess to not having liked
him. They resented his attitude to his family and to their own culture, and this, in
their eyes, put him beyond the pale. Fran Storm remembers that he 'was one of
those people you avoided because he was talked about'. By contrast, his father
Ulric was remembered with affection. But Leo was a fighter.

Avoiding this 'respectable' society, he had then 'gone Bramblewick, down bank'.
He had not at first been sure if he wanted to go on writing. He had taken the lack
of interest in his writing by the Skeapings rather hard, especially as he reckoned that
they cheerfully sponged off him. Yet he soon came to see himself as 'lying fallow,
absorbing Bramblewick'.[4] He tried to live as a 'down banker', emptying his own ash
bucket, gathering driftwood, helping to launch and recover the cobles and sitting
among the crowd of gossipers in a favourite meeting place in the gas-works. His
cottage fell short of Bay standards, showing a new bachelor carelessness. He took
great pleasure in roaming the local countryside as he had done as a child.

He was still in debt, and, although he could get credit, this could not go on
indefinitely. In *Phantom Lobster*, he refers to writing a 'pot-boiler' to earn money,
although without success. Fortunately, he still had his small invalidity pension.

For therapy he turned to sea angling. The challenge and physical effort needed
helped him to take his mind off his troubles. It was by offering his catch of a large
cod to the Dukes after one such expedition that started his friendship with them
and he passed from being a bystander who sometimes helped to haul up the
cobles to becoming virtually a member of one of the two fishing families.

This at last fulfilled one of Leo's childhood dreams. He recalls in *The Golden
Waterwheel* on meeting Tommy Peck that they should have been friends at
school, for they were both outcasts. But Leo had always wanted to be friends
with the fisher lads although his offers of friendship were always rejected. The
friendship with the Dukes developed although Henry had grown diffident when
Leo had 'started hobnobbing with the queer folk at the laboratory'.[5] Despite his
reputation, the Dukes were quite happy to have Leo around; after all he was a
'foreigner like them'. His practical ability was admired by Elliot, although with
some reservation.

> 'It just beats me why a chap of your education and ability should be wasting his time in
> a spot like this. In these days education counts above everything. It's my belief there's
> nothing you couldn't do if you gave your mind to it. Look at the way you took that
> magneto of ours to bits the other day and put it right and how you mended that compass
> card. You can take photos and draw likenesses of folk. You know more about fish and
> things that live in the sea than any chap I ever met. You know all about fossils, and
> history and flint implements.'[6]

Just how much Leo went to sea we do not know. He gives the impression that
he regularly accompanied the Dukes and became 'quite adept at making lobster
pots'. It was during this period that he became so involved with the difficulties
facing the Dukes that he enthusiastically turned his hand and mind to inventing a
device, described in the next chapter, which he was sure would solve their problems.
He would accept no payment for his help except an occasional fish, despite his
getting deeper into debt with his landlord and grocer. Possibly accepting the
Dukes' offer would have meant losing his war disability pension. The late Richard

Duke (Steve Lunn in his stories) always said that Leo did not fish regularly in the Dukes' coble but did spend a lot of time hanging round them — and never ever wore socks!

Despite the fact that he had not been in a fishing coble before, he picked up the business and its details as well as the physical feeling of going to sea very quickly, and his accounts have definite authority. Quite a few local boats have been named after his books, *Three Fevers*, *Marney Lunn*, and *Bramblewick*. The power of Leo's writing is revealed in this simple tribute: if the books had not reflected reality they would not have been so named.

The Dukes themselves were surprised how thoroughly he understood their business. Leo could always concentrate on what he enjoyed and being caught up in the fishing lifestyle with the Dukes' 'zest for life' and optimism he was 'completely happy'. After his loss of confidence, it was good to be accepted, and, in the making of pots, proffering some useful return for this. He was able to give his readers a very clear picture of the fishing situation as sail and oar gave way to motor. The two families made the most of their money from lobster fishing in the spring and summer, hence the temptation to start early, with salmon another possibility, and cod fishing in winter.

The inshore fishermen were able to make a living because their catch had a higher value than that caught by steam trawlers and there was a very good price to be had for lobsters; also their overheads were less. Materials used for fishing were cheap; they swapped crabs for hazels used in making lobster pots with a local farmer and driftwood often supplied pot bottoms. Although the twine used for various jobs including netting cost money, they did not cost out their labour which could be considerable. Their wives were involved, often in baiting the lines, making and mending garments and simply keeping the household going. They also suffered severely when a fleet of pots was smashed up in a gale, wasting all their laborious work in making them and valuable fishing time until they could be replaced.

But the worst risks could not be so easily shared. In *Three Fevers*, the brave words of one of the characters, Marney, 'If you're born to be drowned worrying about it won't help' hid a very real possibility. Fishing is inherently dangerous; going to sea was the least of the problems. Accidents happened with pots, hooks and lines lashing about out of control, a sudden change in the weather could leave them vulnerable and help was a long way off. The Dukes might well be tempted to take a chance as bad weather might keep them ashore for weeks. Weather forecasts were less reliable then than now. The absence of a harbour at Bay combined with the hazards created by the scaurs or reefs across the landing area meant that the boats could be launched and recovered only at certain states of the tide thus limiting fishing time. If the weather suddenly changed for the worse, a coble could not return through the surf breaking over the scaurs. Those ashore might light a fire to warn the crew to stay at sea. They might then try to get to Whitby or Scarborough — neither easy places to enter — or otherwise ride out the storm at sea, no easy option in a small open boat.

Risks had to be taken if a decent living were to be made, but even then a catch might be worthless if there was a glut of fish at the market. Leo had tremendous admiration for the Dukes' ability to keep going and to accept with stoicism reversals in fortune, such as the loss of gear, and to risk their lives for no reward. That was 'the true splendour of these men'.[7]

Leo did not gain an entry into the Storms' world so easily. His living with the Dukes gave him some insight but he and they were still 'foreigners' and he was even more suspect to the Storms because he was, for all practical purposes, one of the 'opposition' and they would not discuss their business in front of him. Fran Storm observes that the rivalry was never terribly serious and a lot of it was jesting. Leo was not able to take such things lightly as he had suffered too much as a child from being a 'foreigner'. The two families had to work together for either to be able to work from Bay but there might be some competition for the best fishing grounds, and, of course, there was always family and village pride to uphold.

In his stories, Leo's picture of the Storms is not sympathetic and it is not surprising that, with such a view, his character Luke Fosdyke should be portrayed as 'a grim hater', and the Storms as hard and jealous of newcomers and fiercely loyal to all their old ways. This was in contrast to the optimistic and forward-looking Lunns, who were based on the Dukes. There is some truth in this as the Storms were still using their old pulling (rowing) and sailing coble and were probably not doing as well as the Dukes. But they were certainly not the blind reactionaries portrayed. The Storm brothers were no longer young, nor had they sons to follow them. Investing in an engine would take capital that they needed for retirement. Their working lives were nearly over. On the other hand, Elliot and George Duke were still young enough to look ahead and Henry had three other sons to consider, as well as his daughters.

No doubt there was a fundamental difference in outlook, whether by heredity or environment. A photo taken in 1927 of a shipwrecked crew and local lifeboatmen shows a smiling, cheerful Elliot Duke and a tall, grim suspicious-looking Oliver Storm. The photograph sums up much of the plot of *Three Fevers*. Yet the Storms did have friends, and visitors remarked that Reuben and William Storm were 'lovely people'. Leo did not know this side of them, it seems, and does not report on it, but his respect for them was genuine, unforced and creditable.

Leo's concern in his writing was for the story and he did not pretend to be a documentary writer. He was concerned with showing the real issues rather than detail, and in the concept of 'foreigners' and family rivalry he had an effective theme. The setting was incomparable but the bedrock of his Bramblewick stories came from his love of marine biology, the early influence of Darwin and his acceptance of Shaw's notions of 'the life force' driving the world along. To him, it made more sense of the world and his experiences than the conventional, respectable Christianity he had been brought up to know.

While his books were very much 'man against the sea', he was both enough of a believer in progress to want to show how man could beat his environment and improve his life and enough of a believer in humanity to want to show how, despite their differences, men and women of different backgrounds and natures could work together. He showed, too, that hard work could be fun if there was a purpose to it. While he believed that progress through technology was genuine, he also perceived that the Dukes' life in Bay, although full of hard work and near poverty, was preferable to life within industry. His tribute in a letter written to his friend Sam Wilson states:

> 'I'm all out for the alleged lower class against the middle class because I think a man like Henry Duke is worth any two of us.'[8]

The fact that so many Bay folk would have sourly agreed with Leo's judgement must make us grateful to the Dukes for braving village opinion in having Leo as a friend and to Leo for making such good use of his time with them. His portraits of them, bold, clear, true, understanding, sympathetic and yet unsentimental, are not only good social documents, but wonderfully atmospheric and warm stories, which show the best in man in his ordinary environment. No scope for vast heroics, just a dogged determination in the daily struggle. Leo said in 1946 that, while he had altered a lot of detail in his books, he had been concerned with 'ultimate truth'. To a greater extent than most writers, he achieved just that.

George Featherston

CHAPTER 10

The Brainwave

TOWARDS the end of Leo's sojourn in Robin Hoods Bay, he involved himself, probably to his own surprise, in what most people would consider an unusual project. It engaged almost the whole of his energies for the best part of two years, and he set great store on its successful outcome. Like so many of the best-laid schemes of mice and men, it all ended in crushing disappointment. The failure was a body blow which he never seemed to have quite forgotten. A few years afterwards, he wrote a book, *Phantom Lobster*, in what looks like an attempt to get the whole episode out of his system. It evidently did not do so because he often referred to it in subsequent writings. The story was to have been retold in a chapter of a later novel, *Love In The Sun*, although this portion was for some reason edited out of the published version.[1] There is another reference to it in his play *Sally Lunn* and also in the autobiography *So Many Loves* and yet again in his last book, *Angler's Moon,* with some additional detail. There is no doubt that he also liked to talk about it. On a day in 1930 Dr Hugh Maingay was travelling by train from Crewe to London on his way to an interview for his first job and Leo happened to be in the same compartment, possibly bound for Fowey. On finding that the doctor was himself a Scarborough man, Leo took the opportunity to unburden himself and kept the young man enthralled during the whole journey. Hugh Maingay, who later corresponded with Leo but never met him again, was left with a fascination for him and his invention which has lasted for sixty-five years. What was it all about?

Of all the unlikely things, the project was the attempted launch of the Walmsley Collapsible Lobster Pot, which, it was hoped, would revitalise the inshore fishing industry.

To savour the full drama of this adventure, for that is what it was, the reader is earnestly advised to turn to one of Leo's own accounts of it. His experiences with the lobster pot were among the elements in an episode which formed a turning point in his life and his writing career. If the invention failed to revitalise the inshore fishing industry (at least at that time), it certainly proved to be one of the things that revitalised Leo. Apart from his own prolific writings about the pot, the only surviving 'hard' evidence that it actually happened at all is one letter from the Ministry of Agriculture and Fisheries, and a reference to it in a private letter from the late Margaret Walmsley (his second wife). After sixty-five years it is unlikely that any other written evidence will be discovered.

In the foreword to *Phantom Lobster*, Leo asserts that it is not a novel, intending to convey, no doubt, that it is a true history. This has led to some debate with his publishers and reviewers, who included Phyllis Bentley and Compton Mackenzie. There is a fair element of his usual 'artistic licence', and some things are left out for reasons that seemed good to him at the time, such as Margaret's involvement, but it is mainly true. Leo himself volunteered that it was ninety-five per cent so, but preferred to present it as a novel.

Leo was occupying one of the summer-letting cottages in Littlewood Terrace, fending for himself in his own way. His method of deferring the task of washing-up by accumulating a week's soiled crockery in a bucket of formaldehyde seems to suggest a certain lack of application. Now and then he forced himself to attempt a story or article as a 'pot-boiler', but the cottage was, as he put it, not suitable to work in. Probably it was too cold and it may have smelled too much like a mortuary — formaldehyde is an embalming fluid. Also, the walls were thin, and the neighbours and seagulls were noisy. In his own words, he was at a loose end, and the very inclination to write dried up. His lifelong passion for fishing and his intimate knowledge of Bay sustained him somewhat. He would spend long hours alone with his rod, or indulge his old love of fossicking about along the cliff-foot for firewood and suchlike treasure swept inshore by the high tide. At this time, about 1928, his parents and his sister Sheila were still living up bank, but there is scant reference to them in his writings and Margaret recalled that he seldom saw them.

There can be little doubt that Leo was hard up financially at this period: not actually destitute, as he still drew his war disability pension, but it would not have amounted to much. Despite having enjoyed a period of comparative prosperity while working in London, he was quite adaptable enough to revert to habits of strict frugality when the need arose. Fortunately so, as the need was to arise at intervals throughout his life. It was a time of recession, and millions of his fellow countrymen were in similar predicaments, and at least he at that time had no family to provide for. Even for those in work, two or three pounds a week was the sort of wage offered at the lower end of the job market. Labour-saving devices and central heating were not yet to be found or even expected in the homes of the masses. Had some seer predicted holidays with pay (abroad) or universal car ownership, he would have been laughed to scorn as much as if he had promised another world war. Leo, at thirty-seven, could remember a time when there were virtually no cars at all, no aeroplanes and no wireless either. On farms, which were difficult to let at a pound an acre, horses and steam engines were still more common than tractors in most areas. Perhaps most significantly of all, the establishment was firmly controlled by Victorians, and their moral attitudes prevailed as much among the poor as among the wealthy.

Despite this almost universal penury, a mood of innovation and technical awareness was gaining ground among men and women of all classes. Clerks and council workers were interesting themselves in motor cars, photography or chemistry. Schoolboys, having mastered the use of the 'cat's whisker', were taking the new thermionic valve in their stride, and progressing to superjets. Engine drivers, having bought a treadle lathe for a couple of guineas, were building coal-fired miniatures of their own locos. Amateur experimentation was growing and improvements were being thought out in all sorts of areas. At the back of their minds was the knowledge that an ingenious device, if it 'caught on', could make a fortune. It need be only simple so long as it would sell by the million, like safety razors or a ladies' hairgrip with little kinks in it. When Newnes began to

publish *Practical Mechanics* in the thirties, edited by that prolific but rather
opinionated designer F J Camm, its pages were full of novelties and gadgets of
which their inventors had high hopes, and a section was devoted to advice on
patenting and marketing. With all this going on, perhaps it is not surprising
that Leo, articulate, educated and well-travelled, should be moved to contribute
something on his own account towards progress.

He had recently struck up a close acquaintance with fisherman Henry Duke
and his family, later to become familiar to readers of Leo's books as the Lunns.
He had this in common with Henry, that they were neither of them natives of
Bay. Henry had migrated from Flamborough in about 1906, with a young family
and his father, old Elliot Duke. Two or three other families including the Knaggs
and the Screetons had made the same move. Flamborough had become congested,
the two small landing beaches no longer able to accommodate all the boats. Also,
both beaches were a long way from the village, involving a tedious daily portage
of gear and catch. In Robin Hoods Bay, by contrast, the former large fleet
(historically Bay had exported great quantities of dried fish) had dwindled to very
few, mainly owned by the Storm family, notably William, Reuben, Oliver and
Thomas. Cottages were plentiful and cheap, handy to the narrow creek that served
the landing. The catch could be consigned to Whitby fish market from the railway
station up bank.

During the First World War, while his elder sons were in the mercantile marine,
Henry skippered the mule *Dora Anne*, owned by the Smith brothers, out of Whitby,
in fearless disregard of the enemy mine-fields and raiders. It is said that after the
war he could have bought the mule, a decked boat which, as its name suggests,
was a hybrid, something between a yawl and a coble, and which, being too large
to haul up into Bay Dock, would have forced then to move to Whitby. Mrs. Duke
preferred to stay where they were. Henry fished with the coble *Providence* for a
year or two, but when his father retired and returned to Flamborough (the other
families had gone back as well), Henry was obliged to take a job ashore. For four
years, he ran Bay's little one-man gasworks — and hated it. In 1926, sons George
and young Elliot, opting to be their own masters, left the merchant service to join
their father in the twenty-four foot (7m) coble *Iris* WY 107, formerly *Felicity* of
Hull. In 1928, she was fitted with a second-hand seven-horsepower Kelvin paraffin
engine, giving them a great advantage over the Storms, whose boats were 'pulling
and sailing' only. Elliot also had a small salmon coble, *Alpha*, which his
youngest brother, the late Richard Duke of the RAF, said they used to love sailing
for fun.

Leo had known both the Dukes and the Storms (Fosdycks in his books) since
before the war. Not until now, however, did he begin to know them intimately,
and it proved to be something of a revelation. The inshore fishermen of the rock-
and reef-bound coast were by nature and tradition something of a breed apart.
Stern, devout (for the most part), and incredibly hardy, they kept themselves very
much to themselves and Leo in his younger days seems to have been in constant
awe of these dour, forbidding coblemen. Now, on closer acquaintance, he began
to appreciate their warmth and wisdom, their strict personal integrity and superb
professional skill. Not least, he noticed their inbred courtesy and sort of wry,

fatalistic humour in the face of endless dangers, difficulties and frustrations inherent in their calling.

Leo says that the friendship began when he offered them a cod, caught with a rod and line from the scaurs, which was far too large for him to use himself. Impressed, they invited him to 'go off' with them the next day, generally a rare favour. The Duke's warehouse was a shed on a patch of ground only a few yards from Leo's cottage. One of the Storm family remembers that he regularly attended at the landing, along with other impecunious gastronomes, when the cobles had landed and the fishermen were gutting fish on the scaur. Cod roe in particular, usually regarded as offal, must have seemed too good a delicacy to be consigned to the gulls.

However the association began, it grew into a sort of loose partnership based on mutual liking and, on Leo's part, a deep and genuine respect. Henry Duke was a man of vast experience and quiet authority, while his wife was an attractive lady of striking looks and great strength of character. George and Elliot were lively and cheerful young men. According to Richard, there was never any formal commercial partnership. A coble crew was three and a fourth partner, while useful occasionally, would not have brought larger catches, and returns were too low to split four ways, or rather five, as one share belonged to the boat for maintenance. Nevertheless, Leo would sail with them sometimes and always be glad to lend a hand with the gear or the fish boxes, and to help launch the cobles on their carriages up or down from the 'Dock' in those seasons when it was not safe to leave them at anchor. Some years later Leo wrote:

> 'I was not what Henry Lunn would have called a good fisherman. At best I was no more than their apprentice. I had pulled my weight, however, and this, together with the fact that I could speak their language, that I was as poor as they were, had slowly broken down the reserve which is so characteristic of their attitude to the sophisticated landsman.'[2]

It must have been an interesting period for Leo, one might say an education. He observed their skilful management of a boat and learned how to be aware of changing winds and seas. Elliot, an artist at the craft, taught him how to make lobster pots, and how to net them. Best of all, there was the talk of fish and fishing and gear. One day Henry Duke in a conversation mentioned that it was a pity that a lobster pot could not be made to fold flat.

The subject of collapsible pots may have been a perennial one, but it seems that it was new to Leo. He could see the point of it, though. It would mean that they could carry far more of them in a coble, and with greater safety. The Dukes depended heavily on crab and lobster fishing in the spring and early summer, before the short salmon netting season and subsequent long-lining for cod. The lobster is a curious animal, plentiful in several varieties along rocky coasts worldwide. The female lays vast numbers of eggs which she carries about with her; she is then known as 'berried'. When they hatch, they do not resemble her at all until they have moulted several times. As larvae, they are creatures of the open sea and the prey of many predators, but enough of them reach adulthood to return to their native haunts closer inshore, where they lead a comparatively sedentary life. Poor swimmers, during rough weather they shelter in holes and crannies or in weed beds. It is said that the best time to catch them is after several days of storm when they are really hungry. The design of traps ('pots' or 'creels') varies round our coasts.

The traditional Bay pot was the parlour pot, consisting of a ballasted wooden base with four hazel hoops, the 'bows', which, when covered with netting, made them a three-bay cage. A straight rod joined the tops of the bows to form a ridge: two more, the side sticks, formed what might be called the eaves. Entry spouts on opposite sides gave access to bays one and two, the bait being secured between them. A third internal spout led to bay three, the parlour. This was a delaying device. Having devoured the bait, most lobsters will, given time, contrive to find their way out of the pot. The parlour spout induced some of them at least to go farther in under the impression that they were getting out, useful if the hauling up of the pots was delayed for any reason. Ideally pots are not left down too long but hauled, emptied and re-shot as soon as it is judged that they are reasonably full. The Dukes used a similar but simpler pot of the Flamborough pattern, having only three bows and no parlour. They may still be seen in great numbers on the Yorkshire coast although plastic rod and cord has usually replaced the hazel and tarred twine formerly used. Fishermen invariably made their own pots of locally found materials, a skilled and companionable job for the snug warehouse while winter gales whipped the North Sea to a fury and the cobles were safely secured in the shelter of the 'Dock'. Nevertheless, the job was time-consuming and Henry reckoned that each pot cost them five shillings to make.

Being inherently fragile, the pots, despite being ballasted with scrap iron, needed a week's soaking in the comparative safety of deep water to reduce the buoyancy of the new wood before they could be expected to sit at all firmly among the rocky haunts of the lobster further inshore. Even then, if a heavy sea arose suddenly, which it often does, they would be smashed and lost before they could be hauled up and either taken ashore or to the usually safer deep water and a mud or sand bottom. They were laid out in 'fleets' of about twenty, each attached by a short 'strop' to a stout rope known as a 'tow', at sufficiently wide intervals to ensure that, when hauling, only one pot was being lifted at once, for hauling is a heavy job. A small anchor, marked by a buoy, secured each end of the tow. A team of three men in a motor coble could handle three fleets, shooting and hauling perhaps twice in a day's work. Pots are bulky: one fleet takes up a lot of room in a boat, two fleets stacked up make a high and unstable load if the weather is at all rough. A third fleet might be carried in reliably calm conditions, or it might be towed in the small boat. If a pot *could* be made to fold flat, a coble might carry half a dozen fleets in comfort and safety, but there was a complication. The boat must be moving at a fair speed while shooting pots overboard so as to keep the tow straight, and each successive pot in turn must go over the side at the right moment to avoid injury to man, pot or boat. A folding pot must be capable of being erected and locked upright instantly, without fear of pause or failure, and preferably with one hand.

It was obvious to Leo as it was to Henry that the hazel pot as it stood could never be re-designed so as to fold up. He considered it and felt that there must be a solution and wished that he might be the one to solve the problem. It would be his contribution to the 'partnership'. He longed to do something for the Dukes, for *all* inshore fishermen. He had been appalled at the difficulties that they so patiently bore. Apart from the competition from the larger boats from Whitby and elsewhere, the hazards of storm, tide and fog reduced the number of days that they could work annually. Bay's landing was narrow and had a dangerous bar; there was no proper jetty or pier for shelter. Bait such as mussel had to be bought and was costly; if bad weather kept them ashore it was money wasted. Fish boxes that should have been returned from market went missing, involving more expense.[3] There was wear and tear on men too. Bitterly cold wet conditions at sea, hands raw from hauling the sand-embedded tow, cuts and salt-sores slow to heal, and the misery of knowing that usually prices were good only when there were no fish. Leo wrote :

'These men, I perceived, were being slowly but surely beaten in their struggle to earn a livelihood from the sea.'[4]

If ever there was a time for the application of lateral thinking, this was it. He went home and immediately set about making a model. It was a challenge, it gave him a purpose in life to counteract the descent into an aimless, beach-combing sort of existence. It might make money, bring recognition, give new hope to hard-pressed fisherfolk all over the world. Factories to make the pots! Canneries to process the new, tenfold catch! It could have been the start of something big.

There was a tiny wash-house across the alley from Leo's cottage which became his research and development department. The first need was to verify the geometry, so to speak, of a folding pot. He had only a few cheap hand-tools, and for materials he furtively raided the local rubbish tip. It yielded an old parrot cage which, after it had put up a valiant resistance to being dismantled, provided strong enough wires for the bows. He set about the construction of a working model. One end bow was joined to the middle one by a short stay at the top or 'ridge', and both were hinged to the wooden base with the aid of picture-frame screw eyes, so that they fell flat together. The other end bow also fell inwards on top of the other two, but when erected was firmly clipped to the middle bow by means of another short stay. He now had a collapsible frame and felt able to tell the Dukes what he was doing. They had reservations about it. For one thing, side sticks could not be fitted, and this, for them spoiled its looks. However, Elliot netted the frame and it looked more like a proper pot and was capable of being collapsed and re-erected quite well. Leo was elated; the Dukes admitted that they were impressed, at least so far. A full-sized working prototype was now needed.

The need for secrecy added excitement to the task. Leo could see that the pot would be stronger and simpler if metal was used throughout, discarding the wooden base in favour of one of riveted angle iron with drilled holes in which the bows could pivot. Metal strips or even wire netting could form the floor. No ballasting or soaking would be needed, and the pots would still be lighter to haul than the old ones. He walked across the fields to Fylingthorpe, where the local blacksmith made, to Leo's drawings, iron rod bows and locking stays for a few shillings. The blacksmith was not told what these items were for and Leo hastened back to his cottage, fearful of being seen. A nocturnal foray to the rubbish tip produced stout bedstead iron of the right weight and section. The gas-works man lent him a breast-drill and a bit.

In *Phantom Lobster*, Leo gives a detailed account of how he fashioned the frame of the lobster pot from the scrap metal, using the most basic tools. His doggedness and inspired effort somehow overcame the difficulties of using a hacksaw to cut the metal when the 'high-pitched rasping' sound sent shivers down his spine. He continued 'frenziedly sawing away at the old bedstead', refusing to give in.

> 'Yet I found an ever growing satisfaction in my labour … and as I laboured a profound revelation came to me. I was creating something which if it fulfilled the promise of the first small model, would put new and vigorous life into the moribund inshore fishing industry, that would remove the blight of unemployment from the young men of the coast, and save the magnificent breed of them which the sea had fostered from extinction.'

He decided that inventors were of more importance than writers and artists as they could offer a greater service to humanity.

> 'I was not a writer. I was an inventor, an engineer, a potential captain of industry. And the sudden realization that the pot boiler was no longer on my conscience, that I need not give another thought to the worrying complexities of my unstarted book, brought a great joy to my heart, a new energy to my aching muscles.'[5]

Overcoming pain and fatigue, he laboured through the night and at last, exhausted but triumphant, he gloated over a strong, solid pot base produced entirely by unskilled labour. Elliot again netted the new frame. It looked brilliant. They released the latch. The pot refused to fold up.

After lengthy experimentation, the fault was identified and a technique of netting was arrived at which allowed the pot to be erected and locked, one-handed, in three seconds. The Dukes included it in a fleet of their own pots and it caught lobsters. They pronounced it 'Champion!' The 'easy' part of the project was over.

Leo realised that for his collapsible lobster-pot to be a success, it would have to be mass-produced, the only way in which the costs could be brought down to an economically viable level. With this in mind, he decide to follow the advice of contacts and travel to the industrial Midlands to obtain estimates of the likely cost of manufacture. It proved to be a traumatic experience. His first interview ended in bitter disappointment. Not only had he to face the fact that the final cost of the pot would be far in excess of what the fishermen could possibly afford, but he was in an environment which he hated. The huge conurbation of Birmingham with its gloomy narrow streets and 'murky atmosphere' of factories and warehouses was totally alien and abhorrent to him. However, he persevered and decided to look for another manufacturer, hoping to obtain a more acceptable estimate. His search led him through an area which repelled him with its stench of burning metal and acrid fumes from the furnaces. He entered a grimy building and announced himself as an inventor. The inside of the factory was even more horrendous than outside. Leo gives a wonderfully graphic description of it in *Phantom Lobster.*

'... I felt that I had been transported into a nightmare world. I felt that the only living things in the room were the machines. They were alive. They breathed and moved, and their noises were coherent. They had strength and knowledge and purpose and fertility. There was rhythm and beauty in their lean moving pistons which glistened with oily sweat like the limbs of a straining athlete.'

He left the factory, still dejected, with his problem unsolved. All that he saw around him served to intensify his mood of depression; groups of poverty-stricken women and children, filthy fumes and sulphurous smoke. A place where 'the machines were alive and the people dead'. Leo's reaction to what he saw on that occasion gives us an insight into a little-known aspect of his character. He was no stranger to poverty, aware of the shortage of money amongst fisherfolk when catches were low. But they retained their self-respect and hope, qualities which had been lost in the industrial heartland. Leo's deep concern for those suffering social deprivation remained with him always.

He longed for Bramblewick, where the wind blew fresh from the sea and the men were masters of their lives. He caught the first train back home, but even this was not straightforward and resulted in him having an overnight stop in Leeds. Here, by one of those remarkable coincidences, he found a firm which was able to supply the pot frames that he required at a price which would be affordable.

Leo managed to get a dozen sample pots made by the unidentified firm in Leeds. He had them galvanised, which was expensive, but it was believed that they could be mass-produced for around five shillings each, excluding the netting. He thought that the fishermen would prefer to do this part themselves — but there might have been difficulties here as a special technique would have to be used. Before serious production could begin, finance had to be secured. First of all, official approval by the fisheries division of the Ministry of Agriculture had to be sought.

In *Phantom Lobster*, the official demonstration is described as taking place in Bay, using the Duke's coble. Whether or not this actually happened, a letter has survived from the ministry in London, dated the 6th May 1930, asking Leo to supply 100 of the new pots to be used, with others, in the exploration of new lobster grounds near Beer in Devon during the following month. It invited him to attend to advise on the use of his pots, offering a fee of two guineas a day and third-class return railway fare to Beer. The Royal Navy was to supply the vessel.

Leo went, of course, although it is doubtful if he could supply as many as 100 pots at such short notice, if at all. Later he said that the ministry bought one fleet and the Dukes another, implying about forty in all. Accompanying him on this mission was Margaret Bell-Little, who was later to become his second wife. Margaret, in a letter written years later, recalled that the pots behaved perfectly. They had netted the frames themselves in the back garden of their boarding house, and Margaret mentions their embarrassment at appearing in that impeccable establishment heavily contaminated with tar from the twine.[6]

The quest for financial backing involved a long period of many months in London, during which time Leo supported himself by taking odd jobs. Despite the contacts he had from his earlier period living in St Johns Wood, his efforts proved to be in vain. Carrying a specimen pot, he sought interviews with bankers, captains of industry and philanthropists, none of them identified. One of them may have been Sam Wilson, his old friend and mentor from marine biology days. He dined at the House of Commons with a sympathetic member of Parliament, but sympathy was all he got; there was to be no government subsidy. Many people were impressed, all wished him luck, the obvious fervour of his enthusiasm secured that much, but none could see his way to putting up the money. Why?

One reason for his failure must have been that money was tight, there was a recession with the likely prospect of an absolute slump. Also, after all, it was a bit of an off-beat proposition. City bankers are not necessarily very familiar with the problems of fundamental prime producers. It had not occurred to Leo that he should research his markets, assess the likely demand for the pot. He must have assumed that its benefits would be so obvious to professional fishermen that it would be eagerly adopted, but this was not so for they are a conservative people. Had he tried to promote his invention, he would no doubt have been disappointed. Even his friends the Dukes eventually lashed their metal pots permanently erect, not bothering to fold them. Various types of folding pots have been developed since the Second World War, notably those of Mr R D Leaky of Settle. He started in about 1958, and actually met Leo and gave him a few of his pots. Writing to Hugh Maingay in 1972, Mr Leakey despaired of the uphill struggle to interest commercial fishermen in folding pots; in many cases they would not have them as a gift. Leakey's customers were yachtsmen and other part-timers who were more open-minded and often did very well indeed with his pots.

Then there was the curious matter of the 'provisional patent'. Leo said that he had one but so far no record of one in his name has been found in the files of the Patent Office.[8] In reality, there is no such thing and what he meant was a 'patent for a provisional specification'. This provides cover for about six months, by which time application to patent a fully detailed specification must be made. At this stage, the Patent Office will make a thorough search to ensure that nothing in the invention infringes anything else that has been patented in this country during the previous fifty years. If the device is ingenious, useful and above all entirely original, it can be protected. One cannot patent an idea, but only the means of putting that idea into effect. The fee at that time for a 'provisional specification' was only a pound or two, but the application was invariably left to a professional patent agent and Leo was almost certain to have approached one of these specialists. It is well within the bounds of possibility that the agent would have felt bound to advise him that the folding pot was not patentable.

The new pot was essentially no different, in use, from the traditional pot. It was the same size and shape and caught crabs and lobsters in exactly the same way. The difference was that it folded and there is nothing novel in a hinge. Hundreds of common articles may be made up in such a way that they fold up for convenience in carrying or storing and anyone, presumably, may freely carry out such a modification, certainly for his own use and, providing the article itself is not covered by a current patent, for commercial purposes. It might fairly be said that it was an improvement to make the pot in metal, but the mere making of a traditional design in a non-traditional material does not appear to be patentable. If the locking catch had been of a new type specially fitted for the purpose, it could have been protected on its own, but in fact it was apparently of a standard engineering type. An alternative to the patent would have been the registration of the design, which would have given a degree of protection for several years, but Leo nowhere mentions this option.

Subject to the possibility of a patent, or design registration, being discovered at some future date, it seems likely that the lack of either was a major element in the failure to find a financial backer. Both the person lending the money and the manufacturer setting up the production line would have needed the security not only of a proven market but of exclusive rights to make and sell. One would have expected that these matters would have been pointed out to Leo, but however kindly it was done, it would have added humiliation to disappointment. By his own account, he ended the affair by pitching the specimen pot into the Thames, and whether that is true, or an example of his artistic licence, it can be assumed that he abandoned the project in sheer exasperation.

By this time, his financial position was desperate and his creditors converging. He mentions five county court writs in one week. The total debt was probably not so very great and so far as can be ascertained, the bills were eventually honoured. In addition, one detects that a certain disregard of conventions in his personal relationships was earning him a level of local disapproval. He left Bay to settle rather precariously in Fowey in Cornwall, where Margaret later joined him. It may be that the visit to Beer had given them a taste for a milder coast, otherwise not entirely unlike that of North Yorkshire. At least, it was a long way from his creditors. Nobody knew them and the fishing was good. At last, feeling impelled to write, he produced the books *Three Fevers* and then *Phantom Lobster*, the story of the collapsible lobster pot, both based on the real characters of the Dukes. The latter meanwhile had acquired the old motor mule *Faith* and migrated at last to Whitby to a cottage in Argument's Yard. When the mule foundered in 1935, they set up in the Anstruther-built keelboat *Easter Morn*, and Leo later wrote *Sally Lunn*, based on their further adventures.

With hindsight, one feels that the failure to put the collapsible lobster pot into production was all for the best, however much it hurt at the time. For one thing, the trend to larger fishing boats has made the stowing of bulky items less critical. If folding pots had resulted in even four or five times more of them being put into use, the lobster stocks could have been seriously depleted. Although the pot had briefly been a consuming passion, never entirely to be forgotten, the real significance for Leo was that it brought him for the first time in his life into close contact with the remarkable fisherfolk of his home village. Realisation of their daily difficulties and dangers probably put his own problems into perspective, and at the same time gave him a fascinating and worthwhile subject to write about. One need only compare the 'ripping yarns' written earlier, in a slightly self-conscious and rather contriving sort of style, with those written afterwards. In later years, Leo himself was content to let the world believe that *Three Fevers* was really his first novel. His true genius lay in his gift for telling stories of his own life or of other people's (and not particularly in making up purely fictional ones). It is as if a new and more confident hand grasps the pen. The reader is captured and enthralled, never quite knowing how it is achieved.

The Dukes alone were not responsible for Leo finding himself, or for the 'new man'. There was Margaret, the new love, and there was soon to be at last a young family of his own, for whom he must work to the utmost of his ability. Most of us change, hopefully to mature and improve, at around mid-life. Perhaps he always had the gift of being able to spellbind his readers with plain and homely tales told in simple language and an uncontrived and unassuming way, and this was the time it chose to appear.

Could it be that at some time during those long-ago winter days, as he chatted beside the Dukes' driftwood fire and watched his unsophisticated friend Elliot's darting netting needle deftly fashion the magically diminishing meshes of a perfect pot spout (which he was never quite able to emulate), it may have occurred to him that, after all, the greatest of all arts is that of concealing the art. While his later and better books may not have brought the rewards his friends and admirers would have wished for him, for writing is a notoriously precarious trade, they did earn him widespread recognition as a master storyteller. There is now a growing element of fame as well. That this did not come during his lifetime is to the sorrow of all those friends he never knew he was to have.

John Watts

PART FIVE

ROMANCE AND REALISM

CHAPTER II

Building Their Eden

'WE reached the bluff, but we had completely rounded it before I observed that we had come into the mouth of a little cove, the termination of a short steep valley with bracken and furze and the brambles on one side of it, rough pasture on the other. A little stream ran down the valley, and a hundred yards or so before it entered the cove was a relatively level path of cleared ground on which was a building I recognised as an army hut.'[1]

This is how Leo describes his first sight of the hut at Lanteglos-by Fowey, the place which was to be his home with Margaret for the next three years.

He had met Margaret Bell-Little at the cottage in Robin Hoods Bay where Dame Ethel Walker had her studio. Margaret, the Dain of *Love in the Sun*, lived with her parents in Fylingthorpe, a village just inland but adjoining Robin Hoods Bay. They had moved there when her father had retired. She was a lively dark-skinned girl with a love of nature and the world around her. According to Leo, her appearance and much that was primitive in her nature was due to a distant female ancestor who was the daughter of a deposed ruler of a 'small maritime tropical state'.[2]

Margaret, writing in later life, tells how she met the artist when playing with Ethel's dog, David, a much-loved companion. Margaret took great delight in visiting her cottage with its big window looking out to sea. Ethel Walker became interested in the girl and asked her to call during the evening and wash her brushes. They became friends and while Margaret washed the brushes, the artist would talk to her about her life in London, the parties and her friends such as Henry Moore. Margaret soon discovered that the artist had a studio in Cheyne Walk, London, and that she had pictures hung in the Tate Gallery.

She also talked about Leo Walmsley, whom she knew quite well, and Margaret recalls how determined she was that Margaret should meet Leo. Ethel was convinced that they would get on as they had so much in common, despite the fact that Margaret was much younger than Leo, fifteen years in fact. Margaret had assumed that he would be 'awfully old' and when she eventually met him, she found that he was quite different from what she had expected.

'As I stepped into Ethel's lovely cottage, bright with bowls of flowers and the sun catching white horses out at sea, I saw Ethel in the studio talking to a man who had his back to me. It was not until he turned I saw he was brown and lean. As he came towards me I saw that he had the most interesting eyes, a lovely sort of brown, as you see in that big seaweed like huge ribbons, with the sun shining on it through the water.'[3]

After this first meeting, Leo walked back with Margaret but, conscious that village tongues would be wagging if he were to be seen near her home, left her to complete the journey alone. Ethel Walker seems to have been a determined matchmaker, suggesting to Margaret at this early stage that they were made for each other. Although Margaret begged her not to link their names together, she was obviously intrigued by this man's charismatic personality. In correspondence and other written material, Margaret reveals herself as a person of diverse views and interests. She had loved to explore the environs of the village either on foot or on her beloved pony, Dick. Beside her friendship with Ethel Walker, she gained admittance to the Duke family circle, where she won Mrs Duke's respect (no easy achievement) by teaching herself how to knit a guernsey, a fisherman's jumper unique in style to the particular village, and furthermore was taught by Henry Duke how to make a lobster pot. So with the meeting of Leo and Margaret, two like-minded people came together, each with strong, individual personalities but with sufficient common interests to form a basis for the passionate relationship which was to develop.

The first occasion on which Leo invited Margaret to spend an evening was certainly a date with a difference! He suggested that they should go poaching trout in a mere on the moors. On the way back, they stopped at an old barn and lit a fire and grilled the catch for their supper. This barn would play an important part in their lives in later years.

Meetings continued at the artist's cottage, with Ethel keeping a benevolent eye on the pair. The evening visits for washing brushes were always a delight for Margaret as she loved to watch her painting. She was thrilled when the artist asked her to pose for a portrait sitting on the window sill with the sea in the background. Ethel questioned Leo about his writing, wanting to know how his book was progressing. Margaret shared his disappointment when he explained that he was having difficulty getting into his latest book. They left Ethel's cottage together and walked down to Leo's small cottage on the other side of the village. It was certainly not as pretty as Ethel's, but on the walls were several watercolours by Leo's father, Ulric. Margaret's attention was caught by the shelves of books, Shaw, Kipling, and Conrad and some of his own. She was particularly interested in *Toro of the Little People* and was delighted when he told her to take it and borrow others when she had finished it.

Leo was going to London and suggested that Margaret should go with him. She shied away from the prospect but while he was away she knew that, should he ask her again, she would not refuse. She was aware that her parents would disapprove if they knew of the association, particularly as Leo was still married to Suzanne, and this worried her. When Leo returned early from London and asked her to go to Dartmouth with him, she could no longer resist and fabricated a story for the benefit of her parents that she had been invited by a girlfriend to stay. They arrived at Dartmouth where they were to stay on a house-boat moored on the banks of the river. By this time, she knew that she was in love with him, and despite the fact that he was still married to Suzanne, she eagerly agreed when he asked her to spend the rest of her life with him.

She greatly regretted the distress that her relationship would cause her mother and father and was well aware that the village community of Robin Hoods Bay would be deeply shocked. Leo, she knew, saw little of his parents, although she never questioned why. Indeed, nowhere in his writing does Leo give any indication as to why he virtually ignored his family. It seems that it will remain a mystery.

They spent two wonderful weeks at Dartmouth, swimming, picnicking, exploring the area; in love and ecstatically happy. Margaret returned home while Leo remained in the West Country, searching for somewhere for them to live. She picked up the threads of her life back home in the village until in January 1931 a letter arrived postmarked Fowey.

The letter was full of plans and he told her that he had rented a cottage. Paint and some furniture would make all the difference, he wrote. The 'cottage' was named 'Higher Cairn' and was on the banks of a beautiful little creek, Pont Pill, off the River Fowey. It was in fact a derelict hut, a First World War army hut. It had originally been moved there from a camp on Salisbury Plain for use as a workshop by a boat builder in Polruan, a nearby village.

There were several reasons why Leo had decided to leave Robin Hoods Bay. He had been finding it increasingly difficult to concentrate on his writing; consequently he was short of money and was getting more and more into debt. He decided that he had to leave the district, and seek somewhere far away from his creditors where he would find peace and seclusion, giving him the atmosphere in which he could work. Also, as the relationship between Margaret and himself developed, it was impossible to keep their secret from the prying eyes of the village gossips. The deeply rooted moral convictions of the community made their position untenable.

Although his literary output prior to this time had been considerable, it had consisted mainly of hundreds of articles and short stories in addition to boys' adventure stories. These brought in an income which was spasmodic and unpredictable. He was dissatisfied with his achievement, being sure that he had within him the ability to produce work of a superior technique. During the last few days at Robin Hoods Bay, when the winter storms swept the coast, it struck him that here he had the theme for which he had been looking. His knowledge of the fishing families and their daily battles against that implacable protagonist, the sea, would supply him with the material which he needed for a novel. His admiration for these men was such that for months, if not years, he had felt a compulsion to recount their exploits to a wider audience, but the way in which to do this had eluded him.[4]

By moving away from the district, he was able to clarify his thoughts, unhindered by close involvement with the men and women and their way of life. He was sure that in the idyllic Cornish backwater he would find the seclusion and inspiration which would enable him to produce the work of the high standard to which he aspired. There were, of course, many obstacles to overcome, not least the necessity of making the hut habitable. Furthermore, while in the process of writing his novel, no income would be forthcoming. The story of how he and Margaret worked together to provide food for everyday existence, their successes and catastrophes, adventures and worries, is told in a later book, *Love in the Sun*.

However, the immediate problem which faced Leo on finding the hut on Christmas Day 1930 was to decide whether he should stay on his own, putting the

Pont Pill, Fowey

An aerial view of the hut and creek

Reconstruction of the hut

building to rights and working on his book. It did not take him long to reach his decision.

> 'I looked at the hut, with my heart pounding inside me. Wasn't it almost the very thing we wanted? We'd imagined a fisherman's cottage, on a lonely beach, or perhaps a little island. It would be primitive and dilapidated, and of course, unfurnished, but we would have the excitement of putting it to rights, of furnishing it ourselves. Wasn't the hut almost as good as such a cottage? Wasn't the place almost as secluded as an island? It was out of sight of the real sea, but was there not an outweighing advantage in having a cove and a waterway one could use in all weathers? Why should we wait? Why should we remain parted.'[5]

So began their life together. They had been drawn towards each other not only by a strong physical attraction, but by mutual interests in nature, the sea, the land and all that was happening around them. Living together in their isolated home with, at first, little company except for each other, they grew closer in thought, sharing a philosophy of life which was near idyllic in its intensity. Close proximity to fertile land and the sea was not only a delight, it was also practical. By clearing the land around the hut, they would be able to plant vegetables and fruit trees and there was a regular supply of fish to be had in the creek, river or out in the harbour and along the coast. If they wanted a variation in their diet, they could make a shopping trip across the estuary to Fowey in the boat which they had bought for £1 from the Slades, the owners of the hut. Most of their basic needs

An internal view of the hut

could be supplied in Polruan, which was only a short distance down the creek. It was here that the Slades had their boat building yard and the Walmsleys turned to them for advice and permission to make alterations and repairs to the hut. The Slades were an easy-going family, content to make a reasonable living, and Leo and Margaret became quite attached to them.

The hut itself was a standard army hut, dirty and dilapidated. Designed originally as a dormitory for soldiers, it had been converted into a dwelling house.

> 'And the conversion had been done apparently with the sole object of obtaining the maximum number of rooms with a minimum of material. Each room in the converted part was small and with only a single window. The room containing the stove measured nine feet by ten.'[6]

They had been given permission to make whatever alterations they liked, so, on examining the construction of the interior, they decided to remove partition walls to make two rooms into one. Margaret's natural exuberance soon produced suggestions and plans regarding how they could attack the problems facing them. The most urgent job was the roof which, as they had discovered in the middle of their first night, leaked. A storm which sprang up had wreaked havoc.

> 'The roar was the wind blowing at least with the force of a gale; the banging I judged to be one of the hut doors; the flapping sound evidently was made by loose felt on the roof; and the dripping needed no explanation, for in addition to the stream that had wet

us, water was pouring in from at least a dozen places in the roof, and the floor, except for one section immediately under the apex of the roof, was practically awash ... It was alarming. The whole fabric of the hut seemed to be loose and shaking. Save that the floor was level, we might have been aboard a storm-tossed ship.'[7]

Afraid that their boat would be torn from its moorings, they dashed to the beach. In the course of rescuing their boat, they saved the life of a tiny, half-drowned kitten. They revived it and it was immediately established as a member of the family. It was given the name Choo-i, a Swahili word meaning 'small thing'.

This version of their early days in Cornwall is taken from *Love in the Sun* but in a letter which Margaret wrote about fifty years later she refers to renting a cottage in Polruan while the hut was being 'cleaned and remodelled'. She recalls that they either rowed up the creek or walked along the cliff-top path then down to their land. They actually took up residence in their new home in the spring of 1931.

Although the roof took priority over all other jobs, it was also vital that a room was prepared in which Leo could write. Until he completed his book, they would be desperately short of money so they settled into a way of life different from anything either of them had experienced before. The practical repairs and painting of the hut progressed; furniture was made from wood washed up on the beach or from any source that presented itself. Chairs and table had to be made with legs of uneven length as the floor of the hut sloped several degrees. The garden was started as soon as the land had been cleared.

They loved to wander along the beach as relaxation from the physical labour of the renovations to the hut, and it was on one of these occasions that Leo was struck by an idea which was to provide a supplement to their very meagre income. Finding an abundant supply of cockles and mussels, his first thought was that it was an ideal source of bait for fishing. Then, remembering his days at the marine laboratory at Robin Hoods Bay when he had discovered that there was a 'definite cash value' in small marine animals required by the zoological departments of universities, it occurred to him that there was likely to be a regular demand. He decided to write to the firm of naturalists with which he had had connections in those earlier years. Eventually, in reply to his letter, he received a list of various small creatures which it required and would pay for when supplied. The list included spiders, centipedes, beetles, cockroaches, earthworms and many others in addition to the marine animals, crabs, starfish and sea-slugs which Leo had been expecting. At a few pence each, it was a mildly lucrative if unusual occupation which brought them an average income of twenty-two shillings a week — a very welcome addition to their sparse funds.

During this very hectic period, writing of the book progressed at all hours. There were times when he was inspired and wrote for hours on end, but worrying periods when he was devoid of ideas. But at last in April 1931 *Three Fevers* was finished. The worst, it seemed, was over, but there was to be a further anxious time when Leo tried to find a publisher who would accept his book. In a letter written by Margaret many years later, she referred to the depression which he suffered as the book 'kept coming back from every publisher'. However, it was eventually accepted by Jonathan Cape Ltd and published on the 2nd February 1932.

A few weeks before publication, Leo sent a copy of the manuscript to Sir Arthur Quiller-Couch, one of the country's most respected literary figures, who lived across the river at Fowey. There was some doubt as to whether he would be able to undertake the reading of the manuscript as his eyesight was failing, so there was yet more anxious waiting. Margaret recalls watching daily for a red boat to sail into their cove, as Quiller-Couch, who had a waterside house, owned a fleet of bright red boats. At last, late on the afternoon of Wednesday, the 9th December, one of the little boats sailed towards their beach. A very nervous Leo, on opening the letter handed to him by the boatman, was overjoyed to read that Quiller-Couch, or 'Q' as he was generally known, had read the entire text. His letter stated:

'I do most sincerely congratulate you upon it. It is the real stuff: well written indeed (if I may say so), but with no literary fake about it.'

In addition, he included the following endorsement for the publishers:

'*Three Fevers* gave me a surprise and a shock of delight. Its story, in itself simple, is so simply and classically told that maybe only those acquainted with inshore fishermen will recognise its accuracy of detail and only those who understand reticence in Art will admire the anatomy of this piece of work as it should be admired.

Talk about "masterpieces" comes easily to the pen in these days. I can only say that I laid down this book with a respectful wonder, as a bright thing sired by Art out of Knowledge.'[8]

Asking Sir Arthur Quiller-Couch to read the text was an inspired choice. He was King Edward VII's professor of English Literature at Cambridge and therefore his commendation drew particular attention to Leo's achievement, helping to promote the book. Other well-known authors and critics alike gave the book glowing reviews. Rebecca West referred to Leo as a 'perfect yarn spinner', comparing him to the Ancient Mariner, saying that readers would find themselves in the position of the wedding guests who 'so long as he went on had to listen'.

The gift of storytelling was not one which had come quickly or easily. It may have been there semi-dormant from his early childhood years, when he had to be quick-witted to produce an acceptable excuse to extricate himself from trouble after his mischievous nature had led him to commit some misdemeanour. It is likely that the skill would have been fostered during the time he spent in East Africa, where the tradition of passing down information by word of mouth from one generation to another had continued for centuries. It is known that he spent much time in the company of his African boys, particularly his faithful servant, Maganga. How many stories were exchanged during those African nights as they sat around the camp-fires? The art of storytelling must surely have been nurtured by these occasions. Africa had cast its spell over Leo and the intensity of his feeling of affinity with that country must have influenced him as he had started to write short stories with an African theme.

The many articles and stories which he had written had not given him the fulfilment for which he yearned. They were in the nature of an apprenticeship. In what might be thought his best short story, 'The Soul of an Artist', published in 1925, Leo reveals some of his own frustration through one of the characters, Grimsdyck, who is recounting the story of a local character:

'He recognised perhaps in Joseph a symbolic parallel of himself, of his own failure to achieve that high and extravagant and ever-soaring ideal which is the aspiration of all creative artists, whether they be painters, writers or musicians.'[9]

It is perhaps true to say that this could also have applied to his father Ulric's ambitions as a portrait painter.

Although in reality he had not entered the literary world with the publication of *Three Fevers*, it was an impression which Leo himself did nothing to correct. He was happy to be judged by the literary ability revealed in *Three Fevers*, hoping to obliterate the memory of his other works. The deceptive simplicity of his style was in direct contrast to the kind of writing which was being developed about this time. It was a time when writers such as D H Lawrence were pioneering works on contentious issues which hitherto had not been offered to the reading public.

Possibly there was a reaction against these controversial books, but there was no doubt that the reviews of *Three Fevers* were full of praise for Leo's achievement. Many well-known names, H E Bates, J B Priestley, and Eric Linklater were amongst the reviewers, several of whom used the terms 'classic' and 'masterpiece'.

Leo and Margaret were naturally overjoyed at the success of the book. The worries and disappointments of the last few years were forgotten and their lives took on new meaning. Leo was already planning his next book, but once the pressure was lifted he was able to divert more of his time and energy to practical matters. Soon the hut had become a home. They spent days cleaning and repairing the interior, swabbing the floor with 'a strong solution of carbolic' then scrubbing hard with soap and hot water.

> 'We worked at fever heat. While the floor dried we set to on the partition between the galley and the corridor ... By the time we had demolished the first partition it seemed that we had enough material for a dozen cupboards, and a door that would make an admirable table. But we did not stop ... We had a room that measured ten feet by twenty-four with a window at each opposite end, and the doors at each opposite side. The ceiling slanted to an apex in the middle. The walls of the original kitchen had been decorated most recently with a dark green paper with a pattern of roses on it, while what paper remained in the other room was imitation Dutch tiles.'[10]

The contrasting papers were removed and in a 'frenzy of labour' they white-washed the ceiling, distempered the walls dove grey and finished making the cupboards and dresser. They left the wood bare, sandpapering and polishing it until it gleamed. They later lined the walls of all the rooms with 'cloth cut from old sails that Joe had given us.' Hard but satisfying work had produced a result of which they were happy and proud. They loved the big room used as a lounge with its large window which they had put in to give them a splendid view of the creek. They designed and built an open fireplace which was a disaster. The fact that they could never get the room warm enough in winter remained a serious problem as Leo was very susceptible to the cold.

The garden was dug and prepared using seaweed as a very effective fertiliser. Having little prior experience of gardening, they had to rely on the instructions on seed packets and gardening books, but they were determined to become self-sufficient as far as vegetables were concerned. They planned to grow strawberries, raspberries and gooseberries and to have an orchard with apples, pears and plums. In addition, they imaginatively made the stream which passed through their land close to the hut into a very attractive feature. It fell in miniature waterfalls into pools with rocks placed strategically to create the effect that they wanted. At the side farthest from the hut they formed a bank and planted 'masses of primroses and foxgloves' which grew wild and in profusion higher up the valley.

During the period of insecurity and uncertainty Margaret, to her delight, had become pregnant. Leo, older and more realistic, had mixed feelings. Although he admitted that he was surprised to find that the thought of becoming a father gave him great pleasure, he was also worried about his ability to support a family. With their improved circumstances, they could look forward to the birth of their first child.

An unexpected meeting had taken place, which resulted in a friendship which was a welcome relief to their hitherto secluded existence. They had been in their boat on a shopping expedition to Fowey when they almost literally bumped into a couple from Robin Hoods Bay. At first, Leo was taken aback as the man had been one of his contemporaries at school and furthermore one regarded as a bully. As 'Grab Fosdyck', a character in Leo's later book, *Foreigners*, he was feared and hated by the young Leo. The chance meeting was an embarrassment for the Walmsleys as their sudden flight from the village had been subject to much speculation and gossip. However, when they openly admitted their reason for leaving, the couple readily agreed to keep their secret. William and Bettina Beedle were living on one of six ships laid up in the Fowey estuary. As first mate of the *Wyndyke*, William was employed to look after all six ships during a period of stagnant trade during the depression. The episode makes a delightful little story in *Love in the Sun*. The basic details have been substantiated by the Beedles' son, Raymond, although there is a little artistic licence in the telling of the tale in Leo's book. The two couples became good friends, which must have been particularly pleasant for the Beedles as their enforced sojourn in such a remote spot could have become very lonely. They eventually left after staying on the ship for a period of several months.

Leo and Margaret had by this time made their hut into a real home in which they could settle quite happily, planning alterations needed to accommodate the baby. Although in *Love in the Sun* Leo recounts an emotional reaction to the birth of the child in the hut with the services of the local midwife, in fact, Margaret booked into the Dawn Nursing Home at Looe. Ann was born on the 7th May 1932 and was registered on the 21st May as Ann Walmsley Bell-Little. As Leo was awaiting his divorce from Suzanne, they were still unmarried. It was not until the 30th January 1933 that they were married at Liskeard Registry Office, his divorce having been made absolute in November 1932.

It is rather ironic that, at a time when they were living the simple life in an apparently happy if haphazard fashion, they should select a nursing home rather than a hospital or home birth for their child. There must have been some remnant of the earlier sophistication lingering on. Further evidence of this is indicated in a letter dated the 27th October 1932 from his solicitor in London. It appears that Leo had requested extended time for payment of an account. The reply is succinct:

Leo Walmsley, with second wife Margaret Bell-Little and daughter Ann

'Without being impertinent, we would also suggest to you that you go to a Hospital instead of a Nursing Home as you will get quite as good treatment, if not better, at half the cost, for your operation. This is what we do ourselves.'

We have no indication of what the operation was, or indeed whether he had an operation. In one of Margaret's letters, she writes of their near-idyllic life in their cove. She had loved:

'... messing about in boats and fishing and going up to the jetties getting the lovely white china clay and going out to sea with the dolphins playing about us- fishing for mackerel in the dinghy behind Amanda[11] with them flapping around my feet, and doing crazy things like taking Anna out at night in the boat and going up the river to the farm which was quite far up. We liked the old grand-mother and loved her tumbler pigeons.'

She recalls rowing from Fowey and how exciting it was with the 'big ships from far away places, Japan, Holland, and all over' coming to the china clay jetties. There were the beautiful big yachts which anchored in the river during the summer months and the boat which had been abandoned, 'quite spooky as people had up and left it with the table cloth on, all the dishes and glasses and food on the plates'.

It was about the middle of November 1932 when Leo started correspondence again with his old friend, Sam Wilson, who had by this time obtained his PhD, a correspondence that was to continue over the years.

Leo, Margaret and Ann

When Leo started writing again after the completion of *Three Fevers*, he used the same 'Bramblewick' setting, but it was to differ quite considerably in content. He had written the story in a previous draft which had not been published. The subject of this story was his invention of a collapsible lobster pot.[12] He was not satisfied with the way in which he had dealt with the story and decided to rewrite it in a completely different form. He called the book *Phantom Lobster*, although expressed doubt as to the wisdom of this at a later date, commenting on the fact that it suggested a ghost story. In correspondence with P Gilchrist Thompson, a director of Jonathan Cape Ltd, he refers to:

> '... a very agreeable memory of our interview when we discussed *Phantom Lobster* and the memory survived your ultimate rejection.'[13]

A reply from Mr Gilchrist Thompson suggests that he considered *Phantom Lobster* (the first draft) 'self-conscious'. The second attempt was written in the form of an autobiographical novel, although Leo denied that it was a novel, insisting that it was a 'record of an actual experience'. The book was eventually published in October 1933.

The year after Ann's birth until and beyond the publication of *Phantom Lobster* must have been a very happy time for the Walmsleys, despite the fact that Leo suffered typically from the depression and exasperation of the creative artist. Their love for their baby and the delights which they shared when they took her on expeditions as she grew older reveal a contentment and joy in their relationship. In a letter, Margaret refers to 'Leo always cooking dinner which they had very late'. Being short of money, a situation that seems to have occurred to some degree throughout his life, they had a great deal of fish, mussels from the rocks and vegetables from their garden and even gulls' eggs, but later she says that 'he always had steak and two veg' and never changed to anything else!

They had few friends at that time, which is not surprising when they were in such an isolated place. However, one person who became a very close friend was Daphne du Maurier, who lived nearby. Margaret in a letter dated August 1988 recalls that they 'saw Daphne every day'. She would join them for cream teas; she was particularly fond of Margaret's scones and home-made jam; and they all enjoyed the walk to each other's homes, a delightful tree-lined path with glimpses of the river and Fowey beyond. An alternative approach was by boat. They had much in common; their unconventional outlook and way of life was far removed from that of most people. The Walmsleys mixed happily with the local people whereas Daphne became more of a recluse as the years passed by. The friendship grew and lasted over the years, with Daphne being very supportive of Leo when, at a later stage in his life, he was to need all the comfort and understanding which only a true friend can give.

Although there was a close comradeship between Margaret and Daphne, there was an additional factor where Leo was concerned. The two authors shared an interest in their literary achievements and aspirations. Letters from Daphne show that she respected him as a 'jolly fair critic' and they were in the habit of discussing their manuscripts. The esteem which she had for his ability as a writer is shown in her review of his book *Angler's Moon*:

'He has written another spell-binder. Every chapter held and I just don't know how he does it.'[14]

The friendship extended to Daphne's husband, 'Tommy' Browning, although due to the length of time he was absent from Cornwall, the bond was not as strong where he was concerned. In a letter dated the 6th January 1943 and headed 'From Major General F.A.M. Browning C.B., D.S.O.', he replied to one of Leo's letters with obvious affection.

> 'Whenever we pass the old hut up Pont, we always look with affection and happy memories of the time when you and the family were there.'

Having just returned from North Africa where he served in the Airborne Division, he comments on the problems with which he had to deal and refers to Leo's exploits in the First World War: 'I seem to remember that you used to perform considerably more hazardous evolutions in the crates which were called aircraft in the last war.'

Obviously companionship such as this was very important to Leo and Margaret. They would enjoy the conversation with two people who, although appreciating the beautiful country around Fowey, also had contact with the cultural circle where art and literature were part of everyday life. It helped them to retain a link with the 'real' world, while living their own idyll, a life designed to suit themselves which served them well for the three years that they were there.

With the publication of *Phantom Lobster* they had high hopes that their worries would be over. It did indeed help, but was not the financial success anticipated. Ironically, although it was well received by the critics with reviews which were enthusiastic in their praise, it had created difficulties for his reviewers and his publishers. In an author's note at the beginning of the book, Leo had written:

> 'This book is a record of an actual experience ...'

He had then proceeded to give an explanation regarding the characters and the setting 'Bramblewick', even going so far as to give the latitude and longitude of the village. The problem thus arose as to whether it should be accepted as factual journalism, autobiography or a novel. Compton Mackenzie recorded that:

> '*Phantom Lobster* ... is described by the author as a true story and I accept the author's word for it without question. However, it is told in the form of a novel, and it is told with so much of that art which knows how to hide itself, that if it were regarded merely as a novel no reader could help fancying that he was taking part in an actual experience.'[15]

The disarray into which the critics had been thrown concerning categorisation of *Phantom Lobster* did nothing to detract from their unstinted praise of the work. Author Storm Jameson, who had also read the manuscript prior to publication, wrote to Leo and said that she had enjoyed it and would review the book in the magazine *Then and Now*, which she did in the winter 1933 edition.

For Leo and Margaret, life went on as before: fishing, gardening, watching baby Ann growing and delighting in each stage of her development. As soon as they could, they adapted the boat so that they could take her on short trips. She loved the sea and it was not long before they decided that they must have a bigger boat — one in which they could go out to sea, travel to Europe by way of the

Rhine and the Danube, see the Mediterranean, Greece, Italy. Plans, in typical Walmsley fashion, became more and more extravagant. When they discussed the possibility of buying a cruiser with the Slades at their boatyard, they accepted reluctantly that it was beyond their means to buy even a second-hand one. However, they were lucky in that amongst the boats recently acquired by the boatyard was a ship's lifeboat, which was offered to them for a mere four pounds. They spent as much time as they could scrubbing the dirt off the boat, then scraping the paint off using a blowlamp. It was a slow laborious job, but they were rewarded in finding it in good condition. They planned how they would fit it out, getting advice from the experts at the boatyard and eventually acquired an engine for the boat. There is some doubt about whether they spent their money on acquiring a brand new engine or obtained an ancient one which was going for scrap. Comments in a letter from Leo to Sam Wilson and remarks made by Margaret indicate that it was a new one, but when he describes it in his book he says that it is second-hand. They called the boat *Samaki*, which is Swahili for 'fish' and, after much hard work, disappointment and painful blisters, succeeded in making the boat seaworthy. They had many happy trips in her, sailing down the creek to the sea and exploring coves along the coast. One excursion almost ended in disaster when exhilaration and impetuosity overcame prudence and they were caught out at sea as fog descended suddenly. All ended well but it gave Leo such a fright when he realised that he had put the lives of his wife and child at risk, that he resolved that never again would he take chances when leaving the safety of the harbour.

By this time, Leo had conceived the idea of a book about his childhood: the village with its characters, school with the headmaster and class mates who had caused him such harassment, his parents, the fishermen and their fight against the sea, all seen through the eyes of a boy. Margaret was relieved when he started writing again. Over fifty years later, she was to comment on her concern when he had abandoned writing in favour of painting. Scenes remembered from his time in Africa were depicted with Mount Kilimanjaro not surprisingly a favourite subject for his painting.

She encouraged him in his writing, confident in his ability to produce work of true literary value. She was enthusiastic about his chosen subject and was delighted when he read the instalments to her as he completed them. Her enthusiasm was generous and spontaneous, but also at the back of her mind would be the knowledge that they, as a family, were dependent on the successful outcome. He needed to build on the reputation he had achieved with *Three Fevers*. He found that writing about 'Bramblewick' and reliving his childhood there through his work made him feel 'unbearably nostalgic' for the village and the fishermen who had been his friends. There were times when they were both torn by the love which they had for both places, the picturesque fishing village with the roar of the sea breaking against the cliffs and the haven of their Cornish cove, safe for their boats in all weathers.

Margaret was pregnant with their second child, so there was a new urgency about their future prospects. It was becoming more obvious that the hut with its inadequacies and remote location was far from satisfactory when considering a growing family. Leo had mentioned from time to time that he was concerned about his parents; they were so far away. Margaret, in another of her letters, disputes this sentiment as she insists that he rarely made any effort to visit his parents, even when living back in Yorkshire. Leo's attitude to them was ambivalent; natural filial affection seems to have been virtually non-existent, yet there is no evidence of a family dispute.

Matters gradually came to a head when, after the birth of their second daughter, Henrietta Statira, on the 11th April 1934 at the Dawn Nursing Home, Looe, they decided that they would have to leave. The recession had been responsible for a downturn in the fortunes of the Slades and they had offered the hut for sale. Leo made an offer to buy the hut and adjacent land but it was not accepted and it was finally sold to a wealthy army major. Although there was no question of him turning the Walmsleys out of their home, they decided that the time had come for them to return to Robin Hoods Bay. The sale of a short story in addition to the proceeds from *Three Fevers* gave them financial security hitherto unknown and enabled Leo to pay off the debts which had been partially responsible for his flight from the village.

Confident that the new book would be a success, they started to plan their return to Bay.

Nona Stead

CHAPTER 12

Dreams and Plans

RETURNING to the village of his youth, the place which evoked such depth of feeling for both Leo and Margaret, must have been a very emotional experience. Having left in haste to escape his creditors and the hostility of many of the villagers, he hoped that he would now be accepted back into the community. He had reimbursed his creditors and achieved some semblance of respectability with the enthusiastic reception of his books.

Leo had learnt, over the years, that he had to be emotionally self-sufficient and not rely on acquaintances for support and understanding. The battles, both physical and mental, which he had fought as a boy because of the ostracism he had suffered as a 'foreigner' had created in him an indifference to local opinion. It was a hurdle he had been faced with at an early age and had dealt with in his own way. He had no option. However, he did not want his children to experience the same unpleasantness. The circumstances of their return to the village were such that he was convinced that past differences would in no way affect his family. To Leo, this was of vital importance. He had a deep, abiding love for his two little girls and as he and Margaret wanted to add to their family, it was essential that they should be surrounded by a warm, friendly atmosphere.

They knew where they wanted to build a house, away from the village but within walking distance and near the sea. On their first date, that illicit fishing expedition, they had spent some time on the very spot. It had been a favourite haunt of both Leo and Margaret before they met and Margaret for the rest of her life clearly recalled the details of that momentous evening. To reach the moorland tarn, they had to wend their way through the woods past Ramsdale Mill, then climb up towards the moors. As they approached an old barn, a favourite stopping place of Margaret's when riding her pony, Leo told her how he loved the place and dreamed of turning it into a house. The story of how their dream became reality is told in *The Golden Waterwheel* published in 1954.

In the book, Leo refers to their first choice as being a site nearer to the sea, slightly to the south, just above Stoupe Beck. As in so many of his books, sifting fact from fiction sets a challenge. The plot of land he describes exists unchanged to this day and can easily be found if one follows the references in the book. The spring and the water trough are still there. One side of the site is on the edge of the cliff and the way down to the shore is steep and hazardous. It would have been a dangerous place for young children and, aware of Leo's devotion and concern for his family, one can assume that this is another example of artistic licence and that in reality the plot where the barn was situated was the place on which they had set their hearts.

When they first returned to Yorkshire in spring 1934, they stayed with Margaret's parents at Fylingthorpe, but this had its drawbacks as Leo did not get on with her father. According to a letter which Margaret wrote when she had turned eighty, Leo could be very rude to her father Edward Little but was always nice to her mother. It seems that they were very relieved when Leo spent much of his time out of the house.

It is likely that it was during this period that he made a tour of the North East. He was deeply disturbed by the state of the area.

> 'The shipyards of Jarrow had been permanently closed under a scheme which had for its object the rationalisation of the shipbuilding industry as a whole. Thousands of skilled men had been unemployed and on the dole for months on end. It was pitiful to see these men standing outside the employment exchanges. They were not starved. The 'dole' at least gave them food. They were not ill-clad or dirty. In fact their cleanliness and the whiteness of their hands were as tragically significant as the expression of boredom and hopelessness in their eyes.'[1]

The vast shipyards of the Tyne and Tees presented a desolate picture with related industries also affected. Referring to this in *Ports and Harbours*, he expresses relief that a few years later on a return visit he saw a marked improvement after government subsidies had been applied, but points out with some irony that it needed a war to produce a boom.

Eventually they took temporary accommodation at a house named 'Hollycroft', Larpool Lane, Whitby, 'an ugly modern villa about a mile and a half from the town and close to the cemetery'.[2] They paid £9 per month although they disliked the place, christening it 'Butcher's Folly' and accepted it as a base while they saved enough money to buy the land and build their new house.

The village of Robin Hoods Bay had lost its immediate attraction for Leo. The Dukes had left to live in Whitby, close to the harbour. They were partners in a 'mule', a boat bigger than a coble but smaller than a 'keeler', which was the type of vessel preferred by the more prosperous Whitby fishermen. Robin Hoods Bay was becoming more of a holiday village and within a few years of moving back to the area, Leo was to write to an acquaintance advising him not to return as there was:

> 'an amusement park in the Dock, slot machines, and a radio playing non-stop. I don't go near it.'[3]

He referred to his book *Sally Lunn* as his 'epitaph on old 'Bay'. This was published in 1937. Despite this statement, his supposed aversion to the village was short-lived. He did, in fact, retain a deep affection for the place and regularly walked from Leith Rigg to meet the local men in the Dock or on the beach. Articles which he wrote about visits made in later years were characterised by a deep nostalgia.

In 1934–5, the main concern was to accumulate money for their new home. The proceeds from *Three Fevers* and to a lesser degree *Phantom Lobster* were required for current living expenses, so he was looking for another successful publication. Despite the financial disappointment of *Phantom Lobster*, it had been widely acclaimed by the critics. Leo was convinced that their future hinged on the success of *Foreigners*, not yet published. He had every hope that it would prove a success as it was a simple story of his childhood. He felt confident that his strength as an author was in writing in his distinctively simple style about the place which he knew and loved so much.

Meanwhile, he and Margaret were making their plans. A 'genial aunt' had agreed to stay with them to help with the children. They had chosen the site for their house, determined to adapt the old barn which appealed to them for its commanding position looking over towards the sea on one side and the moors on the other. They had contacted a builder, Will Cornforth, and discussed their plans with him, going into quite considerable detail, despite the fact that it was still a dream, unattainable until the money was forthcoming.

They did not, in fact, have to wait for the publication of *Foreigners*. A letter from London arrived which read:

'Dear Sir,

Re-Three Fevers.

We have read this book and believe that it contains distinct filmic possibilities — provided that it is treated something on the lines of *Man Of Aran* — but we should like to know from you whether conditions today in any part of Northumberland or Durham are approximately as they are described in your book. We should also like to know if you are ever in Town, or if you are likely to be in Town in the near future, in order that we might have a chat on the subject generally.

Yours faithfully,

FOR NATIONAL BRITISH FILMS LTD.
John Corfield,
Managing Director.'

Leo referred to it as being 'like a dream come true'. Not only was he to have one of his books made into a film, but one of his earlier ambitions was to be realised. Since his contact with the film world when in Africa, he had been convinced that Robin Hoods Bay was a perfect photogenic subject, ideal for the cinema. In addition, he was to be paid a sum of money which would enable him to build his house, and he realised afterwards that he could have held out for a larger sum. After meeting John Corfield, he sent a telegram to Margaret.

'Walmsley Little, Thorpe, Robin Hood's Bay. Contract Three Fevers. Three hundred. Bay. Wednesday five o'clock. Most exciting. Love. Leo.'

Leo maintains in *So Many Loves* that the making of the film in itself would take an entire book to describe in detail.

Nona Stead

CHAPTER 13

Turn of the Tide

'**M**Y desire to make films had always been at least as strong as my desire to make books. I knew that the film was an entirely different medium from writing. I did not imagine that *Three Fevers* as I had written it *was* a film story that possessed anything but … filmic possibilities.'[1]

Unbeknown to Leo, a company, British National Films Ltd, had been formed by a syndicate of wealthy, influential individuals with the express purpose of making quality films showing life in Britain to be good and wholesome. These would counteract those currently emerging in great numbers from Hollywood. As one contemporary press release put it, 'At its inception, the company announced its intention of making only first-class British pictures of outstanding merit, and their present programme includes several Empire themes. The policy of the company is to present British subjects through British eyes, and to demonstrate to the world that British pictures made by British people can hold first place in entertainment value and beauty of presentation with any in the world. The honour of the first picture falls to *Three Fevers* and special pains are to be taken to make it great in every sense of the word.'

The company clearly knew exactly what it wanted to achieve. Driven by patriotism and by an obvious pride in its national identity, it left no one in doubt that it considered 'British' to be far and away the best. It was a film critic by the name of Walter Mutch who recommended *Three Fevers* to British National Films, and this evidently struck a chord with one of the directors, the Hull millionaire J Arthur Rank, who as a young boy went on Sunday school trips to Robin Hoods Bay. Despite his exalted position in the flour milling industry, Rank was a most humble and down-to-earth man, who foresaw great possibilities in film-making for 'spreading the Gospel' in a way not hitherto considered. He had already sponsored the making of a short religious picture, *Mastership*, but he saw in *Three Fevers* the opportunity to make on location a feature film, the like of which he thought had never been seen before in those early days of the film industry.

The £300 he was offered for the film rights was seen as an advance on Leo's promised five percent of the projected net profits from the film, and he was also employed as a technical adviser on a weekly salary of £6. Not having much of a head for business at that time, he did not haggle over finances, and was not to realise until much later that such a sum was quite derisory when compared with that being paid to others on the set. This, after all, was one of his dreams coming true and he was carried along with enthusiasm mixed with a certain amount of naivety.

'All the wisest people agree a novelist should have nothing to do with the filming of his own novel. It has been said that if an author does sell the film rights of a book, he should have the transaction carried out entirely through his agent and bank manager, never under any circumstances meet any person connected with the filming company, and make up his mind from the start that the script writer, the producers, the directors will do precisely the opposite to what he himself would do if he wished to express his story, its plot, characters and atmosphere through the medium of talking moving pictures. Also that if he has any feelings about his story (and it is certain that between some authors and their books the relationship approaches that of mother and child) he will strongly resist any temptation he may have to see the film when it is made. The nervous shock might finish him. But in my case it was different.'[2]

His initial meeting with the company was certainly encouraging. John Corfield was delighted to find that the setting of the novel *Three Fevers* was an actual village on the Yorkshire coast, and that the families featured in it were real people who were still in the area. Leo was introduced to the chosen director for the project, Norman Walker, a fellow veteran of the First World War, whom he liked from the start. They shared the view that the film should not be another attempt at a *Man Of Aran* as Corfield had envisaged it should be, but that it should be better and be more concerned with actual people as they went about their daily lives than purely with picturesque landscapes. Walker had already had several films to his credit and was no beginner where location photography was concerned, hence his recommendations could not go unheeded and had to be taken into account.

The official announcement about the forthcoming film was made in the *Whitby Gazette* on the 15th February 1935, and the film crew duly arrived in the area in early March. One of Leo's tasks for the six weeks that followed was to liaise with the local fishermen and gain their co-operation as extras in the filming. One incident in particular which persuaded his friends the Dukes to play a part was the sinking of their old fishing boat, *Faith*. She had broken her back whilst negotiating a big sea at the mouth of Whitby harbour and sank within sight of the piers. The crew had immediately sent up distress rockets, giving rise to the rumour locally that the decrepit vessel had been set on fire, and the Dukes had to endure some good-natured ribbing from the fishing community over this, which they took in good part. With their livelihood being taken away so unexpectedly, they at least were ready and available to start work on the film, along with a few other local fishermen. Each was paid £5 per week with a further £5 for each coble to be used, whether called upon or not. But being paid for standing around 'doing nowt' went very much against the grain with these normally hard-working men, especially as they were transported daily by Rolls-Royce taxi from Whitby to Robin Hoods Bay, and even up and down the steep Bay Bank, to the amusement of the people they knew in the village, and they soon began to feel that they were open to a certain amount of ridicule.

Further irritations came with the many operational difficulties that the film crew had to contend with. There was no electricity supply in the old village, and a good deal of equipment had to be hired, powered by generators; this would stand idle for hours or even days when the light was unsuitable. The actors arrived. Douglas Fairbanks Jnr had been the first choice for the starring role of Marney Lunn, but he being unavailable, the role was taken by John Garrick, who was released from

Twickenham Films so that he could play the part. A dour Yorkshireman, Wilfred Lawson, was ideally cast as Luke Fosdyck in his first major part and Sam Livesey slipped into the character of Henry Lunn as if born to it. The two other principal actors, Geraldine Fitzgerald and Niall MacGinnis, both relatively new to films, were both outstanding in their roles.

Rumours circulated in the area that the part of the young boy, Steve Lunn, would be given to a local schoolboy, causing one or two young hopefuls to knock on the door of the Walmsleys' home to offer their services, much to Margaret's amusement. The rumours were without foundation as the part had already been allotted to Derek Blomfield, a fine young actor who was to feature strongly in the picture.

The obvious logistical difficulties associated with filming at such a place as Robin Hoods Bay were further compounded by other problems such as the late arrival of the script and the vagaries of the weather. Norman Walker had many headaches like this to overcome. When a north-easterly gale sprang up early in the proceedings, the opportunity was too good to miss. Leo hurriedly wrote some suitable lines of dialogue and the Dukes, tired of having nothing to do, pleased the director by offering to stand in for the actors and carry out the dangerous task of launching a coble into the rough sea, to Leo's consternation.

He was terrified for their safety whilst watching the launch, and the gale was so strong that cameraman Eric Cross had to have his tripod held down with stones on the beach to steady it. However, the task was accomplished without mishap. An exhilarated Elliot Duke, in his usual daredevil way, was all for having another attempt but, to Leo's relief, this was not necessary, and he could hardly believe how good the results were when played back later, the low camera angle making the waves appear quite terrifying.

> 'Never had I felt such an intense admiration and pride for my old friends ... I felt indeed that nothing could stop our film being one of the greatest films of all time'.[3]

He was jubilant, and the mutual respect he and Walker had for each other's work at that point looked set to realise each man's ambitions for the project. Unfortunately relations were never to be quite so good in the making of later sequences.

The shooting script eventually appeared, and Leo was shocked and angry at what it contained.

> 'The writer had converted the whole thing into a melodrama with a sugary love affair settling the almost bloodthirsty feud between the Fosdycks and Lunns, a feud in which the fishermen snarled and fought with each other, cut each other's buoys adrift, cheated and double crossed like gangsters. In the book I had, and I think with success, tried to show the nobility of both my families ... that they had a high code of honour and essential decency. Feuds, hate, jealousies were all sunk when it came to a lifeboat rescue, or any fellow-fisherman being in peril.'[4]

Leo refused even to consider insulting his friends by condoning such a travesty, and fortunately here had an ally on this occasion in Norman Walker. As a result a conference was held in the Victoria Hotel, Robin Hoods Bay, at which heated exchanges took place until the early hours of the morning. The producer, art director and their associates disregarded the fact that the story was a representation of real people, who would undoubtedly be hurt and upset at seeing themselves portrayed in this light. Had the director not backed up Leo's arguments, a serious rift between author and film company would have occurred on that night. Fortunately Walker saw his point and came down firmly on his side, promising that no time or money would be wasted whilst he and Leo focused their minds on producing a script that would be more acceptable.

Three days of rain during which no filming could take place enabled them to work closely on the alterations, leaving them with little time for sleep. Leo began to feel that even Walker was not in complete agreement with him. The director, being a professional film-maker, had the experience and knowledge to visualise that many of the author's ideas for the film were unworkable. Leo, who was tackling this kind of work for the first time, could not see this and in his exasperation became so confused that he even began to lose his grasp of which actor was playing which character.

> 'I had the horrible conviction before we started shooting again from this ill-constructed and uncompleted script that the whole film was destined to be as big a failure as my first African travel and natural history film had been'[5]

Throughout his life, Leo had been very much his own man, living on his wits whilst making his own individual way in the world, and coming up against an equally strong personality with whom to collaborate was not something that he could easily accept. His confidence was not helped when Walker insisted on filming part of the earlier storm sequence, when an offshore gale was blowing, with the sea as calm as a millpond. With his local knowledge, Leo considered this to be the height of foolishness, but the director's skill and undoubted foresight were ultimately endorsed as few picturegoers were likely to pick up on such a thing, and with some judicious editing, this scene turned out to be particularly effective.[6]

Not the least of Leo's worries was that the two Irish actors were having some difficulty maintaining the Yorkshire accents that they were required to adopt; even J Fisher White as 'Old Isaac' occasionally 'slipped into Devonshire'.

Leo's main contention was that his film must be completely authentic. For instance, he objected to the use of a fish-shaped balloon produced by the props department in a sequence where a salmon was required. He thought that this was ludicrous and said so in no uncertain terms. Another argument threatened but when the director saw the result later he had to admit that Leo was right and consequently the whole scene was scrapped, resulting in yet another major re-write.

Norman Walker was very relieved when the location shooting at Robin Hoods Bay, and to a lesser extent at Whitby and Staithes, was completed and he was able to move back to the controlled environment of the British and Dominion Studios at Elstree for the indoor shots. Leo's confidence in the project was temporarily boosted when he realised the amount of work that the company had undertaken to achieve optimum realism. Plaster casts had been taken by Andrew Mazzei, the art director, of street scenes, cobbled alleyways and cottages in Robin Hoods Bay, to be recreated indoors using plywood and plaster in a most skilful way.

Leo began to appreciate that such a degree of care and attention to detail showed a real willingness on the part of British National Films to spare no expense in its attempt to produce a picture of genuine quality. But by this time, he was becoming pessimistic and seriously out of his depth, being required to attend a series of conferences at which professional people appeared to him to tear his work to pieces.

'It was not until we moved to Elstree that I plumbed the depths of despair and had my final bust with Norman Walker and British National Films'[7]

More drama and romance were thought to be necessary to the plot and John Monk was brought in to help with the script, a choice which seemed odd to Leo as Monk had worked on *Man Of Aran,* a film which had no script at all! Leo had admired this film but was sure that he could do better. He had difficulty in accepting that if it was to have any future at all, they had to make a film of sufficient appeal that the renters would see it as being suitable for wide distribution. With this as a priority, it was Monk who suggested widening their scope by using episodes lifted from Leo's recent novel *Foreigners,* resulting in the part of the young Steve Lunn being given greater prominence.

A further annoyance for Leo was the filming of the arrival in the village of an engine for the Lunns' sailing coble. He thought it absurd that a twenty-horsepower Thornycroft engine, which was hired for the occasion, should have been used for such a small craft, and quickly made his feelings known. He imagined that the audience would find this ridiculous, not appreciating that the vast majority of them would not have a clue about such things. In fact, the scene worked well.

Ever the perfectionist, he next pointed out that the actors were 'making an unholy mess of the baiting job' when the scene showed them baiting lines and he argued over this yet again with the director.

Following a string of unsettling episodes, Leo realised that he could not bear to be present at any more studio filming. Walker tried to change his mind but he could take no more, and during one final outburst he resigned from his position as technical advisor and went home to Yorkshire badly disillusioned, certain that the whole idea had been a waste of time, and threw himself once again into the making of a new home at Leith Rigg.

Without his help (or hindrance), the production could carry on apace, the professionals getting down to the exacting task of forming a real work of art from the available fragments of material. With distance between them, he and Norman Walker were now able to correspond in a reasonably civilised manner. The film company did return to Yorkshire in the summer to complete the filming, and he was quietly pleased to see that it was using the very locations along the coast that he had originally suggested for capturing on film the rough seas which Nature fortuitously provided at this time.

Leo had nothing to do with the filming of a steamship aground in the bay in a thick fog, apart from earlier having made the suggestion to simplify it. It was vital that this episode was made to look realistic and hazardous. This the team succeeded in doing, even using the 1,500-ton collier *Plawsworth* as the vessel in distress. The lifeboat being hauled from its shed to go to the rescue was, in fact, a studio mock-up, but the care taken made this quite difficult to spot when viewing the film.

Summer and autumn passed and, hearing nothing more about the film, Leo assumed that the whole thing had been dropped. He was surprised, therefore, when in October he received an invitation to a trade screening of a film, *Turn Of The Tide*. This was the name chosen for the film resulting from a competition run by the popular magazine *Picturegoer* to replace the rather doubtful working title *Three Fevers*. Ironically, he was unable to attend as the invitation arrived at his remote home on the very day of the event, and with some bitterness he suspected the film company of planning this deliberately. This was followed by the premiere at London's Capitol Cinema on Monday, the 21st October, and he heard no more until he bought the Sunday papers and was astounded at the reviews it had attracted.

One critic enthused,

> 'An author everyone knows is not always an asset to a film company, but in this case he has behaved himself with genius.'

Another reported,

> 'If I had a big drum I'd bang on it until the whole twenty million of you went along to see it.'

And so it continued with each reviewer heaping yet more praise upon the film. Leo thought he must be dreaming.

The regional premiere was held in the Empire Cinema in Whitby, where an American film had to be cancelled due to the demand by the public to see *Turn Of The Tide* for themselves, and a special invitation was sent by the manager to the Walmsley family asking them to attend. Unable to afford a taxi, they arrived by bus to the sight of an enormous queue of people waiting to enter the cinema, and Leo began to suffer an acute attack of first-night nerves. He was surprised to see the film beginning with waves washing on to the shore, where names and dates of lost fishermen were carved into the rocks. He thought that this must be trick photography, but in fact a local stonemason, Matthew Hodgson Hart, had been engaged to achieve the effect.

> 'The film was on. And from the moment I surrendered my possessive literary pride in the authorship of *Three Fevers* I forgot my feud with British National Films, my quarrels with Norman Walker, my disillusionment, my fears of what Henry Lunn and the other fishermen were feeling and what afterwards they were going to say to me ... here was reward, a more exciting reward than any money or spoken or written praise the book had brought us.'[8]

Even as he watched, totally absorbed, he did not know how the film was to end, and hoped that his friends would not be upset by their portrayal on the screen, but as it neared its close, he could sense what was coming, a twist in the story completely fabricated and far removed from the truth and his own account of it.

> 'I felt dreadful. I could think of nothing but the last few scenes, especially the last of all showing Luke Fosdyck in command of the keeler, boss of the Lunns, and of course Henry Lunn. I thought that Henry would never forgive me for that insult.'[9]

Elliot Duke, however, was ecstatic, and fought his way through the crowds afterwards to tell Leo so. His father, the stoic Henry, was more restrained but obviously very pleased with the result and was typically generous with his praise, despite referring to the film as 'a lot of daftness'.

Leo made nothing further from *Turn Of The Tide* in financial terms. It had cost over £30,000 to make, and he received regular statements for the next two years itemising the takings against this amount, but in the end not even a third of the cost was recouped, and he never received his five percent of the expected profits. The film was screened throughout the English-speaking world, and it generated a good deal of correspondence from homesick Yorkshire exiles. It suffered heavily from a lack of experience in the distribution side of the business on the part of J Arthur Rank, but the lesson was not lost on the millionaire flour-milling magnate; he learned the expensive way and made full use of bitter experience in going on to build up the great Rank empire and to become a major force in the film world for the next few decades. Norman Walker deservedly took most of the accolades as director, and Arthur Benjamin's stirring music was certainly one of the most imaginative film scores of its day. *Turn Of The Tide* went on to win third prize at the Venice Film Festival that year, but was later relegated to a B-movie status. For such an innovative feature film, it never achieved the recognition it surely deserved.

Leo never mentioned it in future writings but he did have further brushes with the world of films. In 1937, he was engaged to write a script for a thirty-seven minute religious film called *As We Forgive*, in which he had to adopt a moral tale by Canon S N Sedgewick set in a Cornish fishing community. This was later put on general release under a different title, *Breakers Ahead*. Norman Walker corresponded with Leo whilst he was working on his adaptation, offering his help with the script-writing, and he was later to say, 'Leo was a wonderful writer who could turn an ordinary incident into something dramatic and exciting.' And of the Yorkshire fishermen, 'They were a grand bunch of chaps, and helped me greatly in the making of the film.'

Jane Ellis

CHAPTER 14

Between Moor and Sea

D URING the period when Leo was involved with the filming of *Turn of the Tide,* he had to concentrate his attention on other important matters. Buying land and building a house is invariably beset by problems and this was no exception. The fact that he and Margaret had such definite ideas as to what they wanted ensured that they both participated in the planning project. When they made inquiries regarding the purchase of the land from a local farmer, he was at first reluctant to sell. Then he made an offer which was a remarkable example of the truth being stranger than fiction. He stipulated that they should buy all the land including the barn for the sum of £300. They could scarcely believe what they heard — forty acres (16ha) of land surrounding the barn which they so desperately wanted, all for the exact amount of money which Leo had received for the film rights.

A deposit was paid immediately and legal matters were put in the hands of a Whitby lawyer the following day. They could hardly wait to start putting their plans into operation, but arrangements for a mortgage had to be made and that was dependent on the costs negotiated with the architect and builder. This did not stop them from going to explore the land, using a six-inch (15cm) Ordnance Survey map, which their lawyer had lent them. The property that they were buying was called Leith Rigg[1] and included woodland, and a section of Ramsdale Beck as well as grassland and scrub. The view was :

'... magnificent in every direction. There were miles of unbroken moor reaching due west. The whole vale of Bramblewick, with its mosaic of fields, lay below us to the east. The headland of High Batts was foreshortened; and its profile less bold, but there was the whole bay, with the roofs of the village making a red patch at the northern end.'[2]

More than thirty years later this view was to be an important selling point in an auctioneer's specification of the property.

'Leith Rigg enjoys a beautiful unspoilt situation with superb views to the sea over woodland in the picturesque Ramsdale Valley, in a National park area. The scenery is at its best when displaying the natural tints of Spring and Autumn.'

The existence of a water supply was of paramount importance, being in such an isolated position away from the mains supply. Fortunately a plentiful and reliable source of water was found less than fifty yards from the barn and at least thirty feet above it. It emerged from the ground as a real spring 'bubbling up and crystal clear'. When the builder, Will Cornforth, saw it he was convinced that it would be acceptable to the local council. There would be other hurdles to overcome before building could commence as the plans put before the council had to fulfil all the criteria required by the various departments. Early discussions with the builder resulted in a shock which at first seemed to shatter their dreams. Will informed them of the need to have a damp-proof course in the walls. As the building had been used solely as a barn and beast-house, this had not been required but it was essential for human habitation. Leo and Margaret were horrified when Will told them the only possible solution was to pull the building down to its foundations and insert the damp-proof course as it was rebuilt. It was a formidable project and put the cost well beyond their means.

They were fortunate that in Will Cornforth they had found an honest, reliable man. He realised their predicament and was also understanding of their desire to have the house built as they had planned. He put forward possible solutions which, although considerably altering their original ideas, did offer an acceptable reduction in the estimated costs. Originally they had envisaged a second storey being built of matching stone, which would give them four bedrooms. The space on the ground floor would be taken up by a living-room, lounge and bathroom. The roof would be red pantiles to fit in with the farmhouses in the surrounding area. To allow for more space inside the building, Margaret had suggested an outside staircase, covered so as to be protected against the weather.

The suggestions put forward by Will confounded all these plans. To cut costs, he advised using slates instead of pantiles and, moreover, completely changing the appearance of the outside by having a mansard roof. This would be of slate, starting at the first floor and rising at 'a steep pitch, almost vertical to ceiling height …, then a gentler pitch to the roof'. The changed design meant that they would be spared the cost of buying expensive stone. Margaret was disappointed that, because of the changes, they had to abandon her idea of having an outside staircase. However, they saw the sense of what Will suggested and, with typical pragmatism, they were soon enthusing about the new design.

An acceptable estimate was agreed and plans were submitted to the local authority. With plans passed and a mortgage secured, building could commence. Leo was determined to be on site during building operations, partly because of the fascination of watching skilled workmen, but particularly because it was to be their home. Will agreed to him being there on condition that Leo was discreet and refrained from any form of criticism. So began a very interesting and rewarding period of Leo's life. Watching the craftsmen at work, selecting and dressing the stone, he understood why lengthy apprenticeships were required. While keeping an eye on the progress of the building, he busied himself with two of his own projects. He started to clear part of the land for a garden and also decided to build a hut in which he could write free from distraction. He selected a site in a small quarry near the boundary of the wood. It was a suitable distance from the house and had no view of the sea. This was to ensure that there would be no temptation to allow his gaze to wander from his work. The window would be in the roof, like an artist's studio.

Gradually the house began to take shape. The walls rose, although as they grew higher, the house became obscured by the scaffolding. The spaces for the windows appeared in the new walls and they were able to look through and see the views. It was like having several framed pictures, all different. Views of both moor and sea were delightful and Leo had calculated that they would have a visibility range of more than twenty miles (30km) seawards.

The lounge fireplace was planned with much thought. It was to be in the exact place where Leo and Margaret had lit a fire when sheltering from a storm many years before. The main fireplace was not regarded by them as merely a provider of heat. It should be a 'substitute for the living sun, warming the heart as well as the body'.

While Leo was enjoying watching the steady erection of the house, Margaret remained in Whitby caring for the children, only making occasional visits to Leith Rigg in an evening when the aunt took responsibility for the children. The account of the various stages of the building of the house makes compelling reading in *The Golden Waterwheel*. It also gives further insight into Leo's character. The house was always regarded by him as the family home and he emphasised the importance of the surroundings as well as the actual building.

'The place was a paradise for children.'[3]

Yet he seemed quite content to spend the greater part of his time on his own at the site, away from Margaret and the children. Evidence of this dichotomy appears on occasions in his writings, revealing on the one hand the man content with solitude and on the other the family man, a caring father, deeply in love with his wife.

The building of the house was finished by the end of September 1935.

'Of the many stages in the evolution of a house none is more dramatic than when the actual building is finished and the workmen have packed up, and the place stands completely empty and silent. There are no curtains, no floor coverings, no furniture, the walls are bare. This can happen only once in its history for whoever lives in it will make marks on its structure which nothing will ever completely erase and those marks will as inevitably be evidence of the character and behaviour of the occupants.'[4]

Within a few days, they moved in with their limited furnishings and gradually the house became a home. A few months later, on the 24th December 1935, their first son, Simon, was born. An interesting point revealed by the birth certificate is the place of birth — Dawn Nursing Home, Looe, Cornwall. It seems remarkable that a heavily pregnant woman would travel over 350 miles (560km) in the depth of winter in order to have her child at the same nursing home as her previous children. Apart from the hazards of the journey, there would be the considerable expense which they could ill afford. It is difficult to find a logical explanation. Could it have been a desire to retain contact with a place which had meant so much to them both, where they had spent such happy years, or was it merely a whim? It is unlikely that the latter was the reason as two and a half years later she undertook the long journey again so that their fourth child could be born in the same place. This was Dain Patrick, born on the 26th June 1938.

Leith Rigg was a delightful place for children:

'A clear babbling stream ran from the moor through our land, continuing over a twelve-foot cliff and waterfall into an oak wood. The wood was not our property, but we had a right of way. Here, in spring, daffodils grew in profusion at the stream's edge. There were oaks, alders, ash and mountain ash, and on our own land too. In one place we had

Leith Rigg (Adder Howe) (*Photo: Jack Rigg*)

dammed the stream and made a long pool, deep enough to float a small flat-bottomed
boat I had built. There was a patch of clean white sand nearby, and I made a swing from
a branch of a thick gnarled oak which we christened 'The Greenwood Tree'.[5]

Leo built small boats painted in bright colours for the children. According to a
friend who was the same age as Ann, Leo would stand on a little sandy island in
the middle of the pool and 'bellowed instructions while we all rowed and splashed
wildly'. Visits to the Walmsley family were 'challenging affairs and over all were
dominated by the vigour of Leo's personality and inventiveness'.

Leo and Margaret had very definite ideas about how they wished to bring up
their children, not conventional ideas certainly, but strongly held beliefs based on
what they considered best for the children. Their marriage had always been based
on a philosophy of life which they shared and which had provided a solid foundation
for their closely-knit family.

'We believed that it was a good thing to bring children up in the country, and a country
that bordered on the sea: that the most important foundation for their lives was good
health, and a sanity induced by a close contact with nature; fresh air, good food; space,
a garden, woods, lanes, streams, hills, beaches for them to explore as they grew bigger.
The good, simple things first!'[6]

The ideology which they both believed in had not only shaped Leo's outlook
on life, it had also been instrumental in influencing his literary development.

They were able to purchase milk and butter from the nearby mill farm and were self-sufficient with eggs as they had their own poultry, a flock of Rhode Island Reds. Because Leo was proficient with a shotgun, they were able to supplement their diet with rabbits, partridges and wood-pigeons. Fish was frequently served, caught by Leo as had been habitual over the years. His love of angling produced practical results from which his family benefited with a regular supply of nutritious food. It also provided Leo with the opportunity to relax and forget his worries.

A pony was acquired for the children. Annabella became a much loved member of the family, full of character and very good-natured. Leo built a trap so that they could travel round the country lanes. One source of information also refers to a cart made out of a fish box with wheels and wooden shafts. It was big enough to hold two children and Leo could be seen pushing it down to the village. In addition to this, there was a battered old pram which Margaret used, pushing the children down the track from Leith Rigg into the village to do her weekly shopping. When Leo was in the throes of writing, demanding absolute peace and quiet, Margaret was expected to keep the children out of his way. She records how, because he sometimes worked late at night and into the early hours of the morning, there were occasions when she was seen pushing the pram with the children in it on the main Whitby to Scarborough road at 6.30am. Later correspondence suggests that he could be difficult to live with when absorbed with his writing. The occupation of an author is bound to be precarious and with a mortgage to pay and four children to provide for, the worry of failure must at times have been overwhelming.

Relief from worry came when the next book was published. *Sally Lunn,* the third of the 'Bramblewick' novels about the Lunns and the Fosdycks, appeared in the bookshops on the 1st July 1937. It was chosen as the *Daily Mail* 'Book of the Month'. Three weeks later, it was on the bestsellers list and was remarkable for having sold more copies than *Gone With The Wind.* It was indeed an economic success with five impressions between July 1937 and November 1939.

They wished to be as self-supporting as possible and grew a wide variety of vegetables. Although they had moved from the milder climate of Cornwall and had snow and hard frosts which resulted in most crops coming into season a month later, they had some extremely good crops. They no longer had a plentiful supply of seaweed within easy reach but Leo adopted a method of fertilisation using compost from leaves and bracken with the addition of Annabella's deposits!

> 'Our early potatoes were late, but they were clean and free from disease, and had a delicious flavour. We found strains of broccoli that could withstand days of the hardest frost and give perfect heads in early spring and on into the summer ...
>
> We grew broad beans, carrots, swedes, onions, leeks, lettuces both cabbage and the cos variety. We had successions of peas throughout the summer and of runner beans which lasted until the first autumn frosts. We had gooseberries, logans, and blackcurrants. We planted apple and pear and plum trees. Except for a pair of Victoria plums, none of these had yet produced much fruit, for I had not been able to nurse the blossom through the spring frosts.'[7]

They planted flowers on both sides of the stream which came from the spring and made a small walled garden at the southern end of the house. Although unable to emulate the tropical luxuriance of their Cornish garden, they were delighted with the colourful flowers which grew, irises, sweet williams, marigolds, wallflowers and many others. They had always taken a special delight in wild flowers and were overjoyed when they found that near the beck the primroses grew in profusion and clumps of native daffodils appeared in the spring. They increased these by separating the bulbs and replanting them.

As the years passed, the Walmsley family became an accepted, if unusual, part of the district. They made friends with neighbours and became particularly close to the husband and wife who were the principals at Fyling Hall School, a private co-educational preparatory school high on the hill above Robin Hoods Bay and not far from Leith Rigg. Their daughter, Clare, recalled how, as a child, she found Leo's visits more like dramas:

> 'Rather like an imminent thunderstorm you sensed his coming ... Not very tall, stocky, tanned and weatherbeaten, but he moved with great vigour and urgency; he seemed powerfully borne into a room on a wave of an idea, and communication was nearly always prefaced by "My God", causing my father to remark that for a non-believer "Leo gave his poor saviour little peace".'[8]

His visits were never dull. Winter and summer he dressed in a navy blue fisherman's guernsey. A local man who, as a boy met Leo, remembers how he used to stop and chat to the men in the village. On one occasion when the boy was with them at a cafe, Leo paid particular attention to him, asking him what he wanted to do when he left school. He asked whether he collected fossils, remembering the days when he himself had been absorbed searching the shore and cliffs for prehistoric relics. Even to this day, cliff falls of the boulder clay have revealed remarkably well preserved fossilised remains of creatures which lived in that area millions of years ago. Leo's lively interest in the subject never diminished.

Margaret is remembered as being handsome in a gypsy-like way with dark hair and a very brown skin. She was apparently relegated to the domestic area of his life and 'Mabs', the principal of the school, was so concerned that shortage of money meant shortage of food that, on her weekly shopping expeditions when she stopped by the school kitchen, Margaret was given quantities of food to take home, unbeknown to Leo. The unconventional lifestyle of the Walmsleys together with the delightful pool and stream with its waterfall seems to have been a magnet which drew local children. Their love of children would always ensure a warm welcome provided, of course, that Leo was not in the process of writing. The house was also an enchanting place for children, unconventional as one would expect with its wooden floors bare of rugs and wooden chairs without cushions; its wooden staircase up the side of the wall leading to a magical world of miniature furniture. The walls were covered with paintings of birds, flowers and insects. This was Margaret's work as were the pottery mugs and the home-made bread and cakes. It must have been an unforgettable time in the lives of the four Walmsley children.

For Leo, earning a living was rather like a roller-coaster, a series of ups and downs. He was sure that one of his books would be so successful that he would make a fortune, but at the same time he was afraid of being rich, fearful of the effect that it might have on him and the lives of his family. Sometimes he could work at a tremendous pace, knowing the story he wanted to tell and being able to put his ideas into words. But there were black days when despair took hold and he feared that he would not be able to finish the book. There was such an occasion when he was writing *Love in the Sun,* the story of their life together in the hut in Cornwall. It was into the second year before the book had begun to take shape and he could feel confident of completing it. Margaret was thrilled when he read it to her, but he knew it would take another year before it would be ready for publication. After a period of steady progress, he suddenly came to a halt. He struggled on for a while, dreading defeat.

Throughout his life, when facing difficulties or problems, Leo would go out into the fresh air, to the open space of the moors or the seashore. It was the seashore especially that always had a calming influence on him. On this occasion, worried at the prospect of having to abandon his book, he set off late at night and walked down to the village. His thoughts reverted to his boyhood and in his mind's eye he saw those wonderful characters who had lived in Bay. His buoyant personality revived and excitedly he started to consider how he could set them into a book. This would be better than the Cornwall book!

The mercurial changes of mood were typical of Leo and it was not surprising that after a period of highly charged writing, when the latest book seemed to be going well, he once more came to an impasse. Again there was a period of despair followed by a sudden change of mood when he returned to *Love in the Sun,* seeing at last how he could complete the story to his satisfaction. The demands on Margaret during such lapses in his creative periods must have been considerable. These were the times when, overtaken by doubt, he relied on her judgement of his work and needed her encouragement to continue. At the same time, he expected her to ensure that he was free from distractions. It was no mean task to take the full responsibility of running the house, caring for four boisterous children and catering for the needs of a husband in the throes of creativity.

There must be little doubt that Margaret's understanding and the harmony which existed between them gave rise to some of his best creative works. His personal and literary integrity were so linked that he needed harmony in his lifestyle to give him the confidence for his art.

Love in the Sun proved to be all that Leo had hoped for. It was published in August 1939 and was chosen as 'Book of the Month' by the Book Society. It received high acclaim from the critics and public alike and sold 20,000 copies during the first few months. It was also published in America by Doubleday Doran and foreign language editions soon followed. His agent discussed with him the possibility of the book being adapted for a film. He was, in fact, offered £5,000 for the film rights by Alexander Korda and they even considered which actors to employ. But as the month of August drew to an end, so did the Walmsleys' hopes of becoming rich. The threat of war halted both plans for a film and further printing of the book. Within a few days, following the declaration of war, the book trade was killed stone dead.

How unfortunate it was for Leo that this delightfully satisfying book should have appeared on the bookstalls at such a time. It is ironic that the simplicity of the story and style give the impression that it was written with comparative ease and speed, whereas in fact the 'gestation' period was long and difficult. Had Leo been able to complete *Love in the Sun* earlier, instead of being diverted to his 'Bramblewick' book, his life might have taken a completely different course.

The outbreak of war was a blow to Leo's ingenuous belief in man's innate goodness. He had not shared the attitude that Hitler was evil, certain that reports of atrocities were exaggerated. He had lunched with H G Wells at his house in Hanover Terrace the previous year and had been assured by that 'prophet' that there was no likelihood of war as Hitler was 'only a gigantic bluffer'. Now he had to accept the bitter truth. As always, his concern was for the safety and welfare of his family. When his American publishers offered to try to find wartime homes for Ann and Henrietta, he accepted, despite Margaret's expressed wish that the family should not be split up. They travelled down to London and stayed at the Dorchester Hotel so that they could apply for visas and tickets. Fortuitously, as it turned out, Ann had signed her name as Ann Bell-Walmsley, instead of the name under which she was registered, Ann Bell-Little. The delay which ensued meant that the documents were not received in time for them to board the ship on which they should have sailed. The ship was the *City of Benares*, which left the Mersey for Canada on Friday the 13th September 1940, but in heavy seas was torpedoed 500 miles off the coast of Ireland with the loss of 248 lives, over eighty of those being children.

The tragic statistics revealed that, ninety of the children who embarked on a voyage which was to take them to safety, only seven survived. This tragedy caused Leo to accept Margaret's point of view and there was no further argument regarding evacuation of the children. It also served to intensify his fear and hatred of war.

Nona Stead

CHAPTER 15

Shadows of War

DESPITE his peaceful surroundings, Leo had always been concerned about tragic happenings — wars and catastrophes in other parts of the world which Britain could do little about. He liked to believe that all these wars would eventually come to an end and all those responsible would soon realise the senselessness and futility of war.

This blinkered attitude had once caused him to walk out of a film promising to show the horrors of the Spanish Civil War. Also, during the Abyssinian campaign, he and his first wife Suzanne had made a point of not listening to radio news for weeks as they found it so depressing.

> 'It wasn't cowardice nor complacence, but just that I had (and have) a faith in the essential goodness of humanity; that I believed and still wish to believe that the vast majority of men and women are well behaved, honest, compassionate.'[1]

Although aware of the rise of National Socialism in Germany, Leo, like so many of his contemporaries, felt that Germany's recovery depended upon it having a strong leader like Hitler. After the lessons of the First World War, the fears of Germany once again being a threat to world peace seemed ludicrous.

At the time of Munich, he believed Hitler's pledge that he would not lead the German people into an unnecessary war. After all, Hitler, having been a soldier himself, would know the horrors of war, also:

> 'I really believed that Hitler had been sadly misjudged and that the tales we had heard about concentration camps and Gestapo and Jew-baiting were false'[2]

His relief at the time of Munich and his faith that Hitler would 'use his power for good' were finally shattered when the German army marched into Poland accompanied by a vicious and prolonged air attack. The British and French ultimatums expired and once again we were at war with Germany. He was stunned. His immediate thoughts turned to his family, realising that things could never be the same again.

Like thousands of others, he found the first night of the war with its constant radio bulletins utterly depressing. To escape from his gloomy thoughts, he went out for a walk after dark. Normally, during the holiday season there would be a yellow glow in the sky above Scarborough and Whitby and he would have been able to discern the lights of the local villages and individual farms, but:

> 'Now, although the weather was fine, there was not a pin-prick of light anywhere, not even upon the sea. The black-out of which we had heard so much during the "war of nerves" and which I had consistently believed would never happen had come. It was for me the first visible signs that we were at war, the first convincing proof that my optimism of the past few years had been self-deception.'[3]

Leo volunteered for service in the armed forces. The air ministry was quick to inform him that there was no suitable vacancy for a man whose only flying experience had been in the BE2c and Henri Farman aeroplanes. Nor was he accepted for the Home Guard. These rejections were understandable — he was debarred by his age, being within a few days of his forty-seventh birthday at the outbreak of war, and furthermore by his First World War disability.

He had previously volunteered under the National Service Scheme as an auxiliary coastguard watcher but the total complement of watchers was already full when war broke out. This also applied to the Observer Corps, special constables and firemen.

Frustrated and disillusioned by not being allowed to make any active contribution to the war effort, he had to be content with reclaiming the arable land around his home and growing crops.

A further disappointment awaited him at a later date, when he failed to obtain a place in one of the 'small boats' which were to be sent to assist the evacuation of Dunkirk. Margaret confirmed later that:

> 'He stayed on Whitby docks trying to get on any boat going to Dunkirk. But his fisherman friends would not take him and from then on he became more upset about the war.'

The period of Autumn 1939 and the early part of the following year is often referred to as 'the phoney war'. In no way could this term be applied to the experience of the seamen, many of them in defenceless fishing craft, who were being attacked with such savagery from the air. These seamen had provided the manpower for the Naval Patrol Service and had received little public recognition of their hazardous work in commercial fishing, patrolling and minesweeping.

Collins, the publisher, felt strongly that there was a need for both the British and American public to be informed of the invaluable contribution to the war effort being made by this fearless and indomitable breed of men. In the autumn of 1939, being familiar with Leo's writings and aware of his empathy with the members of the fishing community, it commissioned him to write what he often referred to as 'his propaganda book'. The Admiralty offered him every facility and he visited minesweeping bases, made a trip in a minesweeper in the North Sea and flew almost to the coast of Holland in a coastal command aeroplane.

Unarmed fishing vessels were particularly vulnerable to attacks from enemy aircraft, which usually operated singly or in pairs. Their sole protection came from a section of RAF coastal command known as 'the kipper patrol'. A great affection had been established between the air crews and the fishermen themselves. A special device was used for dropping messages such as the position of wreckage likely to foul nets, but often they were merely chatty or informal greetings. One pilot nearing the end of his patrol scribbled, 'Every time we eat kipper we think of thee dear skipper. Love from the R.A.F.'[4]

Fishermen often showed their general appreciation of the RAF by sending regular consignments of fresh and kippered herrings to the station concerned. Boats were at greatest risk when there was cloud cover.

Leo Walmsley, c1939

'These raiders, cruising just above the lowest cloud bank, could dive down into clear air and perhaps spot a victim several miles away. They could take a compass bearing on it, climb back into the clouds and fly on until they were approximately above it; dive down, carry out the attack and then seek the security of the upper air.'[5]

Boats were machine-gunned relentlessly. When bombs were dropped, survival could depend on the skipper's coolness during the action and his good seamanship in avoiding them — as well as an element of luck. When the enemy started dropping thousands of new magnetic mines by parachute at night, there was an appeal to all fishermen to augment the existing patrol services by acting as special constables, who could report the position of any mines spotted. It was the period after the dropping of these mines when aerial attacks on all types of craft, armed mine-sweepers, lightships, Trinity House tenders and trawlers intensified.

Leo's visits to the minesweeping bases resulted in an exposition, commendable for its clarity, of the daily operations of the minesweepers and the adaptation and modifications necessary to meet the new threat of the magnetic mine. All this effort and dedication resulted in thousands of tons of shipping being saved.

Leo did not forget to pay tribute to the valiant service rendered by the RNLI. His account of a particular lifeboat rescue near Whitby in darkness and at the height of a vicious winter storm was a highlight of the book and an example of graphic journalism at its best. This did not escape the notice of one of his reviewers, H E Bates.

The terrible winter of 1939/40 was one of the worst on record but the deep sea fishermen were used to contending with savage conditions — freezing fog, blinding snowstorms, snow-covered decks and bitingly cold north easterly gales.

Leo's knowledge of their character and temperament was made clear when he stated :

'I do know there is not a finer breed on earth. They have their faults: some of them, especially on our northern coasts, are dour, suspicious, seemingly unfriendly. They are superstitious, stupidly old fashioned in many respects, and fiercely independent. But what are these faults against their natural bravery, that imperturbable courage with which in peace time they face the daily hazards of their calling, against their skill in handling their boats: above all against that great quality of kindness, self-sacrifice and brotherhood which is universal among them, and finds its expression so often in times of peril on the sea, when other boats and ships and men (of all nations) may be in need of help.'[6]

Leo's book *Fishermen at War* was published in July 1941, in London by Collins and in New York by Doubleday Doran, although the photographs in the American edition were in some case changed as they were considered 'more appropriate for the American market'. It was generally well received both at home and in America.[7]

John W Stead

CHAPTER 16

The Shadows Deepen

LEO had been away from home for three weeks and his admiration for the fishermen and all the sailors involved in the hazardous operations knew no bounds. Writing this book was a way in which he could repay them personally, by drawing the attention of the Americans as well as the British people to the bravery and sacrifice of these men.

He had been relieved when, on returning home, he had found his family safe and well. They were experiencing a bitterly cold winter with fantastic snowdrifts, which had cut them off from the village for a short period. The beck was frozen and the little waterfalls petrified. The landscape was so beautiful that Leo found some difficulty in reconciling the peace of his surroundings with the horrors which he had recently experienced. But he had only to look across his land towards the North Sea to recall those men in their defenceless craft being attacked so mercilessly. Although he did not expect *Fishermen at War* to be a bestseller, he did hope that it would fulfil the publishers' intention that the true facts of this vital element of war at sea would be revealed.

He worked at his book despite a strong desire to be out clearing his land. It was the time when the population was being urged to 'Dig for Victory' and this slogan was appearing everywhere. Home-grown produce was vital to the life of the nation as anything brought from abroad by sea was jeopardising the lives of those men whom he held in such high esteem. He had made a preliminary attempt to clear more land by burning off the grass and bracken but had been faced by the problem of how to deal with the rocks, some of which were of a white flint-like substance. Despite his early interest in geology, Leo was ignorant of the nature of this rock and was therefore unaware of its significance. He could certainly never have envisaged the disastrous consequences which it was to have for him and his family.

The problem of the rocks had to be shelved for a while as there was a reasonable expanse of ground suitable for cultivation. He had to give most of his attention to his writing as early completion of the book was a priority. Realising that this would entail a considerable delay before he could personally return to preparations for farming his land, he decided to employ labour for the difficult task of removing the rocks. Will Cornforth was again called on and his men started to blast the rocks prior to removal. They were mostly white flint and an underlying bed was revealed. Fortunately it was near the boundary and it was decided to leave that area and plough the remainder of the field. The whole family turned out to watch when a neighbouring farmer brought his tractor to start ploughing the land.

'We were all (except the aunt, who was visiting a friend) there to see the start of the ploughing, for it was an occasion almost as important as the laying of the foundation stone of our house. It was a warm sunny day. The primroses and daffodils were already out. A lark was singing. From the copse and the wood came a chorus of bird song, blackbirds, thrushes, finches, linnets, the cooing of woodpigeons, the harsher notes of jays and woodpeckers, the croaking of crows and magpies. Sam started on the field nearest to the moorland boundary, and first made a single furrow round it, to mark the headlands. Then using all three shares of the plough he came up the middle of the field and began ploughing up and down one half. The children ran after him, shouting excitedly.'[1]

The love which Leo and Margaret had for the earth and its produce never seemed to diminish and remained central to their philosophy of life.

Ploughing was followed by harrowing. Leo benefited from his neighbour's experience and was grateful for any advice offered, determined to follow it in the next few years. They were fortunate to have perfect weather for ploughing and sowing with no late damaging frosts. Hopes were high for a good crop.

'No field ever received more lavish attention than did those fields of ours. We looked at them every day and at first while the soil was dry it did no harm to wander over them.'[2]

Then, one morning in the Easter holidays, the girls rushed down to Leo's hut calling him to 'Come and look. The corn is out.' And there were the first signs, tiny green shoots emerging from the soil. Soon the fields were green with healthy, vigorous corn.

The horrors of war seemed remote until he had a nerve-shattering experience. A lone German bomber dropped a stick of bombs, which landed nearby on the open moorland. Although no damage was done, the effect on Leo was devastating. A few years later, he wrote of his fear for the children.

'I made us all sleep on the floor of the sitting room whenever the raiders came over. I was terrified of course. We had no help if anything had happened. We had proved how difficult it was to get the children downstairs at night.'[3]

He was very conscious of the vulnerability of Leith Rigg as a fire hazard. Part of the house was built of timber, but of more concern was the fact that all the rooms were lined with fibre board, which Leo had discovered to be highly flammable. He referred to a two-storey annexe, which they had added to cater for their growing family. It was built of timber with a flat asphalt roof. It was 'perfect tinder' for an incendiary bomb. Furthermore, the house was surrounded by bracken and furze which, if ignited, would soon be ablaze. The house could be engulfed in minutes.

It is understandable that he was haunted by fear of fire when one remembers that he had almost been burnt alive in his last plane crash in the First World War. As the war progressed into its second year, the East Coast was a target for numerous enemy raids and they lived with the constant fear of being hit by high explosives or incendiary bombs. Many were dropped nearby, some on their own land.

Life continued with some semblance of normality. Farming the land was a priority with them, as with other farmers and landowners in the district. Alongside this, Leo submerged himself in his writing to ensure an adequate income for his family. He was to remark at a later date that this was the first time in his life that he had been free of debt. The land and house had been paid for from his own money plus a contribution of about £150 from Margaret's parents.

The education of the children was a subject about which they were in agreement although their ideas were, predictably, somewhat unconventional. They were impressed by the nearby co-educational Fyling Hall School run by their friends, as their views were similar to their own, and they considered that it would be an ideal school for the children's primary education. In the event, Ann was the only child to attend the school and a series of nannies and governesses were employed for the other children.

Leo and Margaret were determined that the children should have a boarding-school education as soon as they reached a suitable age. They favoured the more progressive schools and it had been their intention to send them to Bedales or Dartington or some similar school. Leo realised that this was an expensive option but here is an example of his earlier sophistication. As in health matters he regarded nursing homes as preferable to hospitals, so in education private schools took precedence over the state system.

Leo's own education must have played a fundamental part in influencing his attitude towards state as opposed to private schools. He hated his primary school and although he appreciated the excellence of his secondary school teachers, he felt very strongly that a different approach would have encouraged him to greater scholastic efforts.

The summer of 1940 was a happy time for the children. There were no more bombs and they were unaffected by the distant war. Leo was too busy with his work to take them on whole-day excursions but at weekends he joined them for picnics and riding on the moors. They never tired of the pool with its boat, the swing on 'The Greenwood Tree' and the profusion of wild flowers for picking.

At last the book was finished and sent off to the American publisher, with the faint hope that it might help Britain's cause. Strangely this was the first time that Margaret had shown little enthusiasm for one of his books. She had always been encouraging and excited about his writing. Leo was later to place great significance on her lack of interest but in 1940 there were many other matters demanding his attention.

He was able to spend more time on his land and returned to the rocks, which had previously defied all attempts to remove them. He again approached Will Cornforth, hoping that he would be able to send one of his men to assist, but he was unable to offer any hope of help for the foreseeable future, and explained why. They were engaged in a top-priority job for the government. Pill boxes and gun emplacements were to be built all along the coast. He gave the additional information that the beaches were to be closed and all roads to them blocked. Leo and Margaret were already aware of military activity near the beach.

'The road leading down to the mill cove was blocked with a stone wall and a number of soldiers in battledress were off-loading coils of barbed wire from a truck. A sentry with a fixed bayonet challenged us at our approach. We were told that unless we had written permission from the commanding officer of his unit we must go no further. The lane leading to Brow Beck Cove to the place where we had first planned to build our house was also blocked and guarded. In a field close by them were a number of military trucks and bivouac tents.'[4]

The war was coming closer.

Shortly after this, Leo was again at work clearing rocks when he saw a man moving along the wall which was the boundary between his land and the moors. Leo had repaired the wall recently using the white flint and he had noticed that it was this stone which had taken the visitor's attention. His attire indicated that he was not a workman and Leo was curious as to why he should be taking such interest in the stone wall. As he came nearer, Leo saw that he was carrying a hammer. When the man looked as if he were about to pull a piece of flint from the wall, Leo, afraid that the wall might collapse, rushed forward. He introduced himself and in return was informed that the man was a government geologist; he was checking rocks in the district as it was known that there were beds of silica rock. When converted into a cement, this rock was used for lining furnaces as it had high heat-resisting properties. At this stage of the war, when furnaces were working at full capacity making munitions, it was of vital importance. The geologist questioned Leo regarding where he had found the white flint and asked if he could take a sample for analysis.

The area had been surveyed before the war and it was suspected that the underlying bed of rock stretched for at least half a mile to the edge of the valley. He advised Leo not to cultivate any more of his land for the time being. This sounded ominous and he questioned the geologist further regarding the quarrying of the stone. To his horror, it appeared that the most likely proposition would be open-cast mining. Leo was aghast at the prospect of his beautiful unspoilt countryside being ravaged by huge excavators. He knew that in times of war the government was omnipotent and he recalled a clause in their conveyance deed stating that mineral rights were 'reserved by the original vendor'.

Worried and depressed, he returned home only to be greeted by more bad news. The moors were to be used as an artillery range. The school owned by their friends was to be requisitioned for staff headquarters, forcing Bill and Mabs to find other premises. What was to happen to Leith Rigg? Was their home to be requisitioned? Was their land to be despoiled by open-cast mining? Leo was distressed when he realised that no longer could his family escape from the consequences of the war. Their lives could never be the same again.

It was confirmed that the white flint which had interested and exasperated Leo was indeed gannister, a precious material required for the war effort. With the beaches closed and the moor likely to become an artillery range, Leo and Margaret made a decision which was to have far-reaching effects on the future of all the family. In May 1941 they left the home they had made with so much love and effort and moved to Pembrokeshire.

Nona Stead

CHAPTER 17

Temple Druid

A T the end of *The Golden Waterwheel*, Leo tells how the war drove him and his family from their beloved home, Leith Rigg ('Adder Howe'), in Yorkshire and how they decided to move to distant west Wales. In outline, this is just what happened to the Walmsleys themselves and is thus autobiographical. But much of the detail is mainly fictional, such as the letter offering them a twenty-room mansion in Wales together with fifty-six acres (23ha) of land and a range of farm buildings, for which the owner 'had paid a ridiculously low price … He was willing to let it go for the same figure, and with a two-thirds mortgage.' In the story, Leo and Margaret jump at the offer — a delightful, surprise solution to their problems — and the book ends on an upbeat note, for Leo was no pessimist and liked happy endings. What really happened at this time was quite different.

Having taken the hard decision to leave Leith Rigg, they faced the problem of where to go, as far as possible from the war. At that time, *The Farmer and Stockbreeder* was running a weekly article by author and naturalist R M Lockley, who had taken on a run-down farm in North Pembrokeshire. He too had been forced to evacuate his home on a remote island off the Welsh coast and was actively helping the war effort by producing food. Here surely, Leo thought, was a man who would understand their plight and would offer advice, perhaps even welcome another like-minded family to join him in his enterprise. What was more, there were close parallels between the lives of the Walmsleys and the Lockleys. He too had been a pioneer, taking the lease of the small island of Skokholm and, with his wife, making a house habitable and a garden productive while earning a precarious living from trapping rabbits and fishing. He had related these adventures in the book *Dream Island* and its sequel, *Island Days*. Early in 1941, *The Way to an Island*, an account of his early days before Skokholm, had been published and the Walmsleys may well have read it at about the time when they could see their life in Yorkshire coming to an end. Nothing could be lost by writing to Lockley, and this is exactly what Leo did.

The reply was gratifying, and commences:

'Dear Leo Walmsley,
Nothing would please me more just now than to have heard from you. I read your "Three Fevers" and "Phantom Lobster" with deep pleasure for I know lobster fishing by heart. Well, now, about your problem. I can appreciate it very thoroughly and should not care myself to be up where you are. I think the best plan is for you to come down here and have a look at our farm and the big rambling old house and we can talk over ways and means of your settling here for the duration. We are in very peaceful and lovely country in N. Pembs. three miles from the sea, where we rarely hear an air-plane or any noise of war at all. We could do with your help. It would be most useful if we could take

turns in running the farm and the island ... I also have a three-roomed bungalow on the
mainland opposite Skokholm, which is a delight to me, as it is in a haven frequented by
lobster fishermen ...'

Like most writers, Leo loved praise and here too was another link with his
correspondent — lobster fishing. Lockley's suggestion exceeded the Walmsleys'
most optimistic hopes and a truly happy ending seemed to be resolving all their
worries, so that they perhaps paid scant attention to the next part of the letter.
Lockley at this point, feeling that his enthusiasm was running away with him,
paused for reflection, and then went on more cautiously:

'But, and it is a big BUT, all will depend on how you and I get on together, and how
your wife and mine do. I like to think I am easy-going and tolerant but "literary gents"
like you and I may not fit. However if two tigers may not live on the same hill together,
perhaps under the present emergency they might work out a condition for living together
in amity.'

He then repeated that Leo should first come and discuss it all. He confronted
the difficulties of education in that remote district, as he had found with his own
daughter, and even suggested 'perhaps we could devise some school of our own.'
Finally he gave some brief details about the farm and the crops being grown that
season, adding 'so we have need for all the help possible'. He ended, 'If you
come, come to Cardigan station G.W.R. and I will meet you with the car.' Although
it is not clear from the letter, it is likely that 'you' in 'if you come' indicated that
Leo should come on his own, making a visit of reconnaissance and then, when
the two men had thoroughly discussed the project and if they agreed as to its
suitability, Leo would return for his family.

This is not what happened. Undeterred by Lockley's cautions, the family vacated
Leith Rigg and, leaving two of their children, Ann and Simon, at boarding school,
moved to Cwmgloyne. It is clear that this was all done in a great hurry, precipitately
in fact, for Lockley's letter was dated the 8th May 1941 and the Walmsley family
arrived at Cwmgloyne a couple of weeks later.

It had been an exhausting cross-country journey from Yorkshire to Pembrokeshire on wartime trains, which, in those days, were noted for being overcrowded
and running late. But at last they were at Cardigan, where the train terminated
for it had reached the end of the land and the Irish Sea lay beyond. A stocky
man in corduroy jacket and breeches came towards them and introduced himself.
He looked somewhat stern and unsmiling but he spoke kindly enough in a gruff
way and helped them to carry their belongings to his car. The drive took about
half an hour, first along a winding road then through lanes which became
progressively narrower and finally down a bumpy track into a farmyard, where the
car stopped on an open area of almost bare rock. On the right stretched farm
buildings, some built of stone and ancient looking, others more modern and
constructed of concrete and corrugated iron sheets. On the left lay the house,
long and low, whitewashed and green-painted. It had a wing running out at right
angles, making it L-shaped.

The family, who by this time were extremely tired, were led through the front
door into a large hall, where Mrs Lockley came to greet them. She was a small,

neat woman with darkish, fuzzy hair and a reserved manner. Refreshments and bed were the first requirements that night. On the following days, they would be settling in and, the Lockleys hoped, making themselves useful. At breakfast on their first morning, they were introduced to the rest of the household. Everyone was summoned to meals by a large ship's or school bell, which hung outside the front door. The farm workers had already done an hour outside, fetching in the cows and milking them, catching the cart-horses and making them ready in the stable for the day's work, and filling up and checking the tractor. They came in hungrily for breakfast and, having finished, were off again about their various duties. The Lockley household of eight had now increased to twelve and Margaret was quick to see where her help was needed. It had already been made clear that the most urgent requirement was help for Mrs Lockley in the house. She was anxious to shed as many as possible of her domestic duties in order to get on with the garden. It had been a wilderness choked with nettles, brambles and slate and stone debris. Workers had been put in to clear it when they could be spared but there was still much to be done.

Margaret, with great goodwill and her customary enthusiasm, accepted the situation. She was, fortunately, used to catering for a large family, but not as dauntingly large as this. She confessed later that 'it all seemed non-stop to me.' The Walmsleys found that the busy farm life was more rigorous and disciplined than in their previous relaxed household, and this generated pressures that added further strain to an unfamiliar situation.

Margaret and Mrs Lockley worked tolerably together but there was little rapport between such different personalities. Margaret was talkative, exuberant, excitable, warm and outgoing, while Mrs Lockley preferred animals to people and very likely found her new partner in the kitchen irritating and wearing.

Margaret did not get any support from Leo. He had made sure of a room of his own where he could do his writing and was apt to escape there whenever he could.

After supper, the children in bed and all work over for the day, Margaret would often sit with the two land army girls and a young farm worker in the great semi-basement kitchen where meals were taken. The Lockleys had their own sitting-room and there was an open invitation for anyone to join them, but the workers seldom did, not wishing to intrude and preferring the independence of the kitchen. Margaret liked young people and they enjoyed her company but she would surely have preferred a few hours of quiet and privacy with her husband at the end of a hard day. He, however, liked to write undisturbed and she respected his wishes.

One of the land girls, Pauline, was very young, not yet eighteen and shy and rather lonely. She was quickly drawn to the warm-hearted Walmsleys, especially as Margaret asked her to let Dain go with her to feed the animals. Dain would greet her on every occasion with the hopeful words 'Baulin! Beed a galbes!' And every day after tea he would walk with her to feed the calves. Henrietta did not join in with the animal feeding and often went off riding with Ann Lockley. Margaret said that they brought 'Henry' with them rather than the younger Simon, because she was so naughty at school and her elder sister Ann got the blame; so Simon became the boarder instead.

Margaret's place in the scheme of things at Cwmgloyne was readily established; Leo's place was more problematic. Lockley appreciated the need of a den for writing and had been willing enough to cooperate - but expected Leo to do his share on the farm. Unfortunately, he showed small interest in this and appeared to have little understanding of farming or the urgency of the work. Lockley himself was a man of great energy and toughness and expected others to be the same. He could be a hard task master and drove his staff, and his wife, to the limits of their endurance. He had little understanding of weakness and no time for passengers in his household. Leo could not expect to moon around all day in his room waiting for inspiration.

Lockley's attitude to writing was professional. He was an early riser and liked to write then. He used to say his articles for *The Farmer and Stockbreeder* were always written before breakfast. After that, he would be out organising the work for the day, sometimes working on the farm himself or in his office dealing with business or getting on with a new book or he would be out attending meetings or making contacts. He was a man who made things happen.

So, from his standpoint, Leo must get outside and work, but the question was what could he do? The answer seemed to lie in his books, where it appeared he was a skilled handyman. Lockley had planned to build a chicken-house but so far no one had been free to do it. Now Leo was surely the man! Unfortunately, the solution did not turn out so well in practice. Leo was used to being his own master, doing what he chose, in the way he chose and when he chose. To him, it was unendurable to be given instructions to do this or that, in this or that way, and to be chivvied out of his sanctum to do it, whether he was in the mood or not. He complained of inadequate equipment and working with unseasoned and crooked timber — the thing was impossible. Lockley simply required a rough and ready job, a frame of birch saplings, walls of corrugated iron, just a shack where the poultry could have safety and shelter and a place to lay their eggs.

There were quarrels. Leo shouted, Lockley stomped off in a huff — acrimony all round. The partnership that promised so well in theory between like-minded families had quickly foundered. The two tigers could not live on the same hill.

*   *   *

The situation was becoming clear within the first week and the Walmsleys began to ask around locally whether there might be a reasonable property to rent or for sale. The only one in the vicinity was a derelict cottage with some land, known as Rhos-y-Bayvil. Pauline, the land girl, recalled,

> 'by the time I met them they had already found Rhos-y-Bayvil. They took me to see it on that first Saturday. It lay between Cwmgloyne and the coast and was within walking distance across country. As I remember it was a smallholding and the cottage a complete ruin. They certainly had ideas of rebuilding it themselves (a mammoth job compared to the chicken-house). One day we actually started building up ruined walls and clearing the site.'

They arranged to rent it on a monthly basis, and at least it gave them a little foothold of their own and somewhere to escape to. There was no question of them being able to make it habitable, at least for many months, and it was obvious for the sake of both families that they would have to move on quickly.

The Lockleys would have no doubt put up with a good deal to secure Margaret's help in the house, but Leo's volatile temperament and quick temper were factors that they were unable to deal with. Laughter would have broken the tension of the situation for it had its ridiculously funny side but neither of the Lockleys seemed to be blessed with a sense of humour. To them, what they saw as Leo's rudeness and abuse of their hospitality must have been deeply offensive. Still, they all had to live together until somewhere else could be found to house the visitors and they settled into an uneasy truce, preserving the common decencies in public as far as they were able.

It was soon apparent that local enquiries to find a new home would produce nothing further so they sought the help of estate agents. They liked the area: the countryside was wild and beautiful and the war had receded to news bulletins on the wireless. They went off for whole days property hunting, hiring a car and driver when buses failed to meet their needs. After one such excursion, they arrived back at Cwmgloyne with cheerful faces, saying that they thought that they had found the very thing. It was a small mansion with farm buildings and some fifty acres (20ha) of land on the other side of the Preseli Mountains, near a village called Maenclochog. They were to go again to inspect the place in detail and discuss purchase, and as the house was in bad repair, although basically sound, Leo hoped that the price would be within the amount he could afford. They went again and finally the purchase price was agreed. At the same time, they were able to arrange accommodation at an inn in Maenclochog, where they could stay while they made some rooms ready for occupation and until their furniture arrived from Yorkshire. They left Cwmgloyne on the 28th June, having been with the Lockleys for about five weeks.

*   *   *

Leo's autobiographical novel *The Happy Ending* was based on their sojourn in Wales. The title indicates that the novel will have a substantial fictional element, and so it does. Written ten years or more after the events that it recounts, he was able to stand well back from his material, select or discard facts as he chose and shape a story with a happy outcome although the actuality had been quite different.

To begin with, he omits the Cwmgloyne episode entirely; it was not an episode he could have taken pride in remembering. Instead of the long, sunny days of midsummer, he describes 'a cold, windy, rainy November night' as the season of their arrival at Temple Druid (Castle Druid in the book). This, and the fiction that they had bought the house without seeing it, gave a more dramatic opening to the novel. There follows the familiar Walmsley story of making a home in difficult circumstances, basically factual, together with a new theme, that of working for the war effort, both by farming the land and by taking evacuees. The first is factual; the second is fictional. Temple Druid was too small to accommodate anything like the number of children he describes and, moreover, he shows no knowledge of the procedures followed for what he calls 'official evacuees'. These

Temple Druid (Castle Druid) (*Photo: Frederick W. Lane*)

children were sent out in batches when certain towns were considered to be vulnerable to German bombing. Their billeting was organised by local members of the WVS and children under a certain age were accompanied by their mothers, not sent alone. What actually happened at Temple Druid was that Margaret decided, without consulting Leo, and much to his annoyance, to take two children from a private charity, one being a baby of eighteen months. They came, bringing head-lice and other problems and although Margaret did marvels with them, they did not stay long. It looks as though it was a short-term arrangement to give a hard-pressed mother a breathing space. It is necessary then to treat *The Happy Ending* with caution when attempting to glean autobiographical material from it.

Another pitfall for the unwary who seek to discover the facts from this book is that the Walmsleys lived in two different places in Wales and he cheerfully conflates them in his fiction.

Temple Druid lay about a mile (1.5km) from Maenclochog, an easy, fairly level walk, following narrow but tarmacadamed lanes. It was, and is, a remote, Welsh-speaking village, set in farmland close to the Preseli Mountains, themselves a low, undulating range of bare hills and moorland, brown for much of the year but glowing purple and gold with heather and gorse in August and September. In the 1980s Maenclochog had two chapels, an Anglican church, three public houses, a primary school, a Police Station, a small cluster of shops and two garages, serving a population of 350 people. A wide street runs expansively through the length of the village, the houses on either side well back from generous verges. At high noon the village is deserted, and in the dusty heat of a summer's day one is strangely reminded of a 'western' township, its populace waiting behind closed doors for the sheriff's posse to arrive ... And then again in the grey of winter, it looks like one of those prints of Pembrokeshire in the horse and cart era of 100 years ago ... 750 feet above sea level, Maenclochog lays itself open to the winds that sweep down from the hills along that two mile long street, so unusually wide because it was once a market ground for sheep and cattle. Streams for the convenient watering of the beasts then flowed on either side, the pens laid out in rows between waters.' The village would have looked much the same forty years or so earlier, when the Walmsleys lived so near it.

Temple Druid is hidden away from the road and there is an account in *The Happy Ending* of the family's first sight of it, which must be very close to what Leo and Margaret saw on that day of house hunting when they found it.

> 'The country was lovely. The valley was sparsely wooded with tall oaks and ash, the stream meandered through it so that here and there one caught the gleam of water ... There were high double stone and earth banks on either side of the road, like those in many rural parts of Devon and Cornwall ... The road banks were still high, hiding the valley, and the road, although now dead level, twisted. Then, coming round a bend, we saw ahead of us on the left side the end wall of a building, partly obscured by a tall horse-chestnut tree.'

Their immediate reaction was one of shock as the building consisted of three very dilapidated cottages, but they were quickly reassured when they realised that the buildings were, in fact, only the farm cottages, and the mansion itself was on the lower ground, completely hidden from the road. The field on which the mansion was built was quite extensive, bounded by a tree-fringed stream on one side and by the road on the other.

> 'The road was lined with tall massive beeches, and there was another gate with big ornamental pillars facing the still, to us, hidden front of the mansion.'[1]

They walked down the drive, then turned to look back at the house.

> 'It was another shock, but this time an entirely agreeable one. Except that there was no paint on any of the windows, the whole building looked intact, and in first class condition ... There was nothing pretentious about it, and it was not, as mansions go, formidably big ... Its height to the eaves, which had an overhang, was about twenty feet, the roof was low pitched, and slanted from the ridge at both ends. There were large multi-paned windows on the ground floor, shuttered from the inside and evidently belonging to the reception rooms; and the bedroom windows, likewise shuttered and smaller, were well spaced. There was a columned flat-roofed portico to the front door which was central to the building.'[2]

The interior, in spite of the dereliction of a house long uninhabited, was to their experienced eyes equally promising. Their belongings in Yorkshire were sent for. They had no need to stay long at the inn in Maenclochog, for their chattels, despite the wartime difficulties, the cross-country route and the remoteness of their new home, were speedily delivered. Kitchen and bedrooms were soon made habitable. The kitchen was comfortably large enough for the family to take their meals and also to sit in and they managed to do without reception rooms until well in to the autumn.

Pauline recalls spending a week in Temple Druid in mid-November, helping with work outdoors and clearing debris from two of the downstairs rooms, one of which was a room known as the Nash Room, for at least part of it was unmistakably the work of that fine architect. Leo described his first sight of it when Clow showed them round the house.

'There was a third door almost opposite that of the big room. He opened it, walked in and opened the shutters of a single window facing the main gate. We followed, stopping at the threshold, and we had another shock, again of mixed dismay and delight. On the floor of the room was another heap of fallen plaster ... And yet, looking round, I thought that it was one of the most exciting rooms I had ever seen, and I knew that Dain (Margaret) was thinking the same. It was unique.

It was square, like the other two, but considerably smaller. The doorway wall, however, was curved, with the doorway central. The door itself, panelled, and an exquisite piece of joinery, was also curved, and on each side of it, following the curve, were built-in cupboards ... From the lintel of the doorway, the plastered wall was scalloped to meet the moulding on the actual ceiling.'[3]

Margaret and Pauline shared a great enthusiasm for riding horses and during the week she was there, they both went to a big fair at a place called Eglwyswrw, when the wild mountain ponies were rounded up and brought down for the autumn sales. Margaret's own ponies, Mary Jane and Lady, had come down from Yorkshire by train as soon as they had acquired Temple Druid. Of the children, only Henrietta had anything approaching her mother's love of horses. The others took more after their father in this respect. Leo did occasionally ride Lady, but was always ill at ease while doing so.

There was a good deal of riding between Temple Druid and Pauline's home at Little Milford, in 1941 and part of 1942. They were sent to Little Milford to graze, which seems rather strange in view of the distance, about twelve miles (20km), but was probably because there was little fencing at Temple Druid and the horses kept escaping.

That first summer at Temple Druid seems to have been a blissfully happy time for the Walmsleys and there was relief that their chief troubles seemed to be over and many problems resolved.

Behind them was the painful sale of Leith Rigg and the failure of the two households to settle into a working partnership at Cwmgloyne. Now once more they had a place of their own. Their possessions were around them, the ponies had arrived and at the end of term Ann and Simon came back from school in the Lake District. They were a family again at last and the parents, with their zest for pioneering, were full of plans for their new enterprise.

Dain's words at the end of *The Golden Waterwheel*, when they have been offered a house in Wales give an indication of the sort of ideas in the air at Temple Druid in 1941:

'It's just wonderful. It's just what we want. A big house. Twenty rooms. We can soon put it right. We could have a governess. Better still, we could have a school, and Amelia and Jane wouldn't have to leave us. We might get Sylvia to join us. And all that land, and

Leo Walmsley early 1940s

the farm buildings. Stables. We could have more ponies and breed them. And the trout stream and the waterwheel. A real farm. But the main thing would be having our children with us, not having to part with them. Do let's take it.'

Pauline, their land girl friend, on her occasional visits, was swept into this ferment of enthusiasm and, writing her recollections long after, is hard put to find the words to express it.

'How to recapture the atmosphere of those early Temple Druid Days? How they come back to me with a kind of magic. There was the old house, solid and four-square, awaking from its sad years of emptiness. Now it was filled with voices, talking and laughter and shouting. People were abustle in its rooms, fires were burning, hot tea was steaming in mugs on the table, saucepans boiling on the stove ... The great trees outside were protective presences and they too seemed to approve of our work on the neglected fields and by the overgrown stream. Leo was in his element. This was what he loved best: to be in his home with his family around him.'[4]

In those early, happy days, they were all full of optimism for their life at Temple Druid. All kinds of plans were being made. Leo and Pauline got on well and she says that he was a fascinating companion and made her feel valued. He consulted her as an equal and took her replies seriously. He loved like-minded people around him and, with his boundless ideas and enthusiasm, he had a natural affinity with young people. He did not care much for conventional socialising, neither did he seem interested in extending his circle of friends. His family, and the few friends who liked to join in and become part of it, were enough for him.

The Walmsleys soon discovered that there was a great deal of work to be done as well as getting the house to rights. As owners of fifty or so acres (20ha) of farmland, they were under the wartime obligation to farm it productively. This was not easy for it had long been neglected.

Leo did what he could himself, and with what help was offered. He managed to clear the gorse and mend the fences that first summer, but for 1942 a more sustained effort would be needed.

'Spring was coming. The days were getting longer. There were golden catkins on the trees down by the stream. The children had found snowdrops and the green shoots of daffodils in the sheltered woods ... I'd had a visit from the Cultivation Officer of the County War Agricultural committee — a panel of farmers and experts whose function was to put into effect the Government schemes for producing the maximum amount of home grown food. It offered expert technical advice to those who asked for it. It controlled a pool of agricultural machinery (largely 'lease-lend' from America) that could be hired out at reasonable terms. It paid the various grants and subsidies that the Government awarded for ploughing up new land and growing certain crops, such as potatoes. It had authority to make financial loans to needy farmers for the purchase of fertilizers, seed, even of stock; to order farmers as to what crops they should grow, and — very important — to displace farmers who were not doing their job efficiently.'[5]

Leo was no farmer but he was learning. He writes briefly about growing potatoes, swedes and mangolds, and the ubiquitous thistles and other weeds that invariably grew amongst them and thrived more lustily than the legitimate crop. In a letter

The remains of the waterwheel at Temple Druid, 1998

of 1943, to a friend, he wrote, 'I've got two fields of oats that I've saved from failure. The potatoes are good as the hoeing will be done tomorrow. With decent luck we'll have about twice as much hay as we had last year.' He also plans to buy some bullocks for fattening and to keep goats rather than cows for milk. In *The Happy Ending*, he describes the tribulations of hay making, the problems of having it just right for harvesting and the worry that rain will spoil it before it can be gathered in and stacked. He also describes the community spirit of the local farmers in helping each other out with harvesting and their worries that whilst helping someone else their own crops were at risk. Margaret and the other womenfolk had their part to play, for as well as helping with the hard physical work, they baked and made beer to feed the workers at the particular farm where they were gathering the harvest.

Leo had given the title *The Golden Waterwheel* to the autobiographical novel that had preceded *The Happy Ending*, but the waterwheel did not materialise in the earlier book. It appeared there as an ambition, a dream, a golden idea that the Walmsleys were always striving after. It symbolised perhaps their desire to be self-sufficient in providing their own power; and because it would need a quantity of water to move it, which meant a dam and a lake, it also symbolised the completion of their paradise, a fisherman's paradise, for in the lake would be fish and on the lake a boat. To Leo especially, country life without fishing and boating could never be fully satisfying.

The Happy Ending therefore is the natural sequel to the earlier book, for one happy ending, even the most significant one, is the achievement of a real water-wheel. The finding of a suitable one at a long-abandoned mill, the dismantling and reassembly at Temple Druid is told at length in the book. Leo and his wife believed that the waterwheel could help the war effort.

> 'The lake should produce a certain amount of food in the way of fish. The wheel, should by producing electricity, save paraffin and candles. If we got a mill, we might grind oatmeal, and if I could pick up a circular saw bench, it might be used for sawing logs for the house fires, and save coal.'[6]

But even dearer to his heart (the authentic voice of Leo can be heard) would be 'the excitement of doing it, the aesthetic pleasure, the trout!'

The great day came when the waterwheel had been installed and everything in order to set it in motion.

> 'Dain and most of the children were already at the lake. I shouted to her that we were going to start the wheel ... and Clow, as I had anticipated, was standing at the sluice gate ready to open it ... I said to Clow: 'You ought to have the honour of opening the sluice itself.' ... We all moved along the sides of the sluice then, watching the water run along it, we were just in time to see it reach the sluice end, pour into the topmost bucket and gush over into the next. And then the wheel began to move.' ...
>
> 'That same evening when all the children were in bed, I suggested to Dain that we should have a stroll around the fields ... The shortest and most agreeable route to the fields was by the lake and dam wall, and a path that branched upwards from that to the quarry. It was natural that we should pause by the wall, have another look at the wheel and gloat over it. 'Isn't it marvellous,' Dain said, 'That we've really got the waterwheel at last.'[7]

Leo's dream of having a working waterwheel had come true at last.

To this day an inscription can be read on one of the concrete mounting blocks supporting the shaft of the wheel. It reads 'Simon Walmsley'.

Amidst all these excitements and demands on their time, an underlying problem beset them: the education of the children. Both parents were strongly biased towards progressive education for they both felt they themselves had suffered in childhood from repressively religious educational regimes and wished their own family to grow up uninhibited in a rural setting which would, they believed, enable their children to grow and develop their potential fully, both physically and spiritually. At Leith Rigg, Leo claimed, 'our first four children got a magnificent start physically. We were agreed too that until they were of boarding school age we should have a governess for them.' He had managed to affect this with a succession of nannies and governesses while the children were very young. The older ones, Ann and Henrietta and later Simon had all started boarding before the family left Yorkshire but when they settled in remote west Wales schooling became far more difficult. At first, they hoped to be able to cope at home. Leo wrote in a letter to a friend, 'We saw in Temple Druid the possibility of getting our family together again by running a school. I knew we couldn't make money out of it that way of course.'

In the event, it proved impossible to find a governess or a teacher. Some came for short periods, none stayed. One left to be married, another was found unsatisfactory and dismissed. If it had been easy in peacetime to find suitable candidates, in wartime it was virtually impossible because of the demands of war work. So it was back to school for the three older children. It was most necessary for Ann to continue her education for she was ten in 1942 and had already made good progress. Largely through Margaret's efforts, a school was found at Llandeilo.

Leo was unenthusiastic for he was inclined to be sceptical about all formal schooling. His attitude to formal education is seen in a letter that he wrote to the headmistress:

> 'I've previously left Jerry to do all the communications with you. She complained that I didn't take much interest in Ann's reports. Frankly reports (I've had to do 'em myself) don't mean a thing to me. If a teacher reports progress then I feel the mistress is paying herself a compliment, if she writes 'Elizabeth' is slow and does not pay attention, then I take it as an admission of her own failings as a teacher. What has impressed me about your school, through Ann and Jerry, is that you've got a fine ideal, and that Ann is acquiring something far more important than a skill in Mathematics or Latin.'

No doubt it was the shortage of money that precluded Henrietta and Simon from being sent away. There was a primary school within walking distance at Maenclochog and, having failed to find a suitable person to teach them at home, the children were entered there. Small county primaries did not always provide a very satisfactory education in those days and it is not known what standard the local school achieved. But the inevitable problem faced by English children then, as now when parents settle in a Welsh-speaking area, is the problem of language. Leo became very heated about it. ' I cordially damn and blast the fate that has put this place out of range of an English school.' With a little more forethought, he could have avoided this because only a few miles to the south was the 'landsker', the imaginary line marking the boundary between the Welsh-speaking and English-speaking Pembrokeshire. Had they taken their house hunting further afield, there would have been no language problems.

To make matters worse, the children were already aliens in appearance and behaviour. They spoke differently and even looked different: big for their age, plump, fair-haired and -skinned in contrast to the dark, wiry Welsh children. It was hard for the incomers. Margaret said later that 'Simon and Henrietta fought their way into the Welsh day school and fought their way home' daily. Henrietta no doubt gave as good as she got for she was a big sturdy girl, with a formidable scowl. Simon, chubby and pale, must have suffered miseries.

How long a period they attended the local school is not clear; perhaps they were removed or perhaps attended only infrequently, for Leo noted at one point that 'all the kids were at home as the local elementary school was vile.'

The war had placed the Walmsleys in an unfortunate position. They had moved from the well-known and loved area of Robin Hoods Bay where they had plenty of friends and acquaintances to unfamiliar Wales, where Leo had quarrelled with the only people he knew, the Lockleys. They had, of course, started their life together in another unknown area, Cornwall, but they were younger then, madly in love and without ties. They could thrive on their hardships because at that moment in their lives anything seemed possible. But now they were ten years older, with four children and consequent responsibilities.

Love on a crust in the 'Garden of Eden' had inevitably been superseded by more sober concerns. Margaret had adapted to the change better than Leo or, rather, she had been imperceptibly changing in time with her growing family. She realised that everyone moving to a new area needs friends and contacts and, although Leo seemed to take little interest in it, Margaret had set about acquiring friends.

They had near neighbours at a farm adjoining Temple Druid and others further afield but in the same vicinity and the indications are that they were on amicable but not on intimate terms with them. Pauline had introduced them to her family, who lived at a greater distance, but the circle needed to be wider than that.

One day at a local sale, about the autumn of their first year in Temple Druid, they fell into conversation with an English couple of about Margaret's age, Betty and Edward Arney. Edward Arney was stationed in the county and connected with the ministry of supply at Aberporth, which was specifically the projectiles development establishment. He and his wife and little boy lived in an improved cottage just on the side of the Preseli range. Why they chose to live in such a remote spot is best known to themselves, but the days must have been long and lonely for Betty while her husband was away. The child was presumably still under school age, but once he was a little older, they would be faced with the same problem that beset the Walmsleys.

Betty and Margaret, drawn together by mutual mothers' concerns, became great friends. When the Arneys visited Temple Druid, they were struck by the Walmsleys' flourishing family life and captivated by the plans and enthusiasm for the upbringing of the children and the cultivation of the 'Good Life'. It was not surprising that they were entranced by being in close proximity to the Walmsleys. Many of their friends in Yorkshire and elsewhere had come under the spell. One of them refers to 'a rare family' and of the relationship between Leo and Margaret as 'so *brave* and so uplifting'. Pauline tried to recapture the atmosphere of those Temple Druid days; her words were evocative, 'They come back to me with a kind of magic.'

The immediate effect upon the Arneys was that they determined to have another child. The friendship between Margaret and Betty developed further and Betty came to stay at Temple Druid, paying something like £2 per week for herself and her little boy, which would have covered expenses but no more. The intention was probably to see how the families got on together, and if happily, to take up the project of starting a school. Betty remained for about six months, her husband coming at intervals, and everyone seemed to get on well at first, although Margaret began to worry about Betty's possessiveness.

Leo said later that Betty did not like him to be alone with Margaret and sulked if they ever went for a walk together. In September 1942 Betty travelled to Southampton for the birth of her second child and there was evidently relief in the Walmsley household. 'Never another red-headed woman for us' was Margaret's comment.

Margaret too had become pregnant again. Leo was displeased at first, feeling that yet another child would compound their problems, both financial and educational, but when Margaret miscarried, they were both upset. The doctor told them that miscarriage was a common occurrence with a mother who had a large family and that, should she become pregnant again, the same thing might follow. Leo felt this to be an added reason for not risking another pregnancy but Margaret, who had been bitterly disappointed at her loss, yearned to try once more. No doubt letters from Betty describing her new baby gave further impetus to Margaret's longing. Betty's letters were also full of matters less palatable. She began to say how she missed all of them at Temple Druid and how she longed to come back. The Walmsleys resisted. They were trying hard to get a nanny and eventually had the promise of one to come at Christmas. Margaret was worried about how to break the news to Betty and tell her firmly that they did not want her to live with them again. There were now further complications as Betty and her husband had split up. Betty told them that she had decided that she could never live with Edward again, as he was such a bore. So deeply had her sojourn at Temple Druid affected her.

*　*　*

The Walmsleys had grave doubts about the wisdom of letting Betty Arney come back to live in their home. But despite these misgivings, she was once again permitted to take up residence at Temple Druid early in 1943.

The reason for letting her return was that they were desperate to find a governess for the younger children and those that they had already found and tried were not suitable. In addition, Margaret's idea of running a small school at Temple Druid had, for her, become an overwhelming aspiration and Betty was to bring her children and help to run it.

If Leo had known what course of events their lives would take by her reinstatement and particularly, the catastrophic effect it would have on him personally, he would most certainly have taken an entirely different course of action.

A few weeks after Betty's return, the whole atmosphere of Temple Druid changed. The two women gradually began to dominate the household, pushing Leo further into the background of family life.

> 'If I dared discipline the children both women went for me. If they were making a noise and I objected, I was a tyrant. Then they started ragging me about my book. They said I ought to be doing war work and not writing about myself. They insulted me in front of the children. Yet when I complained to my wife about this she still said it was Betty's fault. She was jealous of me. Finally there was a scene in which I ordered Betty to leave us. My wife took her side and said if Betty went she would go too … My life was hell during that Spring. Both women did all in their power to break my nerve and prevent me getting on with my book. My wife would flare up at the least provocation. .'[8]

Despite the fact that Margaret had said that she did not want the 'red head' back in her home, she and Betty grew closer together and Leo's exclusion from his wife and children became almost complete and unbearable.

Now began one of the most traumatic periods of Leo's life.

The relationship between the two women grew into a close alliance. How close this really was will probably remain the secret of those involved, but Leo, in a letter written later, even went so far as to accuse them of being lesbians. But when he said this his mind was in a turmoil; he was bitter, somewhat irrational and traumatised by the events which had taken place and which he could not comprehend. He was hitting back in revenge for the intense hurt that he felt had been done to him. He could not understand how this could have happened when he and Margaret had been so deeply in love with each other. He was convinced that their shared experiences should have made the bond unbreakable.

One can only speculate as to why this devastating situation arose. Leo blamed it entirely on Betty and wrote on a number of occasions that he considered her an evil influence on Margaret and that she had 'bewitched' his wife into seeing him as a 'villain' and thereby caused her to leave him. A possible explanation of why the problems might have started was put forward by Pauline, and is probably nearer the truth. It is that Margaret was intensely fond of her children. Her family was her world. Imperceptibly her life had shifted from being centred on Leo to being centered on her children. Basically Margaret was far more conventional than Leo. At first they shared the same ideals on bringing up the family, appearing to be in complete harmony in this matter. But they were both getting older and subconsciously her doubts must have been growing. The coming of Betty with conventional views on discipline, manners and behaviour probably awoke in Margaret a realisation that she shared her views on the education of the children. Leo with his very different ideas had become an obstacle to the way that she wanted the children to be brought up. The subject of contention was one which affected them to the depths of their beings. It was nothing less than the welfare of their children.

Leo held strong and loudly expressed opinions on the matter and was passionately opposed to corporal punishment. He had strong doubts about religious indoctrination of children, particularly in view of his own experiences as a child, preferring to let the children decide about their religious beliefs when they were old enough. When Margaret and Betty decreed that the children should go to church, it was strongly opposed by Leo. So their marriage probably foundered on aims and ideals.

Leo was naturally too deeply concerned for cool reason to prevail; neither did there seem to be much of that quality in his make-up. It was too painful for him to face the fact that their cherished project for an experiment in the good life, the ideal community, had been violated because of disagreements over what the good life might be. Still more impossible for him to comprehend and acknowledge was the thought that Margaret's love had increasingly centred on the children while he had drifted unawares to the outskirts. To the two women he might have been seen as an obstacle, an irrelevance or even a threat. Such thoughts would have been intolerable to him and that is why he seized on the hope that he had been ousted by some irregular passion, for at least it would give him the chance to fight back, to win back his wife and family.

In the early part of 1943 Margaret, having recovered from her previous miscarriage, found that she was pregnant again.

In May 1943 it was agreed that the two women and the children should go on holiday to a place near Cardigan. For three weeks, Margaret did not communicate in any way with Leo and he was left to fend for himself. As it was hay time, he got a man to cut the seven acres (3ha) of hay but said that he had to do all the turning of the hay himself. However, with help from neighbours, it was all gathered in.

Then came the bombshell. A letter arrived from Margaret[9] saying that she would not live with him again as the constant quarrelling was upsetting the children. She also informed him that she and Betty had found a large house, which they were going to run as a school and she asked him to sell Temple Druid. They did not return.

Pauline Burdon

PART SIX

INTO THE WILDERNESS

CHAPTER 18

Despair

WHEN Leo received the letter saying they were not coming back, he was utterly devastated and it brought about a recurrence of neurasthenia. His mind was in turmoil, he did not know what to do, he was desperate. He phoned a lady named Maureen, who was a mutual friend of both Pauline Burdon's mother and Margaret. Maureen drove an ambulance at Scolton Military Hospital housed at Scolton Hall. He told her that he was ringing to say goodbye: 'Jerry' had left him and he was going to take his life. Maureen, with great presence of mind, told him that he could not possibly say goodbye over the phone and that it would be much better to come round and make a proper farewell. Leo arrived on his cycle and was obviously in a state of great distress. Maureen, seeing that it was going to be a difficult situation, enlisted the help of the matron of the hospital. They made him sit down and supplied him with whisky. He talked continuously and told them the story of the separation with his wife. They managed to calm him a little and persuaded him to stay the night to give him time to calm down. Although still in a state of shock, by the next day he had become more rational.

After the break with Margaret, Leo took support from his friends, one of whom was Pauline's mother at Little Milford, where he stayed from time to time. He was trying to deal with the financial problems associated with their farming at Temple Druid. There were some debts from loans to buy stock and it was not until the end of 1943 that he was able to sort these out. His very good friend Daphne du Maurier gave him great support during these difficult times. Her offer of a private loan was of immense material help, but of greater importance was the sympathetic understanding which her letters at the time reveal.

Such was the state of his mind that he even wrote to the person he considered responsible for starting all the trouble. In a letter to Betty Arney dated the 18th June 1943, Leo accepts responsibility for the gulf which opened up between Margaret and himself and adopts a much more conciliatory attitude towards Betty than he had hitherto shown. This was in direct contrast to the serious criticism which he had levelled at her in letters to friends, alleging that she had been instrumental in Margaret's decision to leave him. No doubt he thought that if he ingratiated himself with her, he might have a better chance of patching things up with his wife.

Among the friends to whom Leo wrote during this traumatic time was Elaine Rice who, in the wills of both Leo and Margaret, was named as the guardian of the children should anything happen to them. In a letter dated the 20th June 1943, he tells Elaine what has happened and, in what is something of a confession of his conceived failings, he refers to his marriage as being a happy one, expressing pride in the part he played. In this letter, as in others, he was obviously trying to rationalise the situation which he found difficult to comprehend and even more difficult to accept. He appears to have accepted Margaret's determination to support her children and give them the education which she considered right for them by running a boarding school. He claims that he has accepted the fact that they can never live together again as before but then goes on to say that he will continue trying to patch things up. Clutching at straws, he suggests that Margaret's attitude has been affected by her pregnancy; that her condition following so soon after a miscarriage has affected her psychologically and that all will be well when the baby is born.

> 'I was prepared on her accepting my admission of my faults and wrong actions, to get down to the job of earning money for her and the family in chastened and energetic spirit and felt I could make good the damage I had done and demanding nothing but her good will. But now I am broken. She gave me faith in myself when I was comparatively young. Now within sight of the goal of success she has destroyed that faith utterly and I cannot write again.'

In a further letter to Elaine on the 5th July 1943, he reiterates the hope that a reconciliation will be possible. He is still tending the farm and tells her about saving two fields of oats from failure, hoeing potatoes, milking the goat and that the hay crop should be good.

Leo wrote a contrite letter to Margaret offering to leave Temple Druid and let her go there to have the baby. He received in return a solicitor's letter telling him not to write to her again nor to try to see the children otherwise it would mean police court proceedings. He knew that it was probably a bluff but feared the adverse publicity which might damage his reputation. At this time, he was also trying to sell Temple Druid which was in their joint names. He felt strongly that Margaret was being duped by Betty, who, being estranged from her own husband and 'in love with Jerry', could see the chance of a partnership with Margaret on half of the proceeds of the sale.

Leo was expecting to hear that the women had moved into the house they claimed they had found but in the end it turned out that the house did not exist. Again he offered them Temple Druid but they still refused. He insisted on seeing the children and eventually, after much effort on Leo's part, Margaret agreed. He wrote and said that he would look after the older children until they had found a house, but received no reply.

Then at last, towards the end of 1943, Leo received a letter telling him that his wife had found a large house, where they could start their school. The women and children moved into Bwlchbychan Hall, Drefach, a few miles from Lampeter. They asked Leo to let them have all the furniture that he did not need so he packed up practically everything inside Temple Druid and took it to their house.

He arrived at the house expecting it to be empty and thought that he would take the furniture in and have fires going for them before they arrived but they were already there. Margaret 'went for me like a tigress' he said, and although it was late at night, he left and found a hay barn to sleep in.

At this time, Leo had been offered a lecturing job visiting the isolated gun emplacements on the coast around Milford Haven. He did three lectures a day for three days despite the fact that he had not done any lecturing for many years.

Meanwhile, he was endeavouring to write and keep the farm going while trying to sell it.

The children's ponies were still at Temple Druid and Leo received a pleasant letter from Betty asking for them to be sent over. Hopefully he set off with them on the train and arrived at Llanybythor station, where Betty, Ann and Henrietta met him. To his surprise, they mounted the ponies and left him standing there. Margaret had told him that he could not stay at the house under any circumstances, and as there was no room to be had in the village, he spent the night in the police station.

The next day he went up to the house to see the children. This he achieved but Margaret would not come near him. He said later that he stayed around for a few days and even did some repairs on the house but had to reside at a local inn. This was the Pen Pom Pren Inn at Drefach. Harriet Davies, who owned the inn, and her family were eventually to become his very close friends. He corresponded with Amy and Rita for many years after he had left.

Temple Druid was sold, Leo said, for about £1,600 (it had cost £700). At the end of 1943, probably about September, Leo left Temple Druid for the last time and went to stay in the Pen Pom Pren Inn so as to be near to Bwlchbychan Hall.

On the 11th November 1943, Margaret gave birth to a son at Bwlchbychan. He was named Sean Alasdair.

Leo received a telegram saying that the baby had been born. 'I went over to see. It was grand, but Jerry was like ice.' Then he was told that he could visit again at Christmas. Leo made a 'trap for Mary Jane (Betty's child), a dressing table for Ann, a huge drawbridge for Simon and a garage for Dain. I felt like father Christmas. When I arrived I was greeted by two tigresses.' Margaret told him to take the 'filthy' things away and Betty denied that she had invited him.

The difficult period dragged on, with Leo trying to seek reconciliation and keeping in touch with the children. In many of his letters to friends, the children and their education was uppermost in his thoughts. The two women and the children left Wales probably in mid-1943 although this is not confirmed.

Whilst Leo was staying at the Pen Pom Pren, he helped out doing general work, such as haymaking at a local farm, Maes-y-felin, which was a few minutes' walk from the inn. The owner let him use a room in a barn on the farm as a writing room. It was ideal for his purpose. It was situated away from the road and quiet. It had a first-floor room with a single window overlooking the beautiful countryside. Beneath the window was an old wooden bench, which he probably used as his writing desk. Close to the bench was an old free-standing cast-iron stove with its stove-pipe chimney passing out through the back wall just above the bench. Here he could find peace for a while from the turmoil of his life and a quiet place to write. Just outside there was a stream which had been dammed and a waterwheel had been installed to drive machinery in a small factory. The barn had been part of the factory at some time. It was here that he wrote his autobiographical book *So Many Loves*. On the whitewashed walls he drew sketches, one of which was a view of Robin Hoods Bay and was to become the picture on the dust jacket of the book.

When Leo had written a chapter of the book, he often became bad-tempered. Amy would suggest that he went out and did something like cut a few hedges until his temper improved, which he usually did.

Life for Leo at Pen Pom Pren continued with no solution to the difficult situation which had beset him and his family. His attempts to see the children were usually frustrated. He occupied his time with writing and painting. He expressed his gratitude to the owners of the Pen Pom Pren Inn, now his very dear friends, by presenting them with a picture of the inn which he had painted. They at least gave him sympathy, support and a home. Someone who saw him at the time says he looked much like a tramp and was a forlorn and lonely figure, sitting in the corner of the bar. Eventually he left to return to Yorkshire, with all the main problems unresolved.

Frederick W Lane

CHAPTER 19

Retreat to Yorkshire

PERIODS of unhappiness or mental stress during Leo's life seem to have focused his attention on Robin Hoods Bay, his native place, as he called it. Although he lived elsewhere for the greater part of his life, there was always a sense of belonging, a homing instinct or even stronger than this, a place to which, like a wounded animal, he could retreat and allow time to alleviate his pain.

It would be a natural choice when he decided to leave Wales. Margaret and the children had left and he could see no future in following them. His writing at Pen Pom Pren had brought success with the publication of his autobiography *So Many Loves*. He concluded this on the 14th April 1944 and it was published in the same year. He was struggling with another book, which he had started to write several years earlier when he had reached an impasse with *Love in the Sun*. He returned to it from time to time, but it seems to have been a source of frustration for him over quite a long period. This book was *Master Mariner*, the only book which he described as a novel.

With the commencement of *Three Fevers*, Leo had embarked on an approach to his writing which was autobiographical. In most of his books he features either as himself or as an unnamed narrator. Even in the non-fictional books which he was commissioned to write, he could not resist the temptation to refer to episodes in his own life which enliven the documentary aspect of the works.

It was important to him that he should maintain his artistic integrity which, to him, meant that his characters should be true to life. Perhaps this belief was partially responsible for the problem which repeatedly confronted him throughout the gestation period of *Master Mariner*. After Margaret had left him and his whole world had been turned upside-down, he began to question his integrity both as a writer and as a person. He was bedevilled by self-doubt and was desperate to reassure himself. It was against this background that he was attempting to rebuild his own self-esteem and reassert himself in his own eyes as an author whose artistic integrity could not be questioned. By writing a work of traditional fiction, he hoped to prove that he was, in fact, a creative writer and thus confound those critics who accused him of being unable to create characters from his imagination, but merely record them as a sort of literary photographer.

There is little doubt that the dilemma in which he found himself with *Master Mariner* would have strengthened his resolve to return to Robin Hoods Bay, as once again the village was the setting for his book. Writing about the village had invariably presented Leo with two divergent problems. At times he felt the need to move away in order to obtain an objective view; but conversely, when he was in some distant place, he found difficulty in recalling particular aspects of the area which he considered vital to the story.

The date when he left Pen Pom Pren Inn is uncertain although it is known that he was still there in August 1945. It is assumed that he left during autumn as he was living at Old Fyling Hall, a farm above Robin Hoods Bay, later that year. He retained contact with his friends at Pen Pom Pren. Letters written years later show the deep affection which he had for them. He also asked for their help with Welsh words, including 'swears', when he was writing *The Happy Ending* in 1954.

By moving north, Leo had established a considerable physical distance between himself and Margaret. He put his energy into his writings and it is known that he travelled to London on occasions to visit his publishers. While accepting the futility of seeking reconciliation with Margaret, he never gave up hope entirely that some time in the future he would be reunited with his family. He was allowed to see some of his children and it appears that he met them in London, suggesting that reunions were short and infrequent.

The stay at Old Fyling Hall was comparatively brief and later in 1946 he moved to the Yorkshire Dales. He rented a cottage, 'Dalegarth', in the village of Hawkswick in Littondale. To call it a village is to exaggerate its size, for Hawkswick is merely a cluster of houses with one or two farms in the surrounding area. Its setting is delightful. On the banks of the River Skirfare, a tributary of the River Wharfe, it is almost hidden from sight and is dwarfed by the impressive fells topped by limestone outcrops. Littondale is like a secret valley with the fells seeming to close in, leaving barely space for the narrow winding roads which wander, one at each side of the river, leading further away from the busy world. It was an ideal place in which to find the peace and quiet which Leo needed so he could concentrate his attention on writing.

Another writer had found inspiration a few miles farther up the valley. It was while staying in a house overlooking the river at Arncliffe that Charles Kingsley is reputed to have conceived the idea of *The Water Babies*. Leaning over the parapet of the bridge, watching the river cascading over the rocks, leaving little pools of tranquil water, catching sight of a brilliant flash of colour as a kingfisher darts into the shelter of the overhanging bank, one can well imagine the mind of a writer being stimulated by the scene.

The exact date of Leo's arrival at Hawkswick is not known but in a letter dated the 21st November 1946 to his old friend Sam Wilson, he refers to settling down in his new home, waiting for water to be laid on; 'it's a pump at present'. He liked the people and the country but was never truly happy away from sight and sound of the sea. Perhaps the sound of the river flowing just across the road from his door was some compensation. The prime reason for this self-imposed isolation in Littondale was to concentrate on completing *Master Mariner* free from distraction. He was, however, very happy to allow himself distraction at Christmas when he had hopes of seeing his children. In his letter to Sam, and subsequent letters, he rather incoherently writes about trying to make arrangements for Simon and Dain to stay with him during the Christmas holidays. Apparently agreement had been reached through solicitors that Margaret would send the children to Yorkshire. She would not allow Leo to go and collect them from Cowes, where she was living at the time, insisting that they be met in London. He had been making plans to take the boys to school instead of returning them home. He had been very impressed by what he had heard of Wennington School, where the headmaster was Kenneth Barnes. Leo informed Sam of his somewhat devious scheme, seeking his support, both from the moral aspect and also because the mental strain was taking its toll.

> 'God. What a relief. No sleep for 3 nights. Feeling the devils were going to beat me after all ... I'm really too excited to write clearly. I'll have to take some dope tonight to sleep.'[1]

As it turned out, his plans failed to reach fruition as the Christmas visit did not take place. His letters of the time reveal the turmoil of his mind, his lack of rational thought; his correspondence with Sam supplied the support and encouragement that he craved.

He experienced the terribly severe winter of February 1947 when blizzards struck with alarming suddenness.

> 'High "dry" walls criss-cross the hill tops, and in bad weather the ewes huddle on the leeside of them, and the snow itself will help to keep them warm; and even a week like this would do them little damage, although the shepherd might have to dig them out. But this phenomenal weather was to last for nearly eight weeks: a wind that never shifted from the east; blizzards, and a continuous frost. For a whole week there was no communication at all with the outside world except by telephone and radio.'[2]

Leo assisted the farmers in their grim search for sheep once the thaw had set in. His own limited attempts at farming had given him some insight into the disastrous consequences which the vagaries of the British climate could have on farmers. His involvement with the local people during this period gave him a deep respect and admiration for the hardy men of the dale. He must have been the cause of surprise and amusement during the weeks of deep snow when he adopted a novel method of travel which he had first used when living at Leith Rigg. He made himself skis, but instead of the traditional sticks, he used a single long pole, propelling himself along as if punting on a river.

Although Leo referred only briefly to his sojourn at Hawkswick, a member of a local family, the Spencers, recalled several incidents which throw some light on his life at the time. John Spencer was a young boy of nine when Leo arrived at the cottage and he remembered him as having very striking looks, being rather a gaunt, thin figure in ginger-coloured cord trousers. He was impressed by his abundance of hair, but even more so by his sad face.[3] A friendship developed between Leo and the family, probably prompted by Leo's relish for intellectual conversation, which Mrs Spencer's college education would stimulate. He was regarded as eccentric and was usually referred to as 'Old Leo'.

John Spencer recollected the spasmodic attempts made to improve the bungalow. This no doubt referred to what Leo called his 'summer bungalow', which was a large hut adjoining 'Dalegarth. He expressed the hope of being able to buy it and in a letter to Sam dated the 7th December 1946 states that he had completed the purchase of the summer bungalow for £75 furnished. In a way reminiscent of his pioneering days in Cornwall, he scrounged wood which could be utilised in repairing the woodwork. From Leo's own account to Sam, he was obviously pleased with the result as he compared it with Leith Rigg.

What pleased him did not satisfy the next tenant, Winifred Haward Hodgkiss, who took over the tenancy after Leo left the bungalow. In her autobiography, she describes it as being box-like and very neglected. It rarely seemed to have occurred to him to take a duster to the cobwebs draping the walls and the windows were apparently covered with a grimy film. In addition to the summer bungalow, there was a lean-to shed of corrugated iron and she bought these two outbuildings from Leo for £175. This financial deal was quite apart from the tenancy agreement — a rather peculiar arrangement but obviously accepted by all parties.

In the glorious summer that followed that terrible winter, weeks of sunshine continued unbelievably from early June through August and towards autumn. The longed-for day came when the children arrived for a holiday. Henrietta and the two boys had an idyllic time playing with the local children, usually in the river, paddling and making dams as they had done in those happier days. Their father revelled in their company. He was always at his best with children, sharing their pleasure and rarely showing signs of that short temper which could flare up with adults who failed to meet his expectations. Henrietta must have gone back to her mother on her own as Leo took Simon and Dain on a fishing holiday at Garelochhead in Scotland. It was while they were there that Leo took them to Glasgow to look around the docks. The boys were as fascinated as their father had been on his illicit visit to Liverpool docks as a boy. One of the vessels was a large oil tanker and it was when he was bombarded with questions about this ship that Leo realised how ignorant he was about oil, its derivation, processing and its transport. This ignorance offended his self-respect. From his childhood, he had been interested in the two main topics on which he was being questioned: geology and ships. Unable to give satisfactory answers to his sons, he was irritated by the recurring puzzle as to how he could acquire the enlightenment he sought. His curiosity was to lead him to an intriguing episode in his life.

Master Mariner was progressing slowly and rather painfully. He used to relax from his work by roaming the countryside, talking to the farmers and other local people or sometimes painting watercolours of the beautiful landscape. He was a competent painter and his knowledge of watercolour technique is demonstrated in a delightful passage in *Master Mariner*. One of the characters, Edwin, after an underwater swim on a sunny spring morning, is so elated by the beauty of the sea-bed flora and fauna, that he felt 'a passionate urge to make a picture'. As a student of natural science, he invariably carried a sketch pad and paints when out of doors. He sat on a rock and started to draw, then took out his paints:

> '... charged a smaller brush with pure ultra-marine. He applied this between two of the curving vertical lines on the right-hand side, and helped the colour to spread on the still damp paper with a brush charged with water only. Then here and there he added dabs of light red and a little sepia, helping these to spread too and blend with the blue to form a tint that varied from purple to the paler and warmer grey of a dove's breast ... He added some yellow ochre to the wash and then a little rose madder and let it all spread and blend with the original grey green wash until it became a glowing grey that made a perfect contrast with the darker rock on the right, suggesting that it was sunlight.'

But whatever Leo did during the time he allowed himself for relaxation, or when he was occupied with household chores, his book was never far from his mind.

'One of the supposed advantages of being a novelist is that a man is his own boss. He has no regular hours of employment forced upon him. He can go where he likes, live where he likes, play when he likes, and work only when his mood, or so-called inspiration moves him. The truth is that a novelist is not his own boss. He is the slave of his own conscience, or muse or inspiration, or whatever force it is that compels him to write his book, and from start to finish there is no real let-up from his slavery.'[4]

It was not until much later in the year that he was able to conclude *Master Mariner* to his satisfaction. Once it had been sent to his publisher, he was able to take advantage of an offer which had been made to him a few months earlier.

Nona Stead

CHAPTER 20

A Caribbean Interlude

LEO had returned home from Scotland in much better spirits. Almost immediately he had the good fortune, during a train journey to London, to get into conversation with an ex-tanker captain, now an executive with Anglo-Saxon Petroleum Company, a subsidiary of the Royal Dutch Shell Group. Arising from this meeting, and on the strength of his claims to be a writer on seafaring matters, he was offered a passenger berth on the tanker *Dorcasia*, 8,053 tons gross. It was not an unconditional offer. Leo explains how it was put to him by the company:

> 'Would I care to make a voyage in a tanker out to Curacao, cross in one of the ... "lake" tankers to Maracaibo, have a look at the oil-fields, return to England again by tanker; and if I was impressed by what I saw, write something about it so that the general public might know that the activities of tankers were just as important in peacetime as they had been in war.'[1]

He did not hesitate to accept but his voyage had to be delayed until he had completed *Master Mariner*.

It is significant that this voyage to Curacao required Leo to write another work of non-fiction. Eight years had elapsed since the publication of *Love in the Sun* and since then the troublesome novel, *Master Mariner*, and the adaptation for the stage of his novel *Sally Lunn* were the only fictional works he had produced. Nevertheless, in this fifteen-year period he published five works of non-fiction.

Turning his attention to the oil industry, Leo knew that much more than journalistic skills would be needed if the resulting book was to appeal to the ordinary reader. Not surprisingly, he returned to his somewhat unorthodox habit of introducing himself into the narrative. He had found that only by doing so could he get closer to his characters, get them into focus and control the direction of the story. In this case, it also lent meaning to the 'romance of industry' and his factual account becomes a fascinating story. And herein may lie the problems he experienced in writing *Master Mariner*. Trying to exclude himself entirely from the tale he was telling was something he found increasingly difficult.

With *Master Mariner* out of the way and while waiting for the tanker berth, he did not waste time. There was a great deal to learn about the oil business if he was to understand what he was likely to see. Leo visited the company's laboratories, noted all that he was told and asked numerous questions. He read what was recommended and anything else that he thought might be relevant. This was in no sense a self-imposed task; enthusiasm and curiosity were the motivators.

The awaited summons came early in February 1948, when he was invited to make his way to Falmouth, where the *Dorcasia* would be calling in for a few hours before sailing for Curacao. As she was already making her way down the East Coast, Leo hurried to catch the overnight train to Cornwall to secure his berth. On the pier he was introduced to Captain Byron Jones OBE and made to feel very welcome. Straight away, Leo felt that under this smiling, good-humoured man the ship he was about to join could only be a happy one. And so it proved.

Not without some misgivings, Leo had faced the prospect of being resented as someone head office had imposed on a reluctant crew but he need not have worried. His enthusiasm and the intelligent interest he took in the work of men who themselves took pride in their profession were irresistible. He was soon an accepted member of the ship's company and wandered freely throughout the vessel. He wanted to see for himself the secrets of the ship's design and construction, about which he had heard quite a bit from the company's naval architect before leaving England. Here were all the separate storage tanks into which the hull had been sub-divided and into which the cargo — oil of one sort or another — would be pumped. Then there was all the gadgetry with which she had been equipped. Realising that he would never see the oil when it was being pumped on board, nor while in the tanks, nor when pumped ashore, he conjured up the phrase 'invisible cargo' as an appropriate title for the book that he would write.

But only at sea would he understand how a modern tanker was run. Engaging the men in conversation, he plied them with questions. In his relentless search for facts, he gently picked their brains and later, in the quiet of his cabin, committed to his journal the information gleaned. How it could be turned into a book was a problem that would have to wait.

*   *   *

It was very cold and, once out of the lee of the land, the *Dorcasia* started to pitch and roll. Then, one morning several days later with the fury of the waves spent, the warm sun broke through the cloud. All on board brightened up and the work of tank cleaning and the never-ending job of chipping paintwork and re-painting could begin.

Leo was the only passenger and had the time to spend gazing seaward for whatever might catch his eye. Off the Azores the snow-capped crest of Pico was revealed in all its glory by the rising sun; but not for long. The weather again started to deteriorate and a gale from the north-west brought more squalls to keep the decks awash and slow down work. Approaching the Sargasso Sea, Leo's excitement rose as, from childhood, this strange and extensive, but ill-defined area of floating seaweed had captured his imagination and now he was to see it for himself. He was not satisfied until, with help from one or two of the crew, he managed to collect and examine a bucketful of the sargasso grass. Now it was Leo's turn to enthral those around him. Always happy to share his knowledge of marine life, his enthusiasm for the wonders of the deep must have left them in no doubt that this 'writer chap' saw the oceans as far more than seaways for the world's commerce. Frustratingly, these countless acres of uninviting seaweed made it difficult to see the jellyfish, flying fish and dolphins that Leo was on the lookout for. It also seemed to discourage bird life.

As they edged towards the tropics, the days became warmer and even more pleasant. Leo went happily about his fact-finding mission but was now settling down to enjoy the relaxed atmosphere of what might almost have been a Caribbean cruise. More ships appeared on the horizon and as the *Dorcasia* neared the island of Curacao, the shipping lanes became more congested. The two-week voyage was coming to an end. Curacao's southern tip was cleared and the ship turned north-west to arrive off Willemstad to await her turn to enter harbour.

'It was the colour of that scene which made it so exciting for one whose eyes had gazed on little but the blue of the sea and sky for so long. The walls of the houses were themselves painted in a variety of colours, from saffron to pale blue and pink. The deeply-fluted red pantiles of their steep roofs (bathed in the light of the moon) glowed above the ornamented gable ends, so typically Dutch.'[2]

This was no exotic island landfall but a busy port and oil terminal. Willemstad, with all its refineries, impressed Leo immensely and he wrote, 'it was unlike anything I had ever seen before'. It was not as dramatic or as beautiful as the glimpses he had of the Azores, but he thought it 'infinitely more exciting'. Leo's apparently uncritical acceptance of what was obviously the outcome of industrial and commercial exploitation of a once lovely island would seem to be at odds with his often declared views on the fragile nature of the environment, the need for conservation and his love of the countryside. Yet this response also illustrates one of his strengths. He could see beauty in man's handiwork. To him, ships, aeroplanes, engines and machinery were marvels that he could appreciate and were of practical value. He thought of himself as a bit of a handyman, having spent endless time creating and making many of the things that his isolated and independent lifestyle demanded. And over the years, as his writing increasingly mirrored his day-to-day labours, he had developed a deceptively easy way of explaining intricate mechanisms and describing complicated activities. With a few well-chosen words, he could unravel the complex.

Once ashore, a representative of the company's Dutch subsidiary, Curacosche Scheepvart Maatschippij, met Leo to arrange the next stage of his journey and to spend a few hours showing him some of the island's more attractive sights. There was still much unspoiled beauty to admire and a swim in the warm, clear blue sea to enjoy. Under the dazzling surface, and against a background of shimmering white sands, shoals of brightly coloured fish darted in and out of the coral. Captivated by this fascinating underwater wonderland, Leo was reluctant to leave.

A quick look over the company's latest and largest tanker, the *Helicina*, 12,167 tons gross, was arranged before boarding the *Galeomma* for an introduction to Captain Spanjer, who would take him on the short sea voyage — about 250 miles (400km) — from Willemstad to Maracaibo. At Maracaibo, a port on the lip of Lake Maracaibo, he would be in Venezuela. For Leo, here were more places with romantic sounding names promising yet more adventure.

The *Galeomma* was a tanker specially designed for the shallow waters of the lake. Naturally the accommodation on board was less spacious than that on the *Dorcasia* but to Leo just as attractive. Although a Dutch-registered vessel, all on board spoke English in deference to their guest, which immediately helped to put

Leo at ease. For the *Galeomma*, the voyage was one she did regularly and Leo was saddened to notice that very quickly the clear waters of the Caribbean gave way to cloudy water in the Gulf of Venezuela and seemed to get even murkier as Lake Maracaibo was approached. At Maracaibo, Leo went ashore in the ship's boat as the oil terminals for tanker use were a little beyond the town itself. In consequence, industry had left the town comparatively untouched although the wealth it created was plain enough to see. Nevertheless, Leo was not slow to notice that there were still many poor people and at the bottom of the heap were the aboriginal Indians, reduced to the status of beggars. Yet to Leo the dignity they retained contrasted markedly with the ill-kempt appearance of the street vendors selling newspapers and lottery tickets.

The official of the Dutch company who had met him off the tanker took him to catch the ferry across the lake to Palmarejo the following day. Most of Leo's fellow passengers were the ever-optimistic poor, heading up-country to the oil-fields in the hope of securing a piece of land and scrounging a better living than the town offered. Leo and his guide now journeyed south by car on one of the many very straight roads laid down by the oil companies. These essential communication links had been cheaply made by spraying crude oil on to the scarified surface of jungle clearance and they soon hardened into passable motor ways. Along their length, shanty towns of squatters had taken root but on either side the jungle formed an impenetrable barrier which, to Leo's disappointment, seemed so dense as to be quite bereft of wildlife. Oil and wildlife, his guide told him, did not mix.

Taking two days over the seventy-mile journey, they drove to Mene Grande, a few miles from the eastern shore of Lake Maracaibo. Calling at Lagunillas on the way, Leo was taken by speedboat to visit two of the hundreds of tall oil-drilling derricks dotting the surface of the lake. It struck him as funny that he had yet to see any oil but he had not long to wait. Further on, near the road, ugly seepages of the crude stuff and pools of pitch were pointed out to him. Now, at last, he felt that he might be getting closer to the source of all the mysterious invisible cargoes.

From the Mene Grande, Leo was to catch a plane which would take him to Casigua to witness the prospecting activities of a field survey party working in the jungle near the border with Colombia. Before leaving, he was shown some of the aerial photographs studied by the geologists in their search for oil. These really caught his imagination and reminded him of the many aerial reconnaissance photographs he had taken over the African continent. But the idea of having to fly was one that both worried and excited him. He had not flown since his near-fatal crash in the African jungle thirty years before. He was well aware that aviation science had advanced considerably since those days but it was with some trepidation that he boarded the six-seater Lockheed. Unpleasant memories came flooding back and it was a relief to him to see that the Lockheed had two engines for the trouble with BE2cs, in which he had done most of his flying, was that their seventy-horsepower engines had failed with great regularity. Having survived many crash landings, he could not now help wondering what the country over which they would be flying would be like. He was very nervous but, once airborne, his fears began to subside and he relaxed sufficiently to find fault with the view he had from the passenger seat. Flying as an observer with the Royal Flying Corps, his view from the front cockpit had been magnificent. The feeling of spaciousness and the fresh air had been exhilarating. Now, confined within a cabin, his vision was restricted to what he could see through the windows. It was less fun, he decided.

As they climbed through cloud, Leo's nervousness returned. The swirling mist and bumpiness reminded him of many awkward moments when he worried about what hidden dangers the clouds might obscure. Flying above them, he could see less of the lake and the jungle than he would have liked but he consoled himself with the thought that his fear of flying had at last been conquered. He was certain that he could look forward to future flights but was disappointed to learn on landing that he would have to return the next day.

From Casigua, a rough ride through the jungle to reach the field survey party was necessary. Here the jungle was more open and alive and he began to feel frustrated, and perhaps a little irritated, at being hurried forward to yet another kindly meant reception and lavish hospitality. He would rather have spent time exploring on his own! He managed to persuade his driver to stop a few times so that he could capture the flavour of the jungle and so he came across an ant-eater (dead) and thrilled to see humming birds and some marvellous butterflies. However, having joined the men carrying out a seismographic survey, his enthusiasm for the job in hand returned. Geology was something that he understood and he was intrigued to learn how the team went about its work. The precision necessary and the uncertainty of the results fascinated Leo. He recognised that here was a commercial end in view; so very different from his own amateur dabbling with geology and his search for fossils; yet what else was oil but a fossil fuel?

Time was short and Leo reluctant to leave the site. Strong as was his interest in oil, in these surroundings the stronger instincts of the explorer and naturalist were the forces willing him to stay, to get off the beaten track, to search for strange new plants, insects, birds and reptiles. But the choice was not his; he had to leave the men in their search for a modern Eldorado and be driven to the aerodrome at Casigua for the flight back. It was essential not to miss the *Theobaldus* at Willemstad so he was flown direct to the island of Curacao, a distance of about 350 miles (550km).

On coming in to land, the blue sea surrounding the sunny island was a welcome sight and he was pleased to find that he need not join his ship for a couple more days. He was shown around the oil refinery and the complicated processes involved made him realise the need for much more study. A tour round a phosphate quarry was an experience that he particularly enjoyed because all the work was so much more visible and practical and therefore more understandable than the oil refinery. To his delight also, the manager and many of his men were from Cornwall and knew well the parts of that country dear to Leo's heart. Pleasure had its place in the final hours of his stay and he went hunting lobsters in a beautiful sheltered lagoon.

* * *

Saying farewell to his kind hosts was not easy but as the last day ended he was expected on board the *Theobaldus*. This was a tanker built in America to wartime specifications so lacked the luxury finish given to the *Dorcasia*, which had brought him from England. It was, however, both larger (10,662 gross tons) and faster but no less comfortable. He was soon at home with the master and chief engineer, who were both Tynesiders and, with a crew proud of its ship, Leo was once more congratulating himself on his good luck.

There were, however, still more facts to gather for his notebooks. How different was this American-built tanker from the British vessels he knew, what cargo was she carrying, to what use would it be put and, not without a measure of self-interest, at what port would she discharge her cargo? With 16,000 tons of kerosene and motor spirit in her tanks, Leo started to think about fire risk and explosions. He had listened to many stories of wartime tragedies involving tankers and the eerie sight of phosphorescence glowing around deck fixtures made him a little uneasy.

Every wave now broke over the bows of the deeply laden tanker and flying fish could be collected off the flooded fore-deck. Friendly dolphins and sea birds kept them company and Leo was fascinated to see Portuguese men-of-war, those curious jellyfish, float by and, ever watchful, was lucky enough to catch sight of a very large turtle. With the *Theobaldus* logging fifteen knots and home coming ever nearer, he began to envy the old-time sailormen dependent entirely on the wind and travelling much more slowly. In those days, a sailor saw far more of the natural world surrounding his ship. They had been able to fish and, when becalmed, take out a boat. Leo could only imagine all the opportunities for studying marine life such voyaging must have brought.

After a succession of gales, they approached the more crowded waters off the British Isles and at night the flickering lights told them that land was not far away. Heading up the Bristol Channel for Swansea, they sighted Lundy and for Leo this brought to mind sad memories. On clear days, from their erstwhile home in the Preseli Mountains in Pembrokeshire, he and Margaret had been able to see the island.

Sadly, as the *Theobaldus* neared home, Leo felt the excitement of all on board building up yet knew that he would not be returning to his family. He would again be on his own. Commercial pressures now communicated themselves to the ship's company. An extra knot was added to the speed with the hope of entering Queen's Dock, Swansea, on the flood tide. Fully laden and drawing twenty-nine feet (9m), every minute counted. A pilot was picked up, tugs took over and once through the dock entrance, they towed the ship to an oil terminal. A line was thrown ashore and Leo's voyage to Venezuela had come to an end. It was raining. On the dockside, tears came to his eyes as he saw the youngest apprentice step ashore to be lovingly welcomed by his waiting parents. They were tears for himself.

In front of him lay the challenging task of turning this latest experience into a book but it was to be four years before the publication of his account of the voyage to Curacao and the oil-fields of Venezuela. How to write a book about winning oil from the earth and transporting it across the Atlantic must have posed many problems. How to make it both factual and interesting was a challenge requiring a great deal of thought. He had collected a wealth of material but he needed time to put it all into perspective. Leo admitted that he 'needed time for mental digestion' but this, he explained, was prolonged by illness.

Invisible Cargo is an intriguing and enigmatic title but, as usual, Leo sets the scene by treating his readers to another taste of autobiography. He continues with the events in his own life which led to his decision to undertake the voyage. The whole is welded into a readable story with a successful blend of hard fact and personal reminiscence. It is a book about the oil industry but it is certainly not a text book. With his skill for writing clear and concise prose, he describes the business of winning and transporting oil. The reader is given a considerable amount of technical information without it being difficult to understand. At least as important is that he imparts to his subject a sense of a story well told.

This voyage to Venezuela had come at a critical time for Leo. It stopped him brooding over the unfortunate turn that his private life had taken and having to immerse himself in writing a particularly difficult work of non-fiction enabled him to see more clearly that he must return to writing the semi-autobiographical novels. A fresh start was needed.

Peter Barton

CHAPTER 21

Half a Loaf

DURING the time when Leo was staying in Curacao and Venezuela, he took the opportunity to indulge in his favourite sport of fishing when the occasion arose. One memorable incident was on the day he was due to sail home, when he was taken to part of a beautiful lagoon, noted for its marine life, where he was told that he might be able to catch a lobster. He spent two joyous hours swimming underwater, able to see the marine life at close quarters as he was wearing goggles for the first time. As a child he had longed to be able to see clearly under the sea. Swimming in the warm, clear waters of the Caribbean reminded him of Cornwall, where he had delighted in swimming in the local coves. As he thought about those idyllic years when he and Margaret lived in the hut, the idea came to him that she might be enticed back with the prospect of recapturing that happy relationship.

Thus it came about that one morning in April 1949, Leo, with a mixture of excitement and trepidation stood on the quay at Fowey waiting for the ferry to take him across the estuary towards Polruan. He saw:

'Its more numerous cottages and houses rising up the flanks of a steep hill from an ancient sea wall were tightly packed together, like those of my native Robin Hoods Bay. They were intersected with narrow winding alleys, and flights of cobbled steps. The roofs were grey sun-bleached slate and again their fronts were painted in varying colours. The alleys and flights of steps converged on a steep main street which led to the quay where the ferry landed. Close by were two pubs, the Lugger and the Russell and along the front were the ship and boat-building yards.'[1]

To his relief, it was neap tide. There would be insufficient water in the creek to allow a boat to be taken up to his cove. He wanted to approach it completely alone with no curious eyes watching his reaction to whatever he might find.

Once he had made his decision to return to Cornwall, he had traced the present owner of the hut and had come to an arrangement regarding the lease. He was informed that it was uninhabitable but that the owner was not prepared to sell the property. It was, however, agreed that he could live in the hut for a nominal rent provided he was prepared to undertake repairs at his own expense. He made an application to Cornwall County Council on the 18th March 1949 for 'permission to develop land'. He gave his address as Hawkswick, Skipton, and referred to himself as 'lessee'.

Leo's first excitement at seeing the hut gradually diminished as he suffered one shock after another when he started to examine the building. As he realised the enormity of the task confronting him he was 'seized with a sudden despair'. He gazed unhappily at the scene of desolation, but glancing out of the end window overlooking the cove, the sheer beauty of the view lifted his spirits and he determined not to be beaten, sure that he was right, that here in this lovely part of Cornwall was paradise for his children. In fact, Leo referred to it as 'paradise creek' and years later, when he wrote about this period in his life, he called the book *Paradise Creek*.

However, in April 1949 he had to face reality and that meant a great deal of hard work before the hut was habitable again. One of the living-room walls had collapsed while the other three walls and the ceiling were damaged and decayed. The roof leaked and the state of the floor suggested that the wooden piles supporting the hut had rotted. The 'big room', which measured thirty feet (9m) by twenty feet (6m), had neither ceiling nor floor covering. There were numerous loose floorboards. The fireplace which he and Margaret had built in stone and cement had been replaced by a hideous slow-combustion stove which had fallen on its side. Rust and rot seemed to be everywhere. It was obvious to him that there was far more than he could cope with by himself. He decided to employ local men and with the contacts from those earlier years was introduced to a family of six brothers with a variety of skills in the building trade.

He had been relieved to find that the area was experiencing a resurgence of prosperity. Boat building yards were being equipped with modern machines and the china-clay industry was booming. There was no unemployment and wages had increased. He realised how fortunate he was to have made the acquaintance of Arthur Bate and his brothers at a time when there was a lull in their workload. He had enough capital to pay for the job, provided the costs were kept within limits. He discussed with Arthur, the eldest brother, what his requirements were, putting a provisional limit of £350 on the job. Plans were made and Leo quickly became aware that he had met a man on whom he could rely. He was practical, down-to-earth, and genuinely interested in making a habitable home out of the derelict dwelling with which he was presented.

In a remarkably short space of time, roof and walls were repaired. Leo decided to partition off ten feet of the 'big room' to allow for a bathroom and an extra bedroom. The hut was to be severed in the middle and, by raising one end and lowering the other, the floors would be made level throughout. It was a difficult and delicate operation but the skilled workmen accomplished the task confidently. A toilet and septic tank had been installed by a previous owner or tenant but entry to the toilet was from outside the building. By the simple expedient of moving the door to the wall of the hut, they were able to gain entry from the inside - an improvement which would be greatly appreciated in the depth of winter. A further convenience which was competently effected was the supply of running water. Using a ship's emergency fire engine (purchased second-hand for £12), they were able to pump water from the spring through newly laid pipes to the kitchen sink.

The work progressed apace and within a few weeks, when the brothers had to leave to fulfil other commitments, the renovation had reached a stage at which Leo himself could take over for the final tasks of painting, decorating and all the other jobs, which seemed to be endless.

The garden was also in need of attention, the vegetable garden a priority as it had been when he and Margaret had lived a hand-to-mouth existence. He attended auction sales and bid for furniture going at knock-down prices.

'... a dilapidated looking settee, two easy chairs with hideous upholstery which could be covered up, an antique oak dining-table with a broken leg that I could repair, and two deal chests of drawers which, although I knew I was letting myself in for time-consuming jobs, I could transform with paint.'[2]

A tea-set, a batch of assorted plates and mugs, a Chinese carpet and rugs were bought for a fraction of their value. These were essential items for his home, but typically there had to be one piece of furniture which satisfied the aesthetic and romantic side of his personality. He bid for a Chinese cabinet, which had taken his attention with its beautiful design and exquisitely painted figures, flowers and birds. He exulted in his extravagant purchase.

Once assured that he would have a roof over his head, Leo turned his attention to that other vital requirement — a boat. Its uses were threefold. Not only was it his sole means of transport across the estuary to Fowey for shopping, but it was also essential for fishing expeditions and, of course, a relaxation away from his chores when he could feel part of the sea which he loved so much. Soon after his arrival, he had acquired a dinghy, given to him by his landlord. It had been stored in what had been Slade's boatyard, although it was no longer owned by the Slade brothers, who had gone bankrupt before the depression lifted.

Also, in response to an advertisement, he had recklessly bought, unseen, a sixteen-foot part-decked motorboat from a man living at the nearby port of Par. When it was delivered, he realised that the owner had not been honest with him. It was not a new boat, as he had envisaged, and there were several defects but he fell in love with it and never regretted his purchase. He named the boat *Amanda*, after the first boat which he and Margaret had owned.

It was this boat, or at least its engine, which led him into a friendship which was to last the rest of his life. The engine had been converted from a 1928 Austin Seven motor car. Following a catastrophic incident resulting in the sinking of the boat, he was appalled to realise that the engine might be completely ruined. With typical impetuosity, he stripped it himself, but not having the necessary expertise, found himself in serious trouble. He had to admit defeat and seek help. He was advised to contact a local man who owned an Austin Seven car. This was Bob Shoebridge, who quietly took control of the situation, sorted out the problem of the engine and set the seal on a comradeship which was to play an important part in Leo's life.

As he settled in to his new home, Leo made a number of new friends as well as resuming friendships made in earlier days. Although he was in some ways a solitary person, he needed the company of others and gradually these old and new-found friendships helped him to adjust to his new life. He seemed to have an affinity with the Cornish people, finding their natural openness easier to accept than the more taciturn attitude which he had found both in Yorkshire and Wales. Soon after his arrival, a friendship developed between Leo and Arthur Welsh, who worked on the Fowey-Polruan ferry. One day, when taking his boat the short distance to Polruan, he had passed the ferry and was delighted when the passengers waved to him.

'... he must have told his passengers who I was for some of them waved a friendly greeting. This was Cornwall. These were the people I loved!'[3]

Reminiscing on one occasion about Leo, Arthur described him as always looking rough with hair flying, enjoying the outdoor life either sailing his boat or walking to Polruan if weather conditions made sailing unsafe. He always seems to have had a rucksack on his back. Another notable feature was his voice, which was frequently referred to as being loud and penetrating. He was well known in Fowey and Polruan and, according to Arthur Welsh, was well liked. He would call in at the Lugger pub for company and a chat and, although he would have a glass of beer, he was not a drinking man. He was obviously regarded as a 'character', frequently seen beachcombing, picking up bits of wood for jobs back at the hut and known for not being averse to the odd night's poaching. He enjoyed mixing with the fishermen, and was always interested to hear about local fishing techniques, particularly from the older men. Leo was a man who liked company. Arthur Welsh remembered how he would listen to what others had to say, but also that when Leo had something to say, his companions would always listen to him. His gift for storytelling never deserted him. But he lived in his own way and the local people respected his privacy.

In the early weeks, he was invited to join the Fowey Galant's Sailing Club. This friendly acceptance of him by the local community acted as a balm to his bruised spirit, but he had to deflect questions about his wife and family. Always in his mind was the hope that they would join him and he was loath to allow news of their marriage breakdown to be known. Contact with friends, new and old, and the hard work which faced him in order to have the hut ready for the children's visit served to occupy mind and body. This was essential if he was to overcome his mental anguish. As on previous occasions when he had a recurrence of neurasthenia, he found solace in the close proximity of the sea, experiencing both a calming influence and a gentle stimulation from being in sight and sound of the sea. He had been very badly affected by the shock of Margaret's sudden departure and in the months and years following, had plumbed the depths of despair. Although never accepting the finality of Margaret's decision, he had eventually come to terms with his position and attempted to rebuild his life. The early torment had gradually diminished as he immersed himself in writing. His journey to Curacao had given further mental stimulation. Now back in Cornwall, he was in better shape mentally and physically to benefit from the restorative influences of his surroundings.

Since the Bate brothers had completed their work on the hut, Leo had devoted his time to preparing for the children's visit.

'With breaks only for meals, shopping and sleep, I worked non-stop at garden or house, and already I felt justified in regarding it *as* a house, with its five bedrooms, well-equipped and labour-saving kitchen, bathroom with water h. and c., inside toilet, and its one huge reception room with its magnificent view of the cove and creek.'[4]

It was important that the hut should be in a satisfactory state and that the boats were seaworthy. The garden was by this time showing the results of the efforts made in the preceding months. With tender new vegetables and fish freshly caught from the creek, the children would eat healthily. In accordance with Margaret's stipulation, Leo had made arrangements with a schoolteacher, a mutual friend from Yorkshire, to come and act as housekeeper during the children's stay. He knew that she would meet with his wife's approval.

The final ingredient needed to set the scene for a successful holiday was warm sunny weather. He anxiously watched the sky as the July heat wave continued, convinced that it would break before August, but the perfect days continued. His hope that Margaret herself would bring the children had been dispelled by a letter confirming that she would be sending the eldest four children, trusting him to return them at the end of a four-week period. The day before they were due he awoke to find a telegram informing him that there had been a change of plan and that all five children were arriving that day. Panic at the realisation that the hut was in a state of disarray vied with joy that he was to see his youngest son at last. After a frantic rush to tidy the hut, he sped across the estuary in *Amanda,* steering for the station quay. He dashed along the platform as the train pulled in to be greeted by 'that lovely word, "Daddy!", "Daddy!", "Daddy!"'.

Leo was aware that it was easy for him to be 'the perfect, generous, tolerant, good-tempered, amusing, loving father on a holiday like this'. The children had the freedom to run about in the open air. They could climb trees, play about on the beach and in the water. He had set bounds beyond which they must not go, just as his own mother had done (although to little avail in Leo's case) and, of course, he was nearby most of the time to ensure that they were not put at risk by the capricious sea. The hut with its innovations was an exciting novelty for them and the big room lent itself to romping and dancing.

> 'But it was the cove and the creek and the boats that excited and delighted them most. From half tide (flood to ebb) to high, there was safe water and a hard shingle bottom for them to bathe, swim or paddle. *Amanda* was moored well out in the creek, but except at low tide, the dinghy was available, and I had also acquired for them another war disposal bargain, an R.A.F. inflatable rubber dinghy, complete with hand paddles, telescopic mast and a little red sail. Here, however, I exercised a parental precaution. These ingenious craft which had saved many a ditched airman's life during the war were potentially dangerous for children. With an off-shore wind or current they could move swiftly out to deep water and although there was no such wind or current in the cove or creek, I tethered it with a stout line.'[5]

Ann, the eldest child, was now seventeen and was happy when she could find a secluded spot and settle down with a book. Henrietta, aged fifteen, was easy-going and 'jolly' as was her brother, Simon, aged twelve. Dain Patrick, at ten, was lively with a 'lean brown body' and Leo immediately saw the resemblance in Sean, the youngest, now four years old. He had been careful not to rush things on meeting his young son for the first time. He wanted to let Sean have the opportunity to get to know him gradually and naturally. He was secretly delighted by the little boy's reaction when seeing the hut. With an infectious chuckle he had given his approval — 'I like this.' A mutual understanding developed between the pair as the little boy eagerly showed his father his discoveries on the beach, such as a tiny crab he had found at the water's edge.

It was a wonderfully bittersweet time for Leo. His delight in having his children with him again after the anguish of the last lonely years was tempered by the realisation that time was limited. He tried to keep any gloomy thoughts at bay, making the

most of every hour of every day that the children were with him. There was no need
for him to worry about the possibility of boredom as there was so much to occupy
them in that idyllic corner of Cornwall. From morning to night as the sun continued
to shine, they spent joyful hours around the hut. Ann, when not immersed in her
books, found a passion for flowers, while Henrietta, more practical, would tend the
vegetables. The boys had a blissful time, having been allowed the freedom of their
father's workshop, making, amongst other things, small boats which they sailed in
the stream or at the edge of the cove. They dammed the stream, making pools, and
positioned rocks so that the water fell in miniature waterfalls. They built that dream
of all children, a house in the oak tree, where a swing had already been fixed. They
collected dry wood and lit fires on which to boil winkles that they had gathered in
the cove. The daily shopping trips to Fowey or Polruan never ceased to delight
them, but more than anything they enjoyed boat trips to the various coves along
the nearby coast. Lantic Bay and Lantivet Bay were particular favourites. Here they
could bathe and collect driftwood to make fires for picnics just as their father had
done with Captain Bunny all those years ago at Robin Hoods Bay. They searched
for crabs and anemones and those beautifully coloured sea-slugs which Leo had
collected with Sam when they worked together at the marine laboratory. He
introduced them to fishing, eager that they should experience the same thrill that
had so captivated him as a boy.

> 'Swimming, climbing the rocks, looking for treasures, they were as happy as ever living
> in the present, as children do, yet forging more memories. Perhaps they were not
> conscious of the beauty of the place. Perhaps they would have been just as happy at
> Southend-on-Sea, or fishing for tiddlers in the Serpentine or paddling in a muddy village
> duck-pond. But I could not believe that subconsciously at least, they were not taking
> things in, the shapes and colours of the rocks and beaches, the salty smells, the feel of
> the sun on their bodies, the sound of gulls; all daffodils for remembrance.'[6]

A week before the children were due to go home, the weather broke. A storm
lashed the area, wind roaring up the creek and huge breakers smashing across the
estuary. The rain came down in torrents. Fortunately Leo had prepared for this
eventuality. Whilst living at Hawkswick, he had seen an advertisement in the local
paper. On impulse he had responded to it and thereby achieved his boyhood
ambition to own a model railway. He had a detailed catalogue of items but had
never opened the boxes. So, on that windswept, rainy day at the end of the family's
holiday, he produced three large cardboard boxes, giving no indication regarding
the contents. The children pounced on them and excitedly delved into the boxes,
hauling out bundles of track, engines, passenger trains, goods trains: in fact
everything needed to keep them occupied for hours. The 'big room', with its
recently levelled floor, had come into its own.

The last few days sped by with a return to better weather but inevitably the final
evening arrived.

> 'Late that night, when everyone was in bed, I walked down the path to the cove. The
> wind had dropped. The tide was at half ebb with *Amanda* just aground on the mud.
> The sky was clear of cloud, and mud and water and the opposite banks of the creek were
> lit by the waning moon. Somewhere among the trees an owl was hooting. Two swans,
> gleaming ghostly white in the light of the moon, were moving lazily down-creek on the

ebb. I heard the plaintive cry of a curlew and in the stillness of the night a sound of an
express train on the distant main line, a grim reminder of what was to happen in the
morning.'[7]

It had been a wonderful interlude. The secret hope that hearing the children's
enthusiastic description of the hut and cove would cause Margaret to have a change
of heart came to naught. Although there were further visits in the following years,
none reached the perfection of that wonderful first holiday.

The following year Leo was dealt a shattering blow when his second son, Dain
Patrick, was involved in a shooting accident at Oddington, Gloucestershire, where
his mother and her friend had their school. He was taken to Radcliffe Infirmary,
Oxford, where he died on the 13th August 1950. He was buried in the old
churchyard at Oddington. The cause of death was given as 'laceration of the brain
caused by a bullet wound sustained at his home and was by misadventure'. Leo
received news of the tragedy when a telegram was delivered to his home. He was
devastated, feeling utterly helpless and alone. Nowhere in his writing does he
refer to the tragedy, but a sentence in *Paradise Creek* has poignant significance.

'I never had the whole family again at the same time.'

One can only surmise the anguish suffered by every member of the family, but
for Leo on his own, there was not the comfort of sharing his grief with others.
What effect did the shock have on his susceptibility to attacks of neurasthenia?

Living in such an isolated place, he was bound to be lonely at times and he
refers to enjoying the company of his cat, Choo-i. Ever since the rescue of their
first half-drowned cat, Leo and Margaret called their cats Choo-i and this was no
exception. It had been a present from a friend. A simple kind thought such as this
would have been greatly appreciated. He had made several deep, lasting friendships
since his return to Cornwall, particularly Bob and Joyce Shoebridge, who had
given an open invitation to call at their secluded home any time he wished.
Therefore his loneliness could be alleviated by visits to and from his friends. He
was never bored, enjoying fishing and sailing his boat in the waters around the
creek or listening to music from the shows or the classics on his elderly radio. He
had a collection of records and on occasions would dance around the room with
Choo-i in his arms! He had always been an inveterate reader so his collection of
books were read and re-read. The time came when he was able to apply himself
once more to writing. He had written a guide-book in the 'About Britain' series.
This was No 9 entitled *Lancashire and Yorkshire* and was published in 1951 for the
Festival Of Britain. As in all Leo's later works, its simplicity of style is deceptive.
The detail and descriptive passages flow so smoothly that the reader is unaware of
how much it would have cost the writer in effort to make it sound so easy. During
this period he wrote *Invisible Cargo,* the story of his excursion to Curacao and
Venezuela. This was published in 1952.

In the writing of *The Golden Waterwheel,* he relived his earlier years when he
and Margaret returned to Robin Hoods Bay and built a home on the moors.
Knowing what had happened to the family after this period, one wonders at the
happy atmosphere which is woven into the story, allowing no hint of the sadness
which he must have felt when writing of those near-idyllic days. Could it be that

he had the ability to shut out extraneous thoughts and concentrate totally on the story he wanted to tell? It is a beautifully written book, a simple story of the simple life told in such a way that the demands on the writer to produce prose which reads with such ease are in no way apparent. Few authors can achieve writing of this particular quality.

Eventually Leo put his affairs into the hands of a solicitor, deciding that he had nothing to lose by filing a petition for divorce on the grounds of desertion. He realised that there was a finality about the action, but still had the faint hope that the shock would cause Margaret to change her mind. The children were growing up. Boarding schools would be followed by careers that could take them far away from him, although it would be some time before Sean reached this stage of his life. Reconciliation had been a forlorn hope. Margaret remained adamant and decided to withdraw her defence of the action. This resulted in an earlier hearing, and the divorce was declared final and absolute on the 3rd January 1955.

Nona Stead

PART SEVEN

PARADISE REGAINED

CHAPTER 22

Life with Leo

AMONG my childhood memories, I have one of an elegant, attractive man, a cross between John Le Mesurier and George Sanders. His clothes were immaculate with beautifully cut trousers, velvet smoking jacket and silk cravat. His hair was smoothed back and his eyes were startlingly blue, framed by thick sooty lashes. In one languid hand would be an ebony cigarette holder, in the other a brandy and soda.

This was Sax Romer, handsome, suave, rich and successful. He was the best-selling author of the well-known Fu Man Chu thrillers, and he lived in a large luxurious house in Surrey with his glamorous wife, Rosie. They had acres of land, servants, a Rolls-Royce and a chauffeur. Lavish parties were held at their house and my parents were always invited; sometimes my sister and I went along too.

This was my childhood image of an author.

In those days, I lived with my parents and sister Felicity in a small village in the heart of the Surrey countryside. Both parents were writers and had their own witty column in the *Sunday* and *Daily Express*. My father, Nat Gubbins, wrote a regular feature 'Sitting on the Fence', and became famous for his humorous style and the characters that adorned his page in the *Sunday Express*: The Sweep, Sally The Cat, Man In The Pub etc. When the Second World War came, his popularity increased, making him a household name. He was called the leading humorist; a hero to the Eighth Army and loved by the navy.

Early on in my life, I learned that a writer needs peace and quiet in order to work. Our house was charmingly designed and quite detached. It was surrounded by a large garden with beds of flowers, vegetables, fruit trees and had a grass tennis court. It was ideal for both parents as it meant that Felicity and I, home from boarding school, could be 'lost' for hours while they tapped away on their typewriters.

Desperate to keep the house quiet for my father, Mother would fill a knapsack for each of us with food and entreat us to go to the far end of the garden. 'You can play your mountaineering game, or pretend you are hikers, but KEEP AWAY FROM THE HOUSE.' It fell to my loyal, patient sister to see that we obeyed these rules.

One day I broke them!

'I'm going in to get a drink of water.' Felicity looked stricken.

'You can't! Mummy said we have to stay out here.'

'Well, I'm going to', I said, and I ran back.

Inside the house my father was pacing the front room in his search for new ideas. It was difficult to write something funny each week. I was five years old at the time and I went up to him and asked, 'What would happen if I said 'shut up' to the king?'

After that, a new character appeared in the column — The Awful Child.

When he had finished his work, my father became sociable. Shy of women, nervous of children and dogs, he liked to escape to his local pub for a quiet drink with his friends. But when Mother, who loved parties, filled the house with people, he entered into the spirit of it and enjoyed pouring out the drinks. My favourite job was handing round the food.

All kinds of colourful people came to these parties: writers, newspaper editors, publishers, film critics, singers. On one occasion, an artist came to lunch to do a sketch of my father and me for *The Sunday Express*. Mother was very excited. She made me put on my party dress and had my hair curled with tongs.

'Keep smiling prettily at him', she urged me, and I was happy to comply. Every time I saw him looking at me across the table, I turned on my most angelic, winsome smile.

When the sketch appeared in the newspaper, it was a caricature, showing my father looking gloomy and morose and me with straight hair, sullen and scowling.

My sister and I absorbed a lot of culture in our formative years. We were taken to London to see the best plays, ballet, and the art galleries. We were encouraged to read and love books. We did. Our house was full of them.

With such an artistic background, it was not surprising that I developed a longing to go on the stage. At an early age, I took part in a charity matinee in London in front of the queen mother and at thirteen I sang and danced with other children in a Christmas musical at the Duke Of York theatre. After that, it was ENSA and a thrilling flight to India in a Sunderland flying boat. The war was over but they were still sending concerts and revues out to the East. Repertory and pantomime followed, leading to a decision that was going to shape my destiny.

In the summer of 1952, I heard that a repertory company wanted an actress to join it on its tour of Cornwall. The advertisement appeared in *The Stage* magazine. Out of work at the time and longing to be on tour again, I fixed up right away to join the company and was off on the train to Cornwall the next day. It was a turning point for me and maybe fate had a hand in it.

Coming from the south-east coast, the journey to Cornwall in those days took a whole day. This made it more of an adventure and there were many changes of train on route. As the train went through Teignmouth and Dawlish and I saw again the red cliffs, I was reminded of childhood holidays in Devon.

My destination was Fowey, a small seaport situated close to the estuary of the river which gives the town its name. It made a lasting impression on me as I arrived. The summer season was in full swing and I remember that it was warm with not a breath of wind. I felt that I had come to an enchanted place and was captivated. There were boats everywhere on the blue water and cottages with boats moored at the end of the garden. There were placards advertising pleasure trips out to sea. On the far side of the river, opposite the town, there was high land stretching along to one of the secluded creeks. Holidaymakers made their way to rocky coves to swim and gather prawns.

I had barely settled in to my new surroundings and was still mesmerised by the dream-like quality of this Cornish haven when I met a man who was about to exercise a great influence over me and would, in time, alter the course of my life.

The man was Leo Walmsley. On this occasion, he had rowed his small boat across from the creek where he lived to pay a polite visit to the bunch of actors who had taken over the town hall for a week. After he had introduced himself, I took in his appearance. My impression was of a man who lived rough, perhaps in a tent. His face, tanned by Cornish summers, looked weather-beaten with interesting lines. He had thick, dark eyebrows and deep-set, hazel-coloured eyes. A mass of grey-brown hair grew like a mop around a well-shaped head. He was slim, a little below average height, and I guessed his age as fifty something. His mouth was full and there was an anxious look on his face until he gave a diffident smile. He wore a green jacket, patched at the elbows, over an old pair of corduroy trousers and on his feet were a pair of large sea-boots. My fellow thespians regarded him almost with awe. He was a very unusual looking man.

Our new friend began telling us that he lived across the water and did his shopping by boat. Then looking at me he said suddenly,

'I'm an author.'

'Oh ... are you?' I almost gasped for I found this hard to believe. Again the mental picture of Sax Rohmer.

'Do excuse my scruffy appearance', the man went on, 'but I've just come straight from the mud.'

A snort of giggles came from the girl next to me. This was Doreen. She was like that.

'You see', the man went on, 'I've been digging worms for bait, there's any amount of fish about.'

More giggles from Doreen, then the man eased an old rucksack off his shoulders and introduced himself.

'I'm Leo Walmsley and I write books', he said, and looked round inquiringly. No one said anything, then, 'I don't suppose any of you have heard of me.' This was uttered with an air of resignation. Sadly none of us had. Then he told us that he loved the theatre and had written a play called *Sally Lunn*. He said that many of his books were about the lives of the brave fishermen of Robin Hoods Bay. Conversation was flowing more easily when our producer asked Mr Walmsley how many books he had written.

'Oh call me Leo', he said, and then suddenly exclaimed, 'I've got to go.' His life, he told us was governed by the tide, which was now ebbing and he did not want his boat to go aground. After a hasty goodbye, he was off and away, down to the quay.

From that moment, a friendship was formed between Leo and me. I met him again once or twice in the town, for he came across each day to collect his mail. The first time I went to have tea with him in his hut up the creek, Pont Pill, I was struck by the beauty of the still water and high land on both sides with wild flowers on the banks. It was to be the first of many trips on the river.

Going over to the hut with Leo became an adventure; stepping into the sturdy dinghy, being rowed across the river and sometimes being allowed to take the oars. It was all so new to me: the smell of boats, the squeaking of oars on the rowlocks, the hushed, quiet atmosphere, broken sometimes by a cormorant diving in after a fish.

When I first saw the hut, which was set above the shore at the top of a path, I thought that it resembled a log cabin. It was raised on piles because of the sloping land, and steps led up to a balcony and the front door. How large it was inside! The front room had windows all round, one with a glorious view of the creek. There were paintings on the walls, bookshelves crammed with books and big chunky home-made furniture. Even the kitchen was large with a big table and garden-like canvas chairs.

As the tour of Cornwall continued, taking me farther from Fowey, so did our friendship. Letters were exchanged. I looked for that now familiar handwriting on the envelope. I thought of the man with the strong character face, the funny old clothes and the modulated voice of an actor. I remembered how he had looked at me during our first meeting. Did he like me? I wondered. I thought of that romantic creek and how the boat just glided on the water; of the hut with the giant sunflowers outside. The smell of honeysuckle by the cove.

As a parting gift Leo had given me one of his books. It was autobiographical, the story of his boyhood in Robin Hoods Bay. There was a photograph of him on the jacket looking distinguished with collar and tie, and his hair with a becoming wave. Often I would pick up the book, turn it over and look again at that handsome face.

It was sad leaving Fowey when the week was up, but to begin with, our tour of Cornwall was fairly local and the company settled in villages about six or eight miles away. Sunday was my free day and I caught a bus in to Fowey each week and spent the day with Leo until it was time for me to return. He was always there to meet me and take me back in the boat. Sometimes he would cast a line overboard, hoping to catch a fish not only for us but for his black cat, Choo-i, who would wait patiently on the cove. This weekly routine became dear and familiar to me. If it was raining, Leo would set off in his old cabin cruiser *Amanda* and gallantly offer me his great duffle coat. As we walked along the path and up the steps to the hut, he would throw open the door joyously and exclaim, 'Here we are, home again, all waiting for you.' And that is what it became, my second home.

Autumn came, bringing a lovelier, more delicate beauty with golden sunshine on the bracken and the creek like polished glass, reflecting the turning oaks. And still I went there every Sunday, deserting my actor friends, who wondered what the attraction was and why I was spending all my free time away. It was difficult to explain it to them. Maybe I did not know myself and was under some enchanted spell. Certainly Pont Creek had an air of magic. Even my landlady voiced her surprise.

'Who is the gentleman you keep going to see, m'dear?'

'He's an author and he lives in a hut up the creek ... it's beautiful up there.'

'Well, 'tis none of my business, but I should have thought you would rather be out with your friends.'

Apart from the fact that I enjoyed spending Sundays with Leo, I knew that he looked forward to my visits; they broke up the lonely week for him. There was an anxious wrought look on his face sometimes as he waited at the bus stop for me. I knew that he was lonely. His marriage had broken up and he was missing his family.

In bad weather the cosy stove in the big front room would be lit and we would sit in front of it, warm and with mugs of tea. Leo would have his pipe. There was no electricity in the hut and during a strong wind the Tilley lamp overhead would sway back and forth. I felt as though we were on a ship and loved to hear rain pattering on the corrugated roof. I also loved to hear Leo tell me about his life in the village of Robin Hoods Bay, how he went to the local school and hated wearing a starched collar, how his ears were boxed and how he played truant to go fishing. He described the pantile-roofed cottages nestling together, the narrow winding streets and alleyways, the beach with its rocks and pools, the crashing seas in winter and the dramatic cliffs. He told me of his many crashes whilst in the Royal Flying Corps and casually mentioned that he won the Military Cross.

Sometimes Leo would read aloud from his books and make the characters spring to life from the pages, especially the brave fishermen from Robin Hoods Bay who put to sea in all weathers and laughed at danger. He spoke of the resourceful couple, he and his estranged wife, leading their Robinson Crusoe life in Cornwall. And here I was, in the same hut described in *Love In The Sun*.

Always optimistic and resilient, Leo hoped that his marriage could be saved, but in spite of his efforts to bring about a reconciliation, this was not to be. There were times when he was in the depths of despair, agitated, missing his four children terribly. He talked a lot about them, especially about the youngest, Sean, who came to stay for half of the holidays. The little boy was four years old when Leo had been allowed to see him for the first time since the fleeting glimpse he had of him as a tiny baby. He told me how happy his daughters, Ann and Henrietta were when he went to see them at their school. 'They came running into my arms', he said, and added, 'I love all my kids, I've had a raw deal ... I don't deserve it ... I don't deserve it.' I saw the pain and anguish in his face and my heart went out to him.

Three years from our first meeting, Leo and I were married in Cornwall; a quiet ceremony with just family and friends. Warning me in advance, he said, 'I'm a poor proposition for you, I'm broke ... the world will be against it.' But I did not think about the future.

People often asked me what it was like living on the shores of a lonely creek with a man old enough to be my father. The press had a field day: 'Bride sails to loneliest honeymoon' was how a national newspaper described it after the wedding, while another one announced, 'Her home in a lonely creek; actress marries author.'

Did I miss young company? friends wanted to know. What about the winters? They were surprised that I could settle down quite happily to a life of semi-isolation. During the dark months, the hut could be made cosy and warm with both fires going.

Leo had a strict routine when he was writing a book. He would be at his typewriter from ten o'clock in the morning and work for four hours. If he was stuck for ideas, he would go and make something in the workshop, a fender for the boat, any job that would concentrate his thoughts. I learnt to keep away from

Leo and Stephanie

him until lunch time and often rowed myself across to Fowey. We usually went out together in the afternoon, up river in the boat or out to sea. In the evening, long after I had gone to bed, I would hear the typewriter going again.

Spring came to Cornwall and brought much beauty. On the high land above the creek, flowers appeared: bluebells, mimosa, pink campion. In hot weather the creek became a swimming pool and when Sean was staying with us, he and I would dive into the water from the boat. He was a beautiful little boy with large dark eyes and a wonderfully tanned skin. I was proud to know that he was my stepson. Sometimes the three of us would go for long walks, taking with us the picnic gear, and we would scale down cliffs and find sandy coves where dark blue water gushed in and out between the rocks. Here we would make a fire from driftwood and boil a kettle for tea.

The simple life was good. If I had had any doubts about marrying a man much older than me, they were dispelled by the arrival the following year of a beautiful baby daughter. Weighing eight pounds twelve ounces, she was like a baby doll. The nurses crooned over her and I overheard one say, 'I'd like her myself.' I felt a rush of maternal instinct coupled with a deep glowing happiness when she was put in my arms and the words of the song 'ah sweet mystery of life' suddenly came to me; now at last I knew the secret of it all.

Leo had less attention from me after the baby's arrival, but it made no difference to his affection for her. He knew that I was totally overwhelmed with new emotions. We were united in our abiding love for this child who filled our days and gave us such joy. Caring and supportive, he was always on hand to hold the baby while I straightened the bedclothes in her cot. Then he would gently lower her down. He would fetch towels, soap and baby clothes while I bathed and dressed her. She was never far from his thoughts: 'I'm going across to Fowey … anything the baby needs?'

As she grew bigger, he liked to carry her down to the cove saying, 'Come on baby, let's see if the swans are here.' In the early mornings, woken by the soft sound of chuckling or gurgling, sleep would tug at me. So too did some inner voice which said, 'Don't go back to sleep, these moments are precious. Make the most of them; they won't come again.' I listened to that voice and got up and went into my baby's room. The chuckling stopped. She had heard my footsteps. At once she became alert, looking round and listening. Then she saw me and smiled, a beaming smile of recognition, arms held out. I picked her up and carried her back to my bed, laying her down at my side. I was content to just gaze at her and fold her in my arms, treasuring the moment, marvelling at this precious gift.

These were the idyllic 'Paradise Creek' years. Peaceful, serene, like our baby, who, with her large eyes and silver-blonde hair was at one with the beauty of the place. All was still and quiet there with only the natural sounds; the watercress stream, oars on the water, the cry of a seagull. Leo called this period his second life and was never happier than when he was making things for his child. He made her such things as a canvas bath, a little truck on wheels for her to pull along, a rocking sea-horse, a dolls' house and a bed.

As Baby learned to walk, I had to watch her carefully. She was adventurous and when the tide ebbed, she liked to toddle off to see what was round the jutting headland. I had to dash after her as I saw the small legs making rapid progress round and over the big rocks. She did not like it when I grabbed hold of her and carried her back to safety. Realising that her fun was over, she would pucker her mouth, about to cry.

'Don't frighten her!' Leo would caution, 'She hasn't any fear.' And he would take her from me and carry her up to the hut, shaking his head in mock reproach. 'Your darling mother is getting into a flap about you, baby.'

We named our daughter Selina, which means heaven. This tied in nicely with Leo's new name for the creek. He called it Paradise Creek, the title for a forth-coming book. Fair-haired with green eyes and dimples, Selina was born with a rich sense of humour. Often dressed like her father in dungarees and tiny red

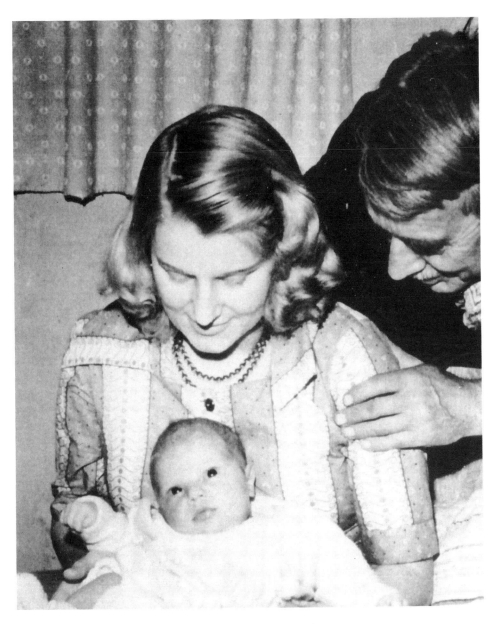

Leo, Stephanie and baby Selina

wellingtons, the flaxen-haired tot would patter down the path after him, to watch while he painted the boat, scraped the barnacles off or made a repair with a lead patch. She might pick up the sandpaper or a box of copper tacks with an intention of helping. Sometimes she was content to squat beside him playing with the pebbles. So happy were the pair of them in their old clothes among the various tools that my mother dubbed them 'Steptoe and son'.

Spurred on by his new responsibilities, Leo wrote *The Happy Ending* (published in 1957). It is a story set in Wales and tells of his conflict with the land and then came *Sound Of The Sea* (published 1959), which is a study of a boy growing up in the Victorian era. Both books were well received by the critics, but it was *Paradise Creek* (published 1963) that put him back at the top again. This was the Book Society choice and headed the reviewers' list. The story was simple and human. It told of the author's efforts to win back his family and recreate his home beside the creek, and finally his meeting with me and the events that gave rise to the last chapters.

During the hot weather, when the creek was like a warm, inviting pool, I took Selina in with me and Leo would watch as I swooshed her up and down in the water, smiling as she shrieked with joy.

Selina was barely three years old when she said, 'Me want to row the boat.' So we sat her down in the dinghy and put her hands on the oars, which were big and heavy. She managed to pull quite well, helped by the momentum, even though the boat was large.

When I rowed across to Fowey to do the shopping, I put Selina in the seat with her reins on and tied her to a nearby ring. Then we would set off in leisurely fashion towards the mouth of the creek and pull across the harbour. As we approached the Albert Quay, I brought the boat alongside the steps, shipped the oars, then jumped up and freed Selina. With my left arm, I lifted her out and held on to her, at the same time grabbing the painter. Then I got out, still holding Selina by the hand, and with my free hand carried the painter along as we went up the steps. Then I made fast to the railings, sometimes with help from the people standing near the quay.

These excursions into Fowey were very agreeable to me for I loved to show off my small daughter and delighted in hearing comments from the locals as they made a fuss of her. 'Hello me 'andsome, going shopping then? She's some fair, isn't she? Like her mother, dear little maid.' Selina regarded them solemnly, sucking her middle fingers. Sometimes a biscuit would be offered her or a sweet.

Leo needed peace and quiet in the mornings for his work, so noisy housework was out. This suited me fine and I took the opportunity to amuse, educate and play games with my little daughter. She loved the swing her father had made for her at the end of the path above the creek, and here we had games about fairies and imps.

Sometimes we went up the path that Leo had made linking up with the one to Polruan and Selina would enter a fantasy world, giving full vent to her imagination. It was a lovely place for a walk as there was an abundance of greenery, trees and bushes. Running on ahead, she would suddenly stop in her tracks, put her head to one side and say,

'Listen!'

'What is it?'

'Ssh.' She put a finger against her mouth. 'Can you hear something?'

I couldn't but I played along. Presently there was a muffled, whimpering noise.

'Can you hear it now?'

'Yes ... yes I did hear something.' Crouching among some foliage, she pretended to lift something up.

Leo, Stephanie and Selina

Leo, Stephanie and Selina (*Photo by Jack Rigg*)

'Oh look! It's a baby. We must take it home, it's all alone.' After putting the imaginary bundle in my arms, she would scamper off again, her imagination soaring. The process was then repeated.

'Listen — I hear another sound.'

'Where are they all going to sleep?' I wanted to know as the eighth 'bundle' was handed to me.

'In your bed', came the cheeky reply. 'Oh look at this one, it's smiling, it loves you already.'

Stepping back to childhood, I became my daughter's companion, sister, animating her dolls and toy animals, giving them different voices. I taught her to read at four years old, to play little tunes on the piano, to swim and float, and to dance.

Sean still came for holidays and did not mind sharing the attention with his small sister, although he was too old to be a playmate. Leo had made him a dinghy, smaller than ours and painted red. Sean and I took turns rowing around in the creek and trying to capsize each other. Sometimes we dived in off an old oil drum. We collected prawns at low tide and gathered blackberries from the land above the hut, making them into jam. We shared jokes, listened to records on my radiogram and danced around the room to the music. This charming little boy had natural grace and rhythm.

Much as he loved Fowey, Leo's thoughts were never far from Robin Hoods Bay, his childhood home.

'Wait till you see my Bay, it will knock spots off anything you have seen before.'

'Lovelier than Cornwall?'

'Ah ...' It was difficult trying to decide the favourite between his 'two loves'.

'You've put me in mind of a poem:

'How can I be true to eyes of blue
When looking into eyes of brown?'

'We'll go there one day', he promised. It was important to him that I should see a beautiful part of his life.

'We'll go in springtime when the daffodils are out. I'll show you the bluebell woods and take the kid on to the scaurs, where I roamed as a boy hunting for crabs.' It was clear where his heart lay. He was a son of Yorkshire.

As time went by, our simple but isolated life had to be abandoned. Although I enjoyed the astonished reaction I got when telling people of our exact location, 'I'm up the creek and round the bend', I realised that in our little girl, Leo and I had a very real responsibility. She must come first. She needed playmates. She also needed a lot of care and protection, for after getting Asian flu at seventeen months old, she could become chesty with an infection. It was essential that we should have the amenities of a town with doctors, chemists, and, of course, a school.

Eventually we found a nice terraced house overlooking the river and moved there in the autumn of 1961. Leo and Selina were sad to go. I breathed a sigh of relief. I had loved it over at Pont Creek and would always remember the happy times, but it was good to feel the security of neighbours and shops nearby. And we still had the boat.

Selina's longing for something 'that's warm and alive that I can hold in my arms and love' didn't stop at puppies and kittens. Next came her yearning for a donkey.

'Please could I have one, please, please.' She was a passionate child and did not give up easily.

'Have you thought any more about me having a donkey? Please let me.'

Being nearer to her age than Leo was, I was in sympathy with her and pleaded her case. But he told me that we had a perfectly good cat and a puppy would make messes. As for a donkey, 'Where would we keep it! It would have to have exercise. How could you keep a donkey living in a terraced house?'

Selina was not to be outdone and sometimes smuggled a hedgehog or a frog into her room and placed it triumphantly beside her bed. Once when she was coming back from school with a couple of giggling friends in tow, I noticed a bulge in her overcoat. Grinning mischievously, she opened it to reveal a bright-eyed guinea pig.

By moving to Fowey, Leo and I made new friends. So did Selina, who joined the Brownies and went to the Saturday morning dancing school, where I had a job as assistant teacher to a lady who held the classes. One Christmas she gave a children's party and asked me to make the jellies, which I did the night before. Leo volunteered to transport all twenty-four of them to the dance hall. The locals that day must have been surprised to see him walking all through the town from our house to the Town Quay carrying a large tray of individual children's jellies. He had to make two trips.

By keeping the boats that were moored at Caffa Pill nearby, we had a link with the past. In fine weather we would sometimes row up the creek and take a look at our old home and remember how lovely it had been to swim in the placid water.

The move had been a wrench for Leo but he felt that it was worth it. Selina and I had given him a new life, a second chance.

In the summer of 1963, Leo felt on top of the world. Collins the publisher gave a champagne party for him, to launch *Paradise Creek*, and invited several influential people. It was a happy occasion for us all. On the day of publication, he signed copies of the book at Smith's shop in Fowey.

Rounding off a memorable year was the crowning of Selina as the fairy queen of the Fowey carnival. There were many attractions during the regatta week in August, floral dancing through the town, yacht racing, the cutting of a giant Cornish pasty outside on the steps of the King Of Prussia hotel on Town Quay. Every child in the town went up and received a free slice.

The carnival was the big event. First the brass band, then the procession led by the queen and her attendants in their decorated float, followed by the fairy queen in hers. Then more floats, scenes from fairy tales like Alice in Wonderland and Snow White, humorous scenes, tradesmen's floats and the fancy dress parade. Everyone wanted to take part in this and would spend months making their costumes. There were also visiting queens and floats from nearby towns and villages and the local shops were closed that afternoon as large crowds gathered and lined the narrow streets.

A few months prior to the big event, a beauty competition for the two queens was held in the town hall, presided over and judged by the mayor of Fowey. Selina was chosen from many other pretty girls, all decked out in their frilly party frocks. I had dressed her in a simple blue frock patterned with ships and stars. When naming her the winner, the mayor lifted her up in his arms and said 'beauty unadorned'.

I do not know what Leo's thoughts were when he saw his daughter in her fairy queen dress of white organza and scarlet cloak sitting on a gilt chair during the crowning ceremony, and later, in the carnival, riding through the town in a splendid coach bedecked with rhododendrons. Opposite her were seated a little page and two small attendants. The procession started at the top of Fowey Hill, Hanson Drive, and went all through the town, ending at the old station.

The idea for his last book came to Leo in 1964. It would be a collection of his fishing adventures under the title *Angler's Moon*. It was published by Hamish Hamilton in 1965 and nicely illustrated with sketches of boats and boys with fishing rods.

At the end of the year, Leo paid what was to be his final visit to Robin Hoods Bay, calling first at Leeds where the *Yorkshire Post* was holding its annual literary lunch. It had chosen him for its celebrity author and Lord Snowdon was guest of honour. They were photographed deep in conversation. While at Bay, Leo visited his old friends and his old school and roamed his beloved scaurs. He came back full of nostalgia. It had been a profound experience for him. Shortly after his return, he bought me a record, 'The Carnival Is Over.' It was soon to have a haunting significance.

It often happens that when living close to someone you don't notice the change in them. But others do, and in that winter of 1965 one or two people in Fowey asked me was Leo all right. 'He's lost weight, hasn't he?' 'He's fine', I said, wondering what they meant.

The following spring, dark clouds began to gather. Leo was ill. The weight he had lost was now noticeable around his shoulders when he wore his jacket. Then suddenly, without any warning, he became unable to keep his food down. He spoke of feeling terribly tired, he hated to give in and he fought this feeling as he went up the many steps to the garden to plant the early potatoes. I felt torn with pity and anxiety to see him; after a few spoonfuls of soup or custard he would have to go straight to the bathroom. Eventually he could not even keep a cup of tea down.

'It's so unfair', I said, 'because you've never been a greedy person.' Far from it. He enjoyed his meals and cakes and the puddings I used to make, but he never indulged himself in excess of food or drink. By now we were both terribly worried and after an X-ray, he went down the road to see his doctor and get the result.

He came back shattered and stunned. He sat down in his armchair and stared up at me for a second or two. Then he managed to speak.

'I've had bloody bad news', he told me, unbelieving, incredulous. He put his hands over his face and his shoulders were shaking. The news had broken him. I put my arm round his thin shoulders. I just did not know what to say and my heart ached with sadness, and love. Just then Selina came into the room. I did not want her to see him so upset.

'We're having a little talk', I told her. 'Just leave us a minute, there's a good girl.' She quickly withdrew. I turned back to Leo, thinking with a pang of how little attention he had ever sought for himself, of how his main concern was for Selina and me; he had put himself in the background. Was this why I had been so slow to notice the change in him? Had I been so blind? I was stung with remorse. Now he would have all my attention. He managed to compose himself a little and I found a clean handkerchief.

'I'm not feeling sorry for myself', he said, gratefully taking it. 'Please don't think that, will you? I'm not thinking of myself. I'm thinking of you and the kid … What's going to happen to you … Oh my God.' I did not think about the frightening future, or what it held for Selina and me. I did not want to think about anything except Leo getting well. Desperately I hoped that this was a bad dream from which I could awake. I wanted life to carry on as we were, for the three of us to go on living in our safe, sturdy house, to go out in the boat, to see our friends. Surely this was not going to be the end of that life. We had been married for eleven years. Tears filled my eyes as I thought of how much Leo had to live for, the plans we had made. We were going to travel one day, when he'd made some money. He would write another book, the outline had already taken shape. A documentary programme about Robin Hoods Bay was already getting underway. Leo would write the script and be narrator. He would find a better house, bigger and with a proper garden.

Presently he told me about his interview with the doctor. He would have to go into hospital for an examination under an anaesthetic. The trouble was in his gullet — a sort of stricture, preventing him from keeping food and drink down. He suggested that Selina and I should go to my parents while he was in hospital. They lived 300 miles (480km) away. I took his hand in both of mine. 'I would never leave you', I said.

In May, Leo went into Tehidy Hospital, which was near Truro and stood in acres of ground. Daphne du Maurier, a true friend to us both, had given him a cheque to cover the expenses of a private room. I had a talk with the surgeon, who confirmed the X-ray report and said that he hoped that, by operating, he would make Leo able to eat again. I then implored him to talk cheerfully to Leo, to raise his spirits, and to deny the evidence of that first X-ray. 'Say anything', I begged him, 'because if he hears any more bad news, it will destroy him, and his will to fight.' Happily the surgeon went along with my idea and I found Leo looking cheerful when I visited him.

'I've got every confidence in this chap', he said. 'I'm sure he's just the man for the job. He's going to put me right.' This was the old Leo talking in a robust, fearless way. He was now very frail and starving through lack of food. But I was told that he was receiving all he needed intravenously in his arm, as they hoped to build him up for the operation. My mother came down to give her support and fixed up for Selina and me to stay with her in a guest house not far from the hospital.

The operation which held such real hopes proved too much for Leo in his weakened state, and he quickly began to deteriorate. I went to see him each day, sometimes with my mother, sometimes alone. Our friends Bob and Joyce came several times. 'Are you going to have a picnic?' he asked us once. I assured him that we were not. I could not bear him to think that we were out there enjoying ourselves during those warm sunny days; days when we would normally be setting off in the boat to some sandy cove. How I hated the bright sun, hated even the beautiful grounds of Tehidy.

Bob and Joyce were our closest friends in those days and had known Leo before I did. Bob would often come to lend a hand when Leo had trouble with his motor boat.

One day when Bob was sitting on the edge of the bed talking to him, Leo looked up, and with something like a smile, as though he had suddenly remembered, he reached out to Bob and said in a quavering voice: 'You're my dearest friend.' 'You're mine', said Bob, quickly grasping Leo's hand in both of his. Tehidy had once been a tuberculosis hospital and because of this, an old rule barring children from visiting still prevailed. This was hard on Leo. But the rapid change that Selina would have seen in her father would have been very upsetting for her. Apart from being emaciated, his voice had lost its resonance and was now little more than a whisper. I managed, however, to catch his last faltering words to me. 'What a joy ... and comfort ... you've been ... during these ... dreadful weeks.'

It was our last communication for, as I hurried along to the hospital next day and was about to enter his room, I was waylaid by the sister in charge. She took my arm and led me away, then she turned to me.

'You're husband has gone to heaven', she said, 'half an hour ago. It was very peaceful and he wasn't in any pain.' I stared at her, hardly able to take it in. Then somewhat to my surprise she added:

'It's the best thing that could have happened. You are a young woman. Now you must look after yourself for your little girl's sake.' Seeing my distress, she led me to a chair and sat beside me. 'He was in poor shape when he came to us', she said, 'and there was little we could do for him: but, as I said, the end was very peaceful ... he just slipped away.' She was very kind and spoke reassuringly for a while. But I was in a daze and only half heard her sincere words of advice.

'Go to your parents, with your little girl, and make a home with them. Your mother wants you to. Go back with her, I believe there is a nice convent school ...' Her words trailed off as I quickly tried to face reality.

'The Carnival is over.' Perhaps, I thought. Life is like a carnival. Leo had loved that song and its final words, 'I will love you till I die.' He died on the 6th June 1966.

Many changes have taken place to Paradise Creek since I lived there. The new owners cut the hut in two with only the front half remaining, but moved to one side, giving space to a large white house, and a road was built to give access.

Last year some friends hired a boat and went up the creek. They looked for the hut, but in vain. It had gone. When I heard this, I felt as though much of my past had been swept away. Life over there had not been perfect and it would not have suited everyone. But it had been a way of life and I had dared to live it.

Memories came flooding back, and with a mixture of sadness and joy, I saw my younger self running down to the cove, holding my baby in the warm creek, descending the precarious cliffs to Lantic Bay, gathering blackberries with Sean.

Paradise Lost? I'm glad I lived there when I did.

Stephanie Walmsley

PART EIGHT

REFLECTIONS

CHAPTER 23

Paradise Remembered

WRITING down some of my thoughts and memories of my father has been a surprisingly difficult task. Not due to any lack of memory — on the contrary, he is still very vivid to me. But a question more of choice, of what to select. There are so many aspects of my life with him, as the father, the author and the man.

In many ways, I was reluctant to stir up sad memories. His death was a great loss to me and one that was harder to accept because his memory was kept alive by the media, by the books, and by the feeling of everyone who knew him that this was someone unique. Therefore, I had the impression of having lost something very precious in my life.

My relationship with him was very close, closer, it would seem, than with his other children. I went everywhere with him. We used to go out in *Amanda* together, go fishing together. He taught me how to bait hooks, how to splice ropes, to saw logs and make things. I remember him having a great sense of humour and found that it was echoed in Sean, whom I met for the first time since childhood in the spring of 1991.

I never knew Leo to be angry — except for once when I ran across the road to leap into his arms and was greeted with a smack! The life at the hut was as idyllic as it is portrayed in *Love in the Sun* and *Paradise Creek*. Even though I was there only until I was five, everything stands out brightly and vividly: the iridescent blue of the creek, the little pebbles and stones on the beach glittering under the water, the gentle rhythmic creaking of the oars in their rowlocks. The chugging of *Amanda's* engine, familiar and reassuring- my infant lullabies!

It was a Garden of Eden and my toys were the flowers that grew in the garden; the big stones on the beach that my father and I would make houses out of; the little twigs and leaves that would, with the help of my mother's imagination, be my 'tea-sets' and pretend meals for the 'fairies' that lived in the cove. I do not know if everyone's childhood feels magical in one way or another, but mine certainly did. It felt as though we lived in an enchanted place, as though the air itself held some spell.

My life was never short of excitement and drama. The fascinating sounds that would issue from my father's lips when he would try and start *Amanda's* engine or mend the water pump. The thrill of catching fish, the boat rocking precariously in rough seas. No need for funfairs — I had it all! In many ways, my father was childlike, which is obviously how I could relate to him. Simple things in life gave him pleasure — the things that most men of his age would be unable to appreciate. He was not world-weary, although his life had been hard and he had lost much of what he had loved. I have never since met someone who could get high on these sort of things. He almost had the ability of a Zen master to live in the present, to be lost in the task at hand, to be fascinated by the 'is-ness' of life. He had a sense of wonder at all the laws of science — electricity, power, acts of creation, the fun of watching things grow.

Yet he was not a simple man. He thought, he wondered, he reflected. He was someone you felt, who had never quite got over being born, being in the world. He wanted to know, he wanted to discover. I see him as someone who was on a quest in life, never losing that taste for adventure and never being made bitter by what he saw, yet not making light of things either. The love of the simple life was not a withdrawal from the outside world. He loved nature but he loved people too and was fascinated by them. He gave me that interest by showing his feelings about the world, by infecting me with his enthusiasm and sensitive awareness.

Leo was, as I remember, a man of strength, a man of action and a man of ideas. He was connected to the physical universe and, through that relationship, he developed a unique philosophy, the closest one, I think, being that of Zen. He was also a very courageous man, all the more so because he suffered anxieties, yet would push through them. Except on one occasion ...

I remember him giving me a microscope for one birthday. It was a real treat for me because I shared his interest in the scientific. The magnification was not that high, but high enough to see the elements of a sample of blood, for example. To produce that sample required an act of courage which my father, whilst being able to ride in flimsy boats on wild high seas and fly aircraft of questionable safety, simply could not muster ... Having wound thread around his finger, he picked up a pin (not bothering to sterilise it — he could cope with a few germs!) and, raising his arm high in the air, Leo, with a grim look on his face, stabbed at the now blue finger. 'Damn, blast and hell!' he said. In the end, it became evident that he would not be able to perform this task and I remember it as being my first lesson in the Walmsley irony.

Yes, a unique man, I think. And the formation of the Walmsley Society has confirmed these earlier impressions. I am more grateful than I can say to everyone involved in the society for their appreciation, their attempts to re-establish him as a writer and for introducing me to aspects of Leo's life that I would never have known about.

Finally, how can I express my happiness at being able to meet my brother again? All my life I had been aware of the existence of my half-brothers and -sisters. Their memory had been kept alive for me in a way that perhaps mine had not for them. As I was an only child, I longed for brothers and sisters. Yet I never really made attempts to see them until a few years ago. Too scared — I am not sure. Maybe I felt that it was too late. I had felt a longing to see them all — they were my family, after all. I needed to know, to trace a feature, a line on a face, to see a likeness to my father, to myself even. And the pool of memories, of information. One drawback was my fear of flying and most of them lived beyond reach.

So it was with the greatest excitement and nervousness that I went to a meeting, knowing that Sean would be there. It was an unforgettable evening: pieces put into place, a sense of wonder and almost unreality. I was not disappointed! I found myself liking him, apart from the fact that he was my brother. It was, as Leo would say, a 'thrilling' evening. And it was a moving experience.

Selina Craze

CHAPTER 24

Reflections on my Father

IT may come as a surprise to many readers of this book that they knew my father better than I did: some of you actually spent more time in his company than I did. Those familiar with the Walmsley history will recall that I was born in 1943, the year my parents separated. I was brought up by my mother, Margaret Walmsley, and her friend Betty Arney, until they parted company and my mother began what was to be a long odyssey through Africa, Canada, and finally the United States. (She lived with my wife, Bonnie, and I, for the last twelve months of her life.) After my mother departed for Africa, I made my home with Sonia and Patrick Bird in Liphook, Hampshire, until I, too, began my own travels from England, first to Ireland, and then to the United States.

What I remember of my father comes from summer holidays spent in Fowey during the 1950s and early 1960s. I am not sure how many summers there were, when they started and when they stopped, but I have vivid recollections of them, and they are permanently embedded in my childhood memories. Until quite recently, I was completely unaware of much of my family's history and if you had asked me how many books Leo had written, I could not have told you. In fact, the only book I remember reading roughly at the time that it was written was *Angler's Moon,* and it was the only one my father sent to me inscribed.

If it were not for the Walmsley Society, I think my memories of my father would have disappeared beyond recall. Because I spent so little of my life in Leo's company and because my mother never really volunteered much about him, I had slowly separated myself from his life and works, to a point where he became a distant and dying memory. Over the years, mostly out of curiosity, I had made an effort to collect as many of his books as I could, but I was ignorant of their significance, and frankly I had little to relate them to. I had even tried reading one or two, but they were set in a place and time that I knew nothing about. (I lived in the south of England and Yorkshire could have been a foreign country as far as we were concerned — an impression that has been put to right in the past few years, as I have travelled extensively in the North Country). As I talked with members of the Walmsley Society, I not only began to fill in some missing pieces about his life, but also started to understand something of him as a writer. This would never have happened spontaneously.

When it was suggested in 1980 that I might like to attend a Walmsley Society function up in Robin Hoods Bay, I was frustrated because I wanted to be there, but I could not take time away from my research and teaching at the University at Albany (in up-state New York, where I live and work). But in 1991, I took a four-month sabbatical in England with Bonnie and our two children, Katharine and Jonathan. Finally, I was able to take a few days off and join the Walmsley Society as it celebrated one of its annual meetings. And there, a wonderful thing happened. I do not really recall the last time I had seen Stephanie and Selina but it was probably thirty years earlier. We had corresponded at various times but it was sporadic — our lives had taken different paths so that it was hard to sustain any genuine communication. But at this meeting, all of a sudden Stephanie, Selina and myself found ourselves in the same place surrounded by a group of people whose common bond that day was the celebration of Leo's writings. Later, as we gathered at the Grosvenor Hotel at Robin Hoods Bay, we remembered over a long dinner the times that we had spent together all those years ago, and we filled each other in on what we had been up to in the intervening years. It was an extraordinary and unforgettable evening. The next day, while the Walmsley Society conducted its business, the three of us took a walk down to Bay again and shared memories of Leo, of our lives and families and future plans. Which brings me back to my memories of Leo. They are brief but memorable.

* * *

I remember the train ride from Hampshire or from London down to St Austell. 'Do Not Lean Out of the Window' (usually changed to 'Do Not Clean Soot Off the Window') was an invitation, not an admonition, to a young boy travelling on his own and, if the guard would let me, I would ride the entire journey standing in front of the open window with my head half out. I would always arrive covered in soot. You cannot do that any more. (It is funny that I write this flying back from Hawaii to New York, and while you cannot open a window on these aircraft, I always book a window seat and peer out. Some habits die hard.) You always knew when you were getting close to journey's end when the earth turned red and the train crossed Brunel's famous bridge.

I remember the 'hut'. It was totally unlike anything I had ever lived in — made of wood, up on stilts (I used to play in the dirt underneath it, and that is where I hid apples that I swore I had not picked from Leo's trees), creaky, and so isolated. I was used to big houses with formal gardens and drawing rooms. This was quite a shock. Leo had cats. They were always called Choo-i (I can pronounce it but have no idea how it is spelled), and so I never remember how many there were, nor if any of them ever died. They ate fish parts and limpets (which Leo cooked, and which stank. I can bring back that awful smell to this day.) My memories of Leo always include Stephanie. I do not remember being with my father except when she was there, although I now know that there were occasions when she was not. I just do not remember them. Stephanie was a bundle of fun (she still is, all these years later) and we had riotous times together. We would laugh so much that it would hurt. Leo was still writing then, so Stephanie and I were thrown together a lot — I always remember her more as a sister than a stepmother, that is the way she behaved.

With Leo, we fished, and it was from him that I learned to love fishing and messing about with boats. My favourite form of fishing was mackerel probably because when you got into them, they would strike a bare hook and always put up a fight: or was it because they tasted so good? I also loved fishing for wrasse off the rocky shore. Leo wrote about my catching mullet with bananas as bait (his inscription in my copy of *Angler's Moon* reads, 'in celebration of a famous mullet'), but that was not my favourite memory, and I think that he took a little artistic licence with that event. I preferred open-sea or rock fishing, but never could find my sea legs to endure anything but the calmest of ocean fishing, something that Leo could never understand, and that persists even today (I will never go on a boat cruise). I do not recall eating anything but fish and mussels all summer long, although I am sure that ice-cream was a major item every time we took *Amanda* across to Fowey. (My wife Bonnie, born in Erie, PA, still does not understand why I cannot stand ice-cream made from yoghurt.)

Leo never revealed to me the agony that he must have felt (and I now know that he shared with Daphne du Maurier) at having me only for the summer and not participating in raising me, and I am grateful for that. It must have been difficult for him to keep his feelings to himself, but I do not think that I could have handled it at that age. Those summers were carefree, great fun, and peaceful. What boy could have found anything but joy living at the water's edge in Cornwall, with boats, skimming rocks, and fishing all day long? Stephanie must take a lot of credit for Leo's self-control during these years, but even Scrooge would be hard pressed to be miserable in the face of her boundless energy and good humour.

Although he never raised me, there is a lot of Leo inside me. I am told that I bear an uncanny resemblance to him, although that is for others to confirm. I certainly have inherited his passion for writing, although my books are — so far, at any rate — works of non-fiction. I write and lecture about education, often with Bonnie, who teaches kindergarten. It is strange to think that Leo wrote and lectured across the United States between the two great wars and had a reputation for lectures that were informative and witty: eighty years later, I lecture across the United States, and have, I am told, a reputation for being informative and witty. And our daughter Katherine writes poetry, some of which is beginning to be published. I still fish, although I prefer fly fishing, but our son Jonathan has the same passion for fishing — of all kinds — that Leo had. He cannot wait for school to end so that he can get out and spend his days by the lake, or up the river. Now, does that sound like Leo's grandson?

Not many of us have a chance to reclaim a lost relationship with a parent other than through old photographs and the memories of aging relatives. Through my father's books, but even more through the writings and recollections of people who grew up with him, and who have studied his life and times, I feel as if I have been given a second chance to know a man whom I barely met. It is a precious gift, and I will cherish it for the rest of my life.

Sean Walmsley

CHAPTER 25

Angling — A Passion

OF all Leo Walmsley's many enthusiasms, there was one which wove as a thread through his life from childhood until his last days. It was constant, never varying in its intensity, always an integral part of his being. This was his passion for angling. It was many things to him — a sport, a hobby, a means of survival, a solace at times of personal distress. So intense was this compulsive urge to go fishing that it would be correct to say that it was a major influence on his lifestyle. It was important to him as a solitary pursuit and as a delight which he could share with his family.

The man to whom the revelation of angling comes in later adult life thinks wistfully of the wasted years. The most fortunate anglers are those who, because they lived close to waters where good fishing was available, discovered the magic of fishing in their boyhood.

Such a fortunate person was Leo Walmsley. The beach and scaurs were but a few steps away from the family cottage in King Street in Robin Hoods Bay.

In the summer season, several old men in the village made a living by taking visitors out into the bay in their dinghies 'for a row', for which they were charged sixpence an hour, or a shilling an hour for fishing at the whiting grounds. It was customary for each pleasure boatman to employ a boy, whose job it was to keep the boat afloat while he touted for custom amongst the visitors approaching the beach. Each boy would help to row the boat while the fishermen baited the clients' lines. Leo became Captain Bunny's boat-boy and a close friendly relationship developed between them.

As we have read earlier, Captain Bunny was always ready with advice and encouragement. The young boy had an insatiable appetite for information. He listened avidly and learned a great deal about fishing techniques and the location and habits of the various species of fish that were to be caught in the bay. It would be fair to say that he served his apprenticeship under Captain Bunny's tutorship.

There was one particularly memorable day in August. Trade was bad as most of the visitors had gone to the Whitby regatta. The weather was good, with a hot sun, so they set off in the small boat for a day's pleasure fishing.

They were soon catching fish — plaice, mackerel, gurnard, whiting, dab and haddock — using a trolling line and spinners from the moving boat.

Then there came a lull in the fishing, so they decided to pull for the shore near Stoupe Beck and have their lunch; also Captain Bunny could enjoy his 'pipe o' baccy'. On the beach they collected some driftwood and made a fire. They boiled water for tea in the Captain's billy-can and two of the mackerel they had caught were grilled in the glowing embers. 'They were delicious'.

This beach barbecue with the smell, the sight and sound of the sea, was for Leo an unforgettable boyhood memory which created a lasting impression. It was to be the first of many beach picnics, particularly in later years with his young family on boat trips to the coves near Fowey.

Suddenly a flock of gulls waiting on the south cliff flew up screaming and made for a patch of water out at sea which had become dark. The sile[1] were in! They pulled out towards it. The billet which had been waiting for the sile were now feeding greedily and the two were soon hauling in a fine catch of fish which were now going for their feathers.[2]

This, of course, was hand-line fishing and not very suitable for fishing from the scaurs, where a rod was more effective. One day, Leo, along with some other village boys, was fishing for pennock. They used hazel sticks for rods, lengths of grocer's string for lines and 'ha'penny hooks' with catgut snoods. Their floats were bottle corks. Suddenly a large conger eel appeared and it seized the bait on one of the boy's hooks and snapped the rod. Then, breaking the other lines with its tail — disappeared. Realising the inadequacy of the tackle that they were using, Leo re-tackled using proper fishing line, which had a much greater breaking-strain, and a large cod hook, which he baited with two limpets. The eel immediately grabbed the bait and, to avoid his rod being broken, he had to resort to looping the line around his waist. The eel rushed past him and darted round the Rocket Post. This made landing it alone impossible. Fortunately, Captain Bunny, who was nearby in his boat, came to the rescue and gaffed it.

An even more exciting and memorable event occurred one day when he was fishing alone on the scaurs. The most profitable time to fish was when the tide was flowing and the big fish lurking in the forest of tangle moved shorewards to feed. The best places to fish were as far out along the scaurs as possible. This could be hazardous as the incoming tide fills gaps in the scaurs before the scaurs are completely submerged. Thus there is the danger of being cut off from the shore. The place that he had chosen was well along the scaur and beyond the bounds set by his mother, but his reckless nature and the excitement of the pursuit of his quarry caused him to ignore or conveniently forget his mother's instructions.

He cast the baited hook into the water in a gap between the scaurs, laid down his rod and went to search for more bait. He had not gone far when, glancing back, he saw the butt end of his rod jerk up, then slither into the water. He dropped his bait tin and ran back.

> 'I looked at my best school boots but I knew that I had not time to unlace them and take off my stockings ... I stepped in and was too excited to notice the shock of the cold as the water came over my knees. I splashed forward ... it was nearly up to my arm-pits, but reaching forward I grabbed the rod end and hung on to it as I started to move backwards with the still invisible fish tugging wildly to get away ... I managed to scramble out on to the scaur. I seized the line and hauled it in. There was a big plop and the next moment the fish was on the scaur. I flung myself on the fish. I managed to get my fingers in its gills and then gave it a whack on the shale and stunned it.'

He had been aware of his mother arriving on the scene as he could hear her screaming and shouting but he held up the fish.

> 'Look!' I shouted. 'I've caught a salmon, a real salmon. Look at its silver scales.'

It was correctly identified by Captain Bunny as a bass weighing two pounds. He told Leo's mother that they were fine eating, better than a salmon.

'You bake it in the oven missus with taties and a couple of onions. I'll lay you've never tasted owt better. And fancy him catching a fish that no Bramblewick fisherman 'as ever set eyes on afore. You ought to feel proud of him.'[3]

Although his mother did scold him for being disobedient and he was sent to bed, she did not take his rod away and had to admit that the fish tasted very nice. Any fish caught were a welcome addition to the table.

Years later he caught his largest fish, a cod weighing twenty pounds, near Ravenscar. It was December and the weather was bitterly cold. His personal experience of fishing under such atrocious conditions enabled him to describe in brilliant detail an incident in one of his books. He conveys to the reader with the utmost clarity the intensity of purpose and physical discomfort endured by the character whose custom it was to fish from the scaur at the dead of night by the light of a lantern.[4]

The reference has a particular poignance when one understands that the incident took place at a time of Walmsley's life shortly after the break-up of his first marriage to Suzanne, and when he was suffering from a recurrence of neurasthenia.

'This was one of the periods of my life when fishing had become an obsession. I could scarcely think of anything else, least of all work. Yet looking back I can see that this in itself was a sort of self-healing instinctive therapy. If I couldn't concentrate on writing I was concentrating less on my misfortunes. Fishing was a narcotic, but even carried to excess it produced no hangover.'[5]

In addition, he was upset by his lack of success in achieving recognition as a writer, feeling that he was a failure. He was fortunate in having such an absorbing passion that he could find solace, anaesthetising his unhappiness and anxieties in physical effort and exhilarating surroundings.

'And the antidote, the anodyne if not the cure, was out on the scaurs, not when the cobles were coming in with their catch, but when they were deserted at dusk or nightfall or by the light of the moon.'[6]

Walmsley insisted that he never did participate in coarse fishing.[7] Perhaps he was only referring to home waters. In his book *Flying And Sport In East Africa* he mentions that on occasions whilst he was in East Africa, he ventured down to the crocodile-infested banks of the river and fished, using a length of bamboo and a hook made of aeroplane bracing wire, which he baited with locust. He caught several species of barbel and electric eel.

It was in his late teens that he first began to take an interest in fly fishing for trout.

His first introduction to the art of fly fishing came when he was about ten years of age. Just above where Mill Beck flows into the sea was a corn mill and farm. Hidden in the woods behind the mill was the mill dam, which was private and was owned by the squire — a fierce, powerful man, also a magistrate who always did his best to have any trespasser or poacher severely punished. In spite of this, Leo's eagerness to catch his first trout there, on a worm, overcame his fear. He wriggled through the undergrowth and was horrified to see the squire fishing from the far bank. He was about to retreat quietly when there was a loud splash. When he realized that the squire had hooked a fish, his curiosity overcame his fear and he stayed to watch.[8]

For Leo, this was a new method of angling — the lightness and action of the rod and the playing of the fish until safely in a landing net rather than simply lifting it out of the water. Nor could he understand why the hook was not re-baited. This mystery was solved later when the hook caught in an overhanging branch and the cast[9] broke. After the squire's departure, he climbed the tree and recovered it. He then realised to his astonishment that the hook was actually an artificial fly.

He often thought about the dam and how wonderful it would be to own his own lake, and stock it with trout, an ambition which he was able to realise in later life.[10]

For his sixteenth birthday, his father presented him with a fly rod and a tackle case full of artificial flies and casts that he had bought cheaply at an auction sale. Early attempts without tuition on the tributaries of the River Derwent were not entirely rewarding but perhaps, at this stage, he had not the determination to master the techniques. He regarded it as:

> 'A makeshift of a sport; something to do when the weather was too rough for the sea and the scaurs'[11]

Later, however, in favour of freshwater fishing he conceded:

> 'Trout fishing, and certainly that of my choice, too is usually found in sylvan surroundings or among mountains or lonely moors, so that if the fish prove elusive you have the many other aspects of nature as a compensation, especially in the spring or early summer when the fishing is at its best; the beauty of the landscape, the singing of a lark, the cry of a curlew or nesting plover, the sight of a water ouzel speeding up and down-stream or perched on a rock wagging its tail, then diving for a caddie grub, into the very pool where you are bent on catching your fish.'[12]

Such thoughts in the early years after the First World War, when he was living in a dreary bedsit in West Kensington, London, spurred him, with spring in the air, to escape to the countryside and fish for trout in a moorland tributary of the River Teign. In later years, when finances permitted, he fished the River Lyn in Devon and, in his native Yorkshire, a tributary of the River Ure. The last expedition was a complete disaster; it was a year of record drought and the stream had dried up completely. Neither did he have much success on his first visit to the Lake District, where he fished Ullswater. One day he decided to climb Helvellyn. Approaching the summit, he sighted a tarn in a hollow below Striding Edge. On investigation, he was excited by the sight of rising fish, which he estimated to be at least three-quarters of a pound in weight. First light the following morning saw him once more climbing Helvellyn, this time with his fishing gear. He tried almost every fly in his collection without success. By afternoon, the sky darkened ominously and he heard the sound of distant thunder. Alarmed at the thought of being caught in a thunderstorm in such a desolate place, he decided to pack up, but at that moment a breeze ruffled the surface of the water. Immediately he had 'a take' and hooked a trout. His 'black gnat' was seized at every cast. He had caught at least a dozen when the storm broke with a vengeance. The rain came down almost vertically, the lightning was continuous and there were crashes of thunder that seemed to shake the ground. The storm seemed to be directly above. With nowhere to shelter and the path now a rivulet, he made the hazardous journey down the mountain side, soaked to the skin.

In 1947, when living at Hawkswick, fishing would have provided a distraction from his worries. The River Skirfare running by his bungalow was teeming with trout. The fishing rights were held by a local angling club, but his application to join the club was turned down. Frustratingly, just in front of his window was one of the best pools but, so far as we know, he resisted the temptation to poach. The water bailiff patrolled it night and day. Discovery could have cost him the tenancy of the bungalow.

Throughout his life, one of his ambitions had been to catch a salmon on a rod and line. The River Esk, which flows into the sea at Whitby, is Yorkshire's only salmon river. In earlier years, the salmon fishing there was even more exclusive and the cost would have been beyond his means.

Opportunity came, however, when he was living by the River Skirfare. One day the postman delivered a letter postmarked 'Eastbourne'. When he opened it, he was astonished to find that it was from the Duke of Devonshire. The duke apologised for writing without a previous introduction and said how much pleasure Walmsley's books had given him. He had read in one of them that Walmsley had never had any first-class salmon fishing. This was followed by an invitation to fish his stretch of the Blackwater in County Cork in the spring of the following year, over a period of ten days. All necessary tackle would be provided. If the duke himself was unable to accompany him, a butler and a cook would be at his service.

'My first reaction to that extraordinary letter was to look out of the window in the hope that I would see one of the Rolls-Royce anglers fishing in that for me, forbidden pool, preferably the one who had rejected my application for membership of the club: to dash down, show him the letter[14] and tell him he could keep his bloody trout. But it was late September, the local fishing season over.'[13]

Unfortunately, he was unable to accept the duke's invitation but met him at a later date by appointment at the duke's club in St James for lunch.

They chatted about Leo's books and in particular about the one he was currently writing. Leo kept his letter and when the duke died, he stated,

'I will always cherish the memory of our meeting, not because he was a Duke and an aristocrat, but because he was a simple, kindly man.'[15]

In his later years, although there was excellent trout fishing in the upper reaches of the River Fowey, he made no effort to avail himself of the opportunity. He made the excuse that he had given his fly rod and reel to a friend, who was going to live in Alberta.

The truth of the matter was that salt-water fishing would always take precedence.

'I hold that salt water fishing has a greater potential for excitement. Half the thrill of angling surely is anticipatory, and in the sea, that emotion is enhanced by mystery.'[16]

When Leo and Margaret first moved into the hut in Cornwall, they were desperately poor and struggling to balance their weekly budget. Unable to afford meat with the exception of the occasional sheep's head, their survival depended almost entirely on the fish that they could catch.

Conditions in the tidal creek, Pont Pill, near Fowey were ideal. When the tide was out, he could dig bait almost at his front door. When the tide flowed, shoals of small bass moved up the creek feeding on the small crustacea. If there were no bass, there were always flounders. In the harbour, plaice, dabs, small skate and whiting provided excellent sport but, even better, out at sea were larger bass and pollack, often running to fourteen pounds, and the most highly prized of all British fish, the red mullet, a fish indeed for epicures.

Many years later, following the break-up of his marriage to Margaret, he returned to the hut, living a solitary existence. The highlight of his life was when the children were allowed to visit during the school holidays. To his joy, the children revelled in their surroundings. It was natural that Leo should wish to introduce the children to his lifelong passion — fishing — hoping that the novelty would create a new interest for them. He need not have worried. On a fishing expedition in his boat *Amanda*, there was soon tremendous excitement and friendly rivalry when, using hand-lines, they began to haul in fish. Leo was content to bait their lines rather than fish himself.

> 'I had no desire to fish myself. I was perfectly content doing what I could to keep the ball rolling. It was a joy to listen to the excited shouts of the children, to know that they were completely happy on this perfect summer afternoon on the shining sea. As such I would remember this, and I believed that they would remember it too.'[17]

Later still, in his late sixties, fishing helped to forge a special bond between Leo and Selina, the daughter of his third marriage. As a child, she delighted in going fishing with him.

> 'Nothing would excite and delight Selina more than to feel the fierce tug on the line, to haul in with the fish darting from side to side, fighting all the way, then to lift it safely onboard; although she would avert her eyes when I unhooked it and gave it the merciful coup de grâce.'[18]

In 1964, an angling correspondent[19] visited the creek at Pont Pill, searching for prawns as bait for his wrasse fishing. He had already read and enjoyed Leo's fishing yarns and hoped to meet him. He was fortunate.

> 'I saw among the dozen or so holiday folk along the shore, a figure which could be no other. It fitted so perfectly with my mental image; a shabby-genteel figure, elderly but spry and so different from the conventional holiday folk. He was sitting, with his young wife and small daughter, against the very rock where I normally rigged up my gear; his ancient dinghy drawn up on the shore nearby.'[20]

When he started putting on his waders, Leo came over and, to his delight, engaged him in conversation. His curiosity had been aroused by the waders which were of an unusual type and very light. They discussed fish and fishing. The visitor then confessed to Leo that he had guessed his identity and had enjoyed his books, also,

> 'I ventured the thought that sea angling, unlike trout and coarse fishing, had not yet inspired a book which might be held up as a classic on the sport. Perhaps, some day, he might fill the gap? He listened attentively but made no comment.'

Pont Pill, near Fowey

They never met again, but the following year *Angler's Moon*, Leo's last book, appeared on the bookshelves.

Today, angling is this country's greatest participation sport. Few sports have such a bibliography. Angling newspapers and journals are in great demand and are read eagerly by thousands of enthusiasts. Writers can make a very lucrative living.

Had these opportunities been available to this extent when Leo was a young man, perhaps he could have confined his writing entirely to the subject of angling.

Had he done so, this poses the question: would he have had the time or the incentive to write the books enjoyed by so many? — a thought that would cause even the most dedicated angler amongst his readers to shudder.

John W Stead

Chapter Notes and References

PART ONE. The Early Years

Chapter 1

1. *Sound of The Sea.*
2. 'Slogger' was Leo's nickname for William Henry Camp, who came from Barnstable to Robin Hoods Bay in July 1876, where he remained as headmaster for thirty-two years. He married a local girl, who rejoiced in the name of Rosetta. When he retired in October 1908, speeches referred to the fact that there had been no complaints of harsh punishment.
3. *Foreigners.*
4. *Invisible Cargo.*
5. *So Many Loves.*
6. Ibid.
7. *Ports and Harbours.*
8. 'Between the Heather and the North Sea' appeared in *National Geographic Magazine,* February 1933.
9. *Sound of the Sea.*
10. Ibid.
11. *Then and Now,* Jonathan Cape 1935.

Chapter 2

1. *So Many Loves.*
2. Ibid.
3. Ibid.
4. Ibid.
5. Ibid.
6. *Lancashire and Yorkshire.*
7. *Sound of the Sea.*
8. *So Many Loves.*

PART TWO. War Service 1914–1919

Chapter 3

1. *So Many Loves.*
2. *Whitby Gazette* the 2nd October 1914.
3. *Whitby Gazette* the 16th April 1915.
4. *Invisible Cargo.*
5. Unprovenanced.
6. Ibid.
7. Ibid.
8. *Flying and Sport in East Africa.*

Chapter 4

1. Walmsley correspondence the 22nd May 1916.
2. *Flying and Sport in East Africa.*
3. Ibid.
4. Ibid.
5. Ibid.
6. Walmsley correspondence 24th–29th July 1916.
7. Ibid.
8. Ibid.
9. AIR 1. 2195 209/19/4. the 3rd August 1916. Public Records Office.
10. *Flying and Sport in East Africa.*
11. Ibid.
12. AIR 1. 2195 209/19/4. the 3rd August 1916. Public Records Office.
13. AIR 1. 2195 209/19/4. the 19th August 1916. Public Records Office.
14. *Whitby Gazette* the 12th January 1917.
15. *Flying and Sport in East Africa.*
16. Ibid.
17. Ibid.
18. Citation. British Expeditionary Force East Africa Routine Orders, Headquarters, Zomba the 25th June 1917.
19. *Flying and Sport in East Africa.*
20. Speech in London. Quoted by Charles Miller in his book *Battle for the Bundu.*
21. *Flying and Sport in East Africa.*
22. Ibid.

PART THREE. The Whirlwind Years

Chapter 6

1. Suzanne was born on the 13th August 1897 at Holland Road, Sutton Coldfield, Warwick. She died in Hove, Sussex, on the 3rd March 1993.
2. Letter from Harold Brighouse the 1st December 1931.
3. Letter from Harold Brighouse the 8th December 1931.
4. 'Two Exiles in Normandy' published in the *Wide World Magazine*, January 1921.
5. 'Our Adventure in Normandy' published in the *Wide World Magazine*, May 1924 under pseudonym 'March Hare'.
6. *So Many Loves.*
7. Ibid.
8. 'My Misadventures in Finistere' published in the *Wide World Magazine*, September 1922. By Lieut Leo Walmsley MC, FRGS.
9. *So Many Loves.*

Chapter 7

1. *The Globe and Traveller* the 17th March 1919. Evening edition.
2. *So Many Loves.*

Chapter 8

1. *So Many Loves.*
2. Ibid.
3. Ibid.

4. Ibid.
5. Ibid.

PART FOUR. The Foreigner Returns

Chapter 9

1. *In A Teacup* by Arnold Storm.
2. *Phantom Lobster.*
3. Ibid.
4. Ibid.
5. *So Many Loves.*
6. *Phantom Lobster.*
7. Ibid.
8. Letter to Dr S E Wilson, winter 1933/34.

Chapter 10

1. Leo Walmsley's unpublished and unedited first chapter of *Love in the Sun*.
2. Ibid.
3. *Whitby Gazette* the 16th August 1929. Letter from Amicus Piscatorium.
4. *Love in the Sun* as 1. above.
5. Ibid.
6. Letter from Margaret B Walmsley to Jack L W Hazell the 23rd November 1988.
7. Enquiries made independently by Walmsley Society members Muriel Hemingway and Alan Roper.

PART FIVE. Romance and Realism

Chapter 11

1. *Love in the Sun.*
2. Ibid.
3. Margaret Walmsley. Unpublished story.
4. Unpublished first chapter of *Love in the Sun*.
5. *Love in the Sun.*
6. Ibid.
7. Ibid.
8. Letter from Sir Arthur Quiller Couch dated the 9th October 1931.
9. 'Soul of an Artist' appeared as a short story in *Blackwood's Magazine* June 1925.
10. *Love in the Sun.*
11. Name of the boat in *Love in the Sun*.
12. See Part 4. Chapter 10.
13. Letter dated the 10th October 1931.
14. Daphne du Maurier. Review on dust jacket of second impression of *Phantom Lobster*.
15. Compton MacKenzie. Review in *The Daily Mail* the 9th November 1933.

Chapter 12

1. *Ports and Harbours.*
2. *So Many Loves.*
3. Leo Walmsley letter, the 4th August 1937.

Chapter 13

1. *So Many Loves.*
2. Ibid.
3. Ibid.
4. Ibid.
5. Ibid.
6. It is now known that David Lean had an uncredited part in editing the film *Turn Of The Tide*. At the same time, he was a newsreel editor and it was on this film that he gained some of his early experience in feature films.
7. *So Many Loves.*
8. Ibid.
9. Ibid.

Chapter 14

1. 'Adder Howe' in *The Golden Waterwheel.*
2. *The Golden Waterwheel.*
3. *Paradise Creek.*
4. *The Golden Waterwheel.*
5. *Paradise Creek.*
6. *The Golden Waterwheel.*
7. Ibid.
8. Article in *The Walmsley Society Journal*, September 1992.

Chapter 15

1. *Fishermen at War.*
2. Ibid.
3. Ibid.
4. The skipper who picked up this message believed that it was a secret code. When he read the legend 'Urgent return at once to the nearest Port Fishery Officer', it left him in no doubt. He immediately hauled his nets and returned to port.
5. *Fishermen at War.*
6. Ibid.
7. *The Field, Country Life* and *Illustrated London News* devoted full-page spreads to their reviews. The American reviewer Jay Lewis described *Fishermen at War* as 'a book of golden deeds, set in words of silver'.

Chapter 16

1. *The Golden Waterwheel.*
2. Ibid.
3. Leo Walmsley letter, the 20th June 1943.
4. *The Golden Waterwheel.*

Chapter 17

1. *The Happy Ending.*
2. Ibid.
3. Ibid.
4. *A Knight Without Armour* by Pauline Burdon. Private publication.
5. *The Happy Ending.*
6. Ibid.
7. Ibid.

8. Statement by Lionel Walmsley of Old Fyling Hall, Robin Hoods Bay, the 13th June 1946.
9. Margaret Walmsley died in the United States of America on Sunday the 26th February 1989.

PART SIX. Into the Wilderness

Chapter 19

1. Letter dated the 18th December 1946.
2. *Lancashire and Yorkshire.*
3. *Walmsley Journal*, spring 1989. 'Walmsley in Littondale' by Jane Ellis.
4. *Invisible Cargo.*

Chapter 20

1. *Invisible Cargo.*
2. Ibid.

Chapter 21

1. *Paradise Creek.*
2. Ibid.
3. Ibid.
4. Ibid.
5. Ibid.
6. Ibid.
7. Ibid.

PART EIGHT. Reflections

Chapter 25

1. 'Sile' are the miniature herring, from two to three inches long, exquisitely beautiful with dark, green-blue backs and silvery iridescent bellies. In each shoal, all are of the same size and identical in appearance. In a shoal, they are packed so closely together vertically and horizontally that as one moves, its neighbours must move too, making a chain reaction. Their numbers are beyond comprehension. A shoal may be a mile long and across and 100 feet deep, an almost solid mass of fish. (Walmsley's notes)
2. Refers to a billet fly. A white feather tied to a bare hook. It presents to the fish the flashing belly of a sand eel or sprat.
3. *So Many Loves.*
4. The alcoholic Captain Tom Bransby in *Master Mariner.*
5. *Angler's Moon.*
6. Ibid.
7. Coarse fish are those which are not members of the salmon family eg barbel, chub, tench, roach.
8. *Angler's Moon* and *Foreigners.*
9. The cast or leader is a length of fine nylon up to nine feet (2.7m) in length, between the end of the fly line and the fly. It is the weight of the heavy fly line and the flexibility of the rod which enables the fisherman to 'throw a fly'. Formerly horsehair or silkworm gut were used as casts.
10. *The Happy Ending.*
11. *So Many Loves.*
12. *Angler's Moon.*

13. Ibid.
14. The angler would have been impressed by the letter. The vast Devonshire estates further downstream included Bolton Priory.
15. *Angler's Moon.*
16. *So Many Loves.*
17. *Paradise Creek.*
18. *Angler's Moon.*
19. Donovan Kelly. An authority on bass, he was made an MBE for his work. He wrote regularly for *The Fishing Gazette* and other papers. Author of *Forty Anglers* published by Merlin Books.
20. Donovan Kelly, *Walmsley Society Journal*, spring 1986.

BOOKS BY LEO WALMSLEY
(With dates of first publication)

Guide to the Geology of the Whitby District	Horne (Whitby)	1914
Fossils of the Whitby District	Horne	1919
Flying and Sport in East Africa	Blackwood	1920
The Silver Blimp	Nelson	1921
The Lure of Thunder Island	Jenkins	1923
The Green Rocket	Jenkins	1926
Toro of the Little People	Hodder & Stoughton	1926
Three Fevers	Cape	1932
Phantom Lobster	Cape	1933
Foreigners	Cape	1935
Sally Lunn	Collins	1937
Love in the Sun	Collins	1939
Fishermen at War	Collins	1941
British Ports and Harbours	Collins	1942
So Many Loves (autobiography)	Collins	1944
Sally Lunn (play)	Collins	1944
Master Mariner	Collins	1948
Lancashire and Yorkshire	Collins	1951
Invisible Cargo	Joseph	1952
The Golden Waterwheel	Collins	1954
The Happy Ending	Collins	1957
Sound of the Sea	Collins	1959
Paradise Creek	Collins	1963
Angler's Moon	Hamilton	1965

INDEX